Carl Schmitt
between Technological Rationality
and Theology

Carl Schmitt

between **Technological Rationality**
and **Theology**

The Position and Meaning of His Legal Thought

HUGO E. HERRERA

Umberto Boccioni, *The City Rises*, ca. 1910. Oil on canvas. Courtesy of the Museum of Modern Art, Mrs. Simon Guggenheim Fund.

Published by State University of New York Press, Albany

© 2020 State University of New York

All rights reserved

No part of this book may be used or reproduced in any manner whatsoever without written permission. No part of this book may be stored in a retrieval system or transmitted in any form or by any means including electronic, electrostatic, magnetic tape, mechanical, photocopying, recording, or otherwise without the prior permission in writing of the publisher.

For information, contact State University of New York Press, Albany, NY
www.sunypress.edu

Library of Congress Cataloging-in-Publication Data

Names: Herrera, Hugo, 1974– author.
Title: Carl Schmitt between technological rationality and theology : the position and meaning of his legal thought / Hugo E. Herrera.
Description: Albany : State University of New York Press, 2020. | Includes bibliographical references and index.
Identifiers: LCCN 2019030528 | ISBN 9781438478777 (hardcover : alk. paper) | ISBN 9781438478784 (pbk. : alk. paper) | ISBN 9781438478791 (ebook)
Subjects: LCSH: Schmitt, Carl, 1888–1985. | Law—Philosophy.
Classification: LCC K230.S352 H47 2020 | DDC 340/.1—dc23
LC record available at https://lccn.loc.gov/2019030528

10 9 8 7 6 5 4 3 2 1

To
Alicia Guzmán Valenzuela
(September 19, 1926–December 17, 2012)
and
Bernardo Palau Oliver
(February 3, 1925–December 17, 2011)

Contents

Acknowledgments	ix
Foreword	xi
Introduction	1
Chapter 1 Law and Technology	9
Chapter 2 Law and Theology	45
Chapter 3 Juridical Thought	73
Notes	109
Works Cited	173
Index	189

Acknowledgments

As is the case with any book, and especially with those that take years in the making, I have incurred many debts. First of all, I would like to thank my family. Then, Jorge E. Dotti (who unfortunately passed away in 2018), Michael Marder, Rafael Simian, Manfred Svensson, Daniel Mansuy, and Joaquín García-Huidobro, all of whom read and commented on parts of the book. Additionally, let me express my deep gratitude to my graduate students at Diego Portales University (Chile), who took the courses where I taught the ideas presented here. I am also grateful to everyone who attended the congresses, workshops, and seminars in Valparaiso, Santiago, Würzburg, Leiden, Curitiba, and Uberlândia, where I had a chance to discuss my views. I should like to thank the Chilean National Council for Science and Technology (CONICYT), which provided generous resources to bring the book to completion (within the framework of project no. 1190199). My gratitude extends to the Diego Portales University, where I could have enough time to do the research necessary to write this book. I must thank Rafael Simian for his translation work, and he and Cheryl Emerson for reviewing the manuscript. Finally, I should like to thank the State University of New York Press for accepting this work as part of its catalogue and the two anonymous reviewers for their comments.

Foreword

Carl Schmitt repeatedly understood himself as a jurist. In his own view, he thus situates himself between two disciplines: technology and theology. These disciplines hold two extreme positions. They do not sufficiently thematize their presuppositions. Given that, in Schmitt's classification, juridical thought and the extremes of technology and theology exhaust the possible ways of human understanding, juridical thought is, for him, superior to the extremes. Schmitt identifies juridical thought with philosophy. This identification entails broadening the scope of this discipline in unusual ways, beyond juridical science strictly speaking, to include existence as a whole. Such broadening is doubly justified. Besides the fact that, for Schmitt, juridical thought is able to thematize and address problems that the two extreme disciplines cannot properly identify, existence as such is juridical for him. Existence may be described as a tension and a relation between general rules and particular cases. The law, broadly conceived, as a form of rationality that emerges with these original tension and relation in view, seems to be the most appropriate kind of understanding for elucidating existence in a hermeneutical radical manner.

Among the countless interpretations of Schmitt's thought, some link it with technological rationality, while others see it as theologically determined. In a previous book, I attempted to clarify the relation between Schmitt's thought and the tradition of practical philosophy (*praktische Philosophie*).[1] That study concluded that the bases of Schmitt's work must be sought neither in his circumstances, nor in his religious motivations, but rather in a set of very sophisticated arguments and justifications. In the present book, I have restricted and at the same time broadened the scope of my research, to focus upon the interpretations linking Schmitt's thought to either technology or theology. Through the discussion of both readings and the analysis of Schmitt's texts, I will try to establish whether his self-description as a jurist, according to the use he makes of this latter term, is plausible, on one hand; and, if it is plausible, whether—and in what sense—his juridical thought is relevant for elucidating human understanding in general, on the other.

Introduction

Schmitt's Self-Understanding

In his work, Carl Schmitt clearly understands himself to be a jurist. He goes so far as to claim the following: "I have always spoken and written as a jurist, and hence also genuinely only for and to jurists."[1] The same self-definition appears in *Political Theology, The Concept of the Political, The Nomos of the Earth, Ex Captivitate Salus, The Tyranny of Values*, and *Political Theology II*.[2] But is Schmitt actually a jurist? Or is he rather a political theologian, or perhaps a thinker bound to a form of technological rationality, as some have said? And in what sense should one understand Schmitt's words, namely, "being a jurist"?

In *The Nomos of the Earth* there is a strange thesis—repeated in "The Plight of European Jurisprudence," *Ex Captivitate Salus*, and the *Glossarium*—namely, that the law lies between technology and theology.[3] Schmitt advances this thesis in the context of a threefold scheme comprising all available epistemological possibilities. Technology is inclined toward "complete functionalism," whereas theology is inclined, says Schmitt, toward the extreme of a "complete substantialism."[4] The law—and Schmitt as jurist—lies between them. The ideal of technology aims at a calculating and controlling rationality, in which knowledge is attained via the construction of the object or the subsumption of cases under general rules.[5] Theology, in turn, is bound to substantialism in the sense that it entails the wholesale acceptance of a transcendent reality.[6]

The intermediate position held by Schmitt does not follow from a compromise between the extremes, but from a hermeneutical and epistemological consideration. Schmitt criticizes technology for ignoring the exceptionality and meaning of concrete existence. On the other hand, theology is criticized for favoring the "result" over "method"—in other words, for surrendering to an alleged substantial existence without exercising due epistemological controls.

The law's superior position in relation to both technology and theology is what justifies the unusual identification Schmitt defends between the law and human understanding in general, on one hand; and between juridical thought and "a philosophy of concrete life," on the other.[7] Juridical thought is held as the most fundamental way of understanding existence, because it is capable of thematizing existence including its "seriousness" and of reflexively considering the tension and relation between rule and case, the abstract and the concrete, the general and the exceptional.[8]

Two Contemporary Interpretations

Schmitt's thought has been understood either as bound to technological rationality or as theologically determined. Each of these readings bears further consideration. If either were correct, Schmitt's characterization of himself would be false. He could not be understood as a jurist, and the hermeneutical scope of his thought would be restricted. As for the interpretation that links Schmitt's thought to the rationality of technology, I shall concentrate on the works of Jacques Derrida; for the interpretation that sees Schmitt eminently as a theologian, I shall focus on the works of Heinrich Meier. Notwithstanding the fact that the theological interpretation has had earlier exponents, Meier has been particularly successful in placing it at the center of Schmitt scholarship. Because Derrida and Meier have been enormously influential in shaping current studies on Carl Schmitt, singling them out for discussion as representative authors of the interpretations that link Schmitt respectively with technology and theology rests on the paradigmatic character of their readings.

According to Jacques Derrida, Schmitt's thought should be seen as bound to technology. Derrida believes that Schmitt's thought is an expression of a form of rationality that depends on the modern distinction between an autonomous subject and an object determined by an inquiring gaze. The subject is conceived as a spontaneous identity that is invulnerable—insofar as it is active and inquiring—to the irruption of the other.

According to Meier, Schmitt's thought should instead be mainly understood as political theology: "'Political theology' is the apt and solely appropriate characterization of Schmitt's *doctrine*."[9] Political theology is, for Meier, ultimately incompatible with philosophy. Actually, it is incompatible with any attempt to elucidate existence critically, insofar as it is based on religious dogma. Meier affirms that political theology is defined, as a discipline, by the claim that "divine revelation is the supreme authority and the ultimate ground."[10] "Human wisdom,"[11] does not play a determining role in its "foundation."[12] Schmitt's task, then, as a political theologian, is not limited to showing some relations between political or juridical concepts and a certain religious tradition, but consists in an effort to ground politics and law upon faith.

Both interpretations differ in their results, but also in the way their authors proceed. In Meier's case, his starting point is a conception of philosophy according to which philosophy is fundamentally opposed to theology. If philosophy follows the path of argumentative justification and "human wisdom," theology follows the path of "faith."[13] Once these two disciplines are distinguished, Meier locates Schmitt within the sphere of theology. To prove his thesis, Meier collects a number of texts that he interprets as documentary evidence. Meier's proceeding is questionable. It seems unlikely that Schmitt's thought was not only motivated but actually determined by dogmatic theology, if one considers the impressive reception his thought has had, and still has, in both philosophy and the theory of politics and law. Further, this interpretation could end up encapsulating Schmitt's thought, which should be ultimately abandoned as dogma and disqualified for rational assessment regarding its eventual intrinsic validity. On the contrary, Schmitt's texts contain many relevant and differentiated arguments, as well as significant methodological reflections, along with passages where Schmitt justifiably distances himself from theology—passages Meier tends to ignore.

Derrida proceeds in a different manner, though he does take a critical distance from what he sees as an inclination on the part of Schmitt toward a form of technical or manipulative rationality. Derrida acknowledges Schmitt's thought as having theoretical weight. According to him, Schmitt's work is "deeply rooted in the richest tradition of the theological, juridical, political and philosophical culture of Europe," and deserves a "serious reading."[14] The problem with Derrida's interpretation appears on a different level, and it may be seen as twofold. On one hand, there are aspects of Derrida's reading that require qualification. According to Schmitt, neither in the exceptional nor in the normal situation should the law be necessarily seen as a form of manipulative rationality. For Schmitt, the law does not shut itself off from what is to come. Although he plausibly argues in favor of an irreducible "distance" in which the subject must find herself, and in favor of a spontaneous conceptualizing activity she must perform if she is to become conscious, Schmitt does recognize a heteronomous aspect of existence. On the other hand, it should be noticed that there are important similarities between Schmitt's and Derrida's conception of the law. These similarities are particularly clear if one heeds a text Derrida omits, where Schmitt develops ideas that closely resemble those later found in Derrida's "Force of Law."

Despite their differences regarding results and procedure, the theological and technological interpretations agree in a fundamental respect, in that Schmitt's thought is removed from its place within the threefold scheme of human understanding. It is no longer found between the substantialism of theology and the calculating rationality of technology, but tilts toward either extreme. Beyond the merits of each interpretation and the light they shed upon many aspects of Schmitt's thought, I think they do not sufficiently reflect on his conception of the law, and on the different ways in which he tries to legitimize the juridical form of understanding as fundamental.

The hermeneutical superiority of the law compared to theology and technology is ultimately based on the fact that, from the very start, the law considers a tension lying at the ground of all human understanding.[15] This tension is a central subject for juridical science. The problem Schmitt addresses from the beginning (already in 1912) is that of the relation and difference between rule and case, norm and situation; or, more broadly, between the general and the particular—between normality and exception.[16] Taking these aspects into account, and conceiving them as members in tension, are proper to a form of understanding that Schmitt calls "jurisprudence."[17] There are a difference and relation between rule and case, and it is by seeing them and thematizing them that juridical understanding emerges. By virtue of that difference and relation, the validity of the rule appears relative. The case, in turn, seems to be more than a mere instantiation of the rule.[18]

Juridical understanding, for Schmitt, takes on the character of an understanding of existence as such, not only of its juridical aspect. The broadening of juridical understanding is grounded on the claim that the problem of the relation and tension between generality and singularity, implied in the problem of the relation and tension between rule and case, is to be ultimately identified with the problem of the tension and the relation between thought and reality.[19] Thus, the law is a form of understanding that embraces the whole of existence. Its problem and its methodological approach to existence coincide with the question regarding the conditions for human understanding. The law achieves its highest hermeneutical level, and coincides with the "philosophy of concrete life," when it explicitly thematizes this question.[20]

An Argumentative Roadmap

This book is divided into three chapters. The first, in three parts, deals with the relation between law and technological rationality. In the first part, I expound Derrida's interpretation, which links Schmitt's thought to technology. The second part contains an analysis of Schmitt's texts in which he compares the law with technological rationality. For Schmitt, more than mere technique or simple artifact, technology is a manner of understanding that distinguishes itself by prescinding from what is exceptional, from the meaning of experience, from the singularity of the individual (the other), and from the concrete peculiarity of the situation. Juridical understanding, on the contrary, recognizes those aspects of existence. Unlike technology, which does not sufficiently thematize the conditions for understanding, and hence for itself as a manner of understanding, juridical thought does. In the third part of the chapter, I return to Derrida's reading of Schmitt to answer some of his criticisms and to show significant points of agreement between these two authors.

The second chapter is also divided into three parts, structurally similar to the first, but the focus now is theology. In the first part, I expound Heinrich Meier's interpretation of Schmitt's thought as theologically determined. In the second, and based on the analysis of Schmitt's texts, I attempt to mark a contrast between the law and theology. Provisionally, it may be said that, according to Schmitt, theology is characterized by its surrendering to the exceptional without due epistemological control, and to the meaning supposedly emanated from the divine. Moreover, theology is inclined to disregard the problem of the legitimacy of the means, of normality, and the other, for the sake of the end. Juridical thought, instead, recognizes transcendence as transcendence, attending not only to the "result," but also to "method;" that is, it exercises intense epistemological control, yet without overstretching and becoming like technology.[21] The law recognizes a meaning in existence, but with more methodological emphasis than theology. The law concerns itself with the end as much as with the means, with normality as much as with exception, and with the other (it is "*ad alterum*"). Ultimately, unlike a substantialist theology, juridical thought thematizes the conditions for human understanding. In the third part, having all these differences in view, I return to Meier's interpretation of Schmitt.

In the final chapter, based on the analyses of Schmitt's texts and the discussion of the two contemporary interpretations just mentioned, I attempt to determine the main aspects of Schmitt's hermeneutical thought, including the characteristics that he attributes to the law as a fundamental manner of understanding, and to demonstrate how Schmitt's main works are expressions of such hermeneutical thought.

The Juridical and the Political

To determine the scope of my interpretation, it is important to briefly address the relation between Schmitt's juridical thought (taken broadly) and his political thought, as the places they hold within Schmitt's oeuvre are not symmetrical. Even if his political thought is discernible from the juridical, the former is not completely autonomous or independent from the latter, but is rather determined by it. His political thought is part of the juridical in the broad sense as philosophy of concrete life. This is for now a tentative claim, but in this book I strive to establish that the way in which Schmitt understands reality is fundamentally juridical, and this kind of understanding has a general scope; hence, it includes the political. Juridical understanding allows Schmitt to see, moreover, that human existence arises from an abyss of indeterminacy, and that it does not emerge as neutral, but bestowed with meaning. It is within this context that the political finds its proper place.[22] The exceptional character of existence and its meaning function as conditions for politics. The political is affected, then, by the existential determinations Schmitt discerns in juridical understanding. In addition, the problem of human understanding has similar practical implications for both the law in a strict sense and politics. The situation must be understood, but it is also necessary to reach a decision—a right and just one, in the case of the law;[23] a legitimate one, in the case of politics.[24] Further, Schmitt's texts allow for the thought that the manner of articulation of political conglomerates resembles or approaches the manner in which juridical institutions are formed: In both cases, there are certain ideas that actually shape reality (either in the juridical situation[25] or in the political existence of a people),[26] thus giving it stable expression. The political can be characterized as the part of the practical realm that is determined by the intensification of the existential tension. The practical realm is a dimension of meaning. But the tension in it can be more or less intense. At the moment of intensification, when the seriousness increases, the practical becomes political. A difference "of quantity" regarding the tension's degree of intensity results in the fact that "the point of the political is reached and with it a qualitatively new intensity of human groupings."[27] However, the juridical structure of existence remains, as a tension and relation between rules and cases, where human understanding should aim at giving the case an adequate, right, or legitimate expression. The quantity of intensity is the quantity *of a quality*: the meaning of existence, tensioned between life and death.[28]

Chapter 1

Law and Technology

Jacques Derrida's Interpretation

In Derrida's lengthy treatment of Schmitt's thought, the latter appears bound to a calculating and controlling rationality in which the exceptional and the otherness of the other are neglected. Within this framework, Schmitt's thought conceives the individual as a spontaneous subject that becomes involved with the other in an inquisitive and determining manner. In the juridical and political spheres, this conception is expressed by the non-problematized affirmation of a sovereign subject who places the other in front of her and decides in a manipulative way.

Derrida says that Schmitt understands the subject classically, that is, as an active spontaneity, identical to itself and—insofar as it is active and identical—as a "calculable permanence."[1] That spontaneous and permanent "identity" is invulnerable; it is a nonreceptive activity. Such a subject is incompatible with the advent of the "event" and the experience of "the other."[2] The "eventness of an event" and the experience of "the other," if they take place, must overstep the boundaries of the objective or phenomenal order.[3] An authentic event is that which is not predictable based on the initial conditions.[4] And every "other" is an "originary non-presence," which retracts before the attempt of a phenomenalizing determination.[5] Opening to the event and the other, to the possibility of their advent, requires exposition, receptivity, passivity, vulnerability—a ceasing of the objectifying activity and control on the part of the individual.[6] This requirement, according to Derrida, cannot be fulfilled by the Schmittian subject.

The Schmittian subject emerges by establishing a distance regarding the other. This distance has an inquisitive character. The spontaneous subject enters into a relation with the other by putting the latter "into question."[7] By means of this inquisitive attitude, the subject places the other before her. The inquisitive attitude proceeds through a determining language that persists in the general identity of concepts and rules. The individual is thus unacknowledged in her depth of alterity and singularity, and brought into "the order of phenomenology" established by the subject.[8]

The ability to fix existence in definitions subjects the other to stable and general rules. Derrida affirms that "the very definition of the definition" supposes "hostility."[9] The active "putting in front inquisitively" is an operation that is ultimately violent. This inquisitive violence accompanies philosophy from its very beginning. "The history of the question, starting with the question of being, likewise for the entire history governed by it (*philosophía, epistémê, istoría*, research, inquest, appeal, inquisition, requisition, and so forth), could not have taken place without polemical violence, without strategy and without arms techniques."[10] The inquisitive subject's putting into question is not, then, just theoretical, but also—and fundamentally—practical. Thinking that starts by questioning ends up turning the other into someone subjected to the violent activity of questioning.

Yet even if the other is fixed through language, through inquisitive and generalizing activity, and is thus reduced to the "order of phenomenology," her alterity is not thereby abolished.[11] "The other appears as a being whose appearance appears without appearing, without being submitted to the phenomenological law of the originary and intuitive given that governs all other appearances."[12] Questioning, then, amounts to reducing by means of hostile treatment, which nevertheless does not eliminate the other's existential depth. In that depth there subsists an indetermination, a "novelty,"[13] an irreducible "eventness."[14]

With the questioning of the inquisitive subject, the other, unknown in her alterity, ends up being placed in front as a subject brought for questioning, as an "enemy."[15] Inquisitiveness and hostility ultimately go hand in hand.[16] The Schmittian subject of "the theory of the exception and of sovereignty" operates on this basis.[17] The sovereign decision in the state of exception is but the last consequence of Schmitt's conception of the subject. Facing the event, the exception, the sovereign subject takes the initiative by means of the decision that sets the other apart, thus avoiding the experience of her eventness and otherness.[18]

The Schmittian subject is thus doubly invulnerable. First, as the questioning subject, she puts before her, in a controlled phenomenal manner, anything confronting her. To this epistemological control, which impedes the subject from being approached by an event and an alterity that surprises her and alters her identity, another control is added, namely, that of the sovereign subject that makes a decision in exceptional situations. By means of the technical-juridical mechanism, she suppresses the other as an enemy. The correlate of the Schmittian subject's invulnerability is an other that is doubly excluded. First, the other is submitted to "the order of phenomenology." Thus, her alterity, which resists that order, is neglected. Second, the other is excluded precisely insofar as the subject of the decision tries to subdue the "exceptional situation" and abolish the irruption of what is radically other.[19]

For Derrida, the juridical rationality works in an eminently controlling manner not only in the situation of exception, but also in normality. I think it is important to clarify that I use the term "normality" in a relative sense, to allude to the situation generated once the juridical-political exception has been suspended. In truth, total normality never takes place. The singular, the other, are present not just in juridical-political exception, but also during peacetime, bringing into crisis the rules of understanding and law. Derrida shows that the juridical rationality always hosts within itself, even in normal situations, a controlling potential.

In normality there is imposition inasmuch as the singularity and concreteness of the situations are, in principle, heterogeneous from the generality of the rules.[20] Derrida states it thus: "How are we to reconcile the act of justice that must always concern singularity, individuals, irreplaceable groups and lives, the other or myself as other, in a unique situation, with rule, norm, value or the imperative of justice which necessarily have a general form . . . ?"[21] The law as rule is always in tension with the singularity both of the situation and of the other.[22] The problem of manipulation, therefore, is not only a menace to Schmitt's doctrine of the state of exception, where the individual is placed under a violent and hostile decision. The problem also arises regarding the law in the normal situation, for the individual is in a way reified and manipulated by being understood on the basis of rules that reduce her singularity.

In the case of the law of normality, the agent who must reach a juridical decision occupies an ambivalent position, according to Derrida. The normal and continual functioning of the law may lead to a mechanical application of it—a law that is general and allows for calculation regarding the other. In this case, the subject protects herself under the law, merely enforcing it, treading on the other's singularity.[23] The one making the decision acts as a "calculating machine."[24] This way of operating is a form of nonexposition of the subject, similar to that of the sovereign decision or of the active inquiring. In all these cases the subject shields herself with some machinery.[25] But in juridical normality a second possibility opens itself, namely, taking responsibility for the decision and for the search for justice, altering the literal sense of the law if necessary. "For a decision to be just and responsible, it must, in its proper moment if there is one, be both regulated and without regulation; it must conserve the law and also destroy it or suspend it enough to have to reinvent it in each case, re-justify it, at least reinvent it in the reaffirmation and the new and free confirmation of its principle."[26] This way of acting enables an openness to the alterity of the other, because it rests on a noninquisitive attitude, an attitude of exposition and receptivity. To a certain extent, the one making the decision makes it passively, letting herself be approached by the alterity of the advening other.[27]

Derrida submits the conception—which he thinks operates in Schmitt's works—of an autonomous and inquisitive subjectivity to a severe critique. This critique opens the path for a way of understanding, within a juridical context, that makes it possible to grasp the other without reducing her (or at least without reducing her as much). According to Derrida, the inquisitive subject is not ultimately original. He also tries to show that, although the generalizing violence of every concept and of human understanding cannot be completely subdued, it can in fact be relativized.

Human beings come into existence and become conscious through speaking, which refers each of them to an other. Speaking with an other presupposes vulnerability, receptivity—an openness to a previous alterity. The "putting into question" is preceded by an "acquiescence [*Zusage*]" in speaking.[28] That "acquiescence" is "more originary than the question."[29] The acquiescence in speaking entails an openness and a relation to the other, a common participation in language. Derrida calls this relation "friendship prior to friendships."[30] This relation is what makes questioning possible.[31] Before questioning, human beings must already find themselves in language, and such finding-oneself-in-language always entails being found next to an other in language, that is, it entails the experience of an initial heteronomy. "The very possibility of the question, in the form of 'what is . . . ?,' thus seems, from the beginning, to suppose this friendship prior to friendships, this *anterior* affirmation of being-together in allocution."[32] In this sense, it could be said that the other is prior to the self: "The other is the condition of my immanence."[33] The acquiescence regarding the other in language is a requirement for the constitution of one's own immanence. In the beginning, there is no identity, but difference: the remission of autonomy to a heteronomy.

The openness to the other, the acquiescence in language, the friendship prior to friendships, are preceded by a *"perhaps"*—by an indeterminacy.[34] The latter announces what Derrida considers to be a *basis* in the structure of language.

The language with which one thinks and questions is not some set of self-identical meanings in the hands of an already constituted subject. Language is, according to Derrida's interpretation of Ferdinand de Saussure's thesis,[35] a "play of differences."[36] "Every concept"—says Derrida—"is necessarily and essentially inscribed in a chain or a system, within which it refers to another and to other concepts."[37] Saussure illustrates this dependency with the following example: "Within the same language, all words used to express related ideas limit each other reciprocally; synonyms like French *redouter* 'dread,' *craindre* 'fear,' and *avoir peur* 'be afraid' have value only through contact with others."[38] If one of those words disappeared, the meaning of the others would change.

The ideal content is inscribed in the "sign." Along with the "signified aspect" or the "ideal sense," the sign includes a "signifying aspect:" the "material image" of the sign, the grapheme or phoneme.[39] This signifying aspect bestows the sign with a certain stability—a sort of "self-identity." Such stability makes its "recognition and repetition" possible.[40] Besides making recognition and repetition possible, this stability allows the sign to enter into different contexts, to separate itself from the previous context.[41] Due to that independence regarding contexts, the sign can be involved in a dynamic process, where signifier and meaning are modified. The sign, with its signifier and meaning, is inserted within the aforementioned "play of differences." The variation of the signifying aspect from one act of understanding to another, its moving from one context to another, makes it impossible for there to be a fixed context. Given that the signifier is independent of any context, and that in each new context it enters into a relation with other signifiers, there are "only contexts without any center of absolute anchoring."[42]

This play forbids the existence of an invariant meaning, of a "transcendental signified."[43] Rather, meanings are "effects" from the "differential system."⁴⁴ Signs are affected by, and vary according to, the position they acquire in a system of signs. The context of relations between the signs does not cease to vary. Consequently, neither does the differentiating process on which the constitution of meaning depends. This movement of signifiers regarding the different acts of understanding determines that the "signified idealities" or the "conceptual identities" cannot remain "intact," but should vary.⁴⁵ Acts of understanding, under the dynamism and the movements to which the signs are subject, cause the signs to change their meaning.⁴⁶ "The meaning" is enmeshed in the "indefinite referral of signifier to signifier." In this dynamic, the "signified meaning" finds neither "respite" nor "rest," but is affected in such a way that the meaning "always signifies again and differs."⁴⁷

At the basis of the differential game of language and its multiple remissions there lies what Derrida calls "*la différance*"—that is, the movement that makes the differential game of language possible. "*Différance*," says Derrida, "is no longer simply a concept, but the possibility of conceptuality, of the conceptual system and process in general."⁴⁸ It is not a positive principle, an original identity; instead, as its name and the effect to which it alludes indicate, it is a "differing" that includes both the reference to a "distinction" and to a "temporalizing," a "spacing," and an "opposition."⁴⁹

The game of language is inscribed within the movement of *différance*. Within it the purported identity of meanings becomes possible, due to the "repetition" that can be executed in that game, given the relative stability of the sign. Moreover, it is within the *différance* that the formation of one's subjectivity becomes possible.⁵⁰ Derrida reverts the postulate of transcendental philosophy, or of any philosophy that conceives of subjectivity as an original spontaneity.⁵¹ "Language [which consists only of differences] is not a function of the speaking subject. This implies that the subject (self-identical or even conscious of self-identity, self-conscious) is inscribed in the language, that he is a function of the language. He becomes a *speaking* subject only by conforming his speech . . . to the system of linguistic prescriptions taken as the system of differences."⁵² Subjectivity is the product of language.⁵³ "Consciousness" does not allude to an original phenomenon, for consciousness is always achieved via a "determination," as an "effect" of the "*différance*."⁵⁴

If one considers the heteronomy of language, one should recognize an initial alterity. Without language and the other, there is no identity. Thus, the conception of the inquisitive subject as an ultimate, identical, and invulnerable function is dissolved. This thesis also entails the possibility of a nonreductive consideration of the other, within human understanding and within the juridical context.

By attending to the variability of the signs' meanings, two paths are opened. It is possible to understand in such a way that this variability is recognized and made fruitful for adjusting the signs to the alterity and the singularity of the other. This variability also affects the juridical rules, so that juridical decisions may resignify those rules insofar as they heed the alterity of the other. But it is also possible for a manner of understanding to emerge such that it takes refuge in the subject's identity and persists in keeping the clarity and rigidity of conceptualizations, thus realizing an objectifying determination that reduces the other to the phenomenal sphere. In the juridical situation, the emphasis lies on a sovereign decision and on the decisionism of a politics of enmity,[55] as well as on the normative-subsumptive regulation of the singular.[56] This is the position one finds, according to Derrida, in Carl Schmitt.

The Schmittian manipulative effort is clearly shown—so Derrida thinks—not only in Schmitt's conception of the subject, but in his search for "a pure and rigorous conceptual theory;"[57] in his faithfulness to the "rigour of the concept;"[58] in his defense of a clear distinction between friend and enemy.[59] On the contrary, the consideration of the alterity of the other and of the instability of the meanings within language allows Derrida to see that the other cannot ultimately be fixed under the strictness of concepts, including those of friend and enemy. The identification of the other as friend or enemy presupposes the procedure of "putting into question" carried out by the inquisitive, spontaneous subject, who manages to fix the other by determining her.[60] Yet this manner of understanding, as previously discussed, supposes another "logic": that of initial "being-together in allocution." The fixing and inquisitive differentiation appears only later, within a language in which the other first emerges as an other.

Based on this consideration, Derrida detects in Schmitt's distinction between friend and enemy a possibility that seems to make it too unstable to be submitted to inquisitive conceptualization. In its irreducible and surprising alterity, friend and enemy may change roles. Moreover, it should also be noted that enmity involves a possibility for friendship even fuller than friendship itself. The tension of enmity allows for the enemy to be more attentive to the other in her singularity and to achieve a deeper understanding of her than one that results from a friendship resting on general conventions.[61]

Derrida's observations on law unveil an eventual tension, or even an inconsistency, in Schmitt's thought. On the one hand, Schmitt tries to distinguish juridical rationality from the technical; while, on the other, juridical rationality emerges—in the states of exception and normality—as a controlling rationality. Further, Schmitt's thought appears, to Derrida, as a defense "against what is to come"—against the emergency of an indeterminate other. That defense is expressed in his rigorous conceptualizations; in a conception of the subject as inquisitive identity; in the clear-cut opposition between friend and enemy; in a sovereign and decisionist idea of decision in which the advent of the exceptional and the other as the exceptional are precluded.[62] This controlling rationality would be the result of an eagerness to know and control, whose correlate would be "anguish"[63] or "dread"[64] before the exceptional, the new, the event, the other.[65]

Derrida raises the problem of the tension between the law—of the state of exception and of normality—and justice, showing that, in the case of legal exception, as well as in the case of legal normality, the law approaches the technological rationality. He also unveils the conception of the subject that underlies the basis of both forms of understanding and decision. He shows, moreover, the controlling character of Schmitt's thought and the dread and anguish before the exceptional that motivates it. However, the problem of the tension between the law—of emergency and normality—and the exceptional and singular does not go unnoticed in Schmitt's work. On the contrary, it is the subject of many reflections throughout his writings, where he tries to thematize and ease the tension in a way not dissimilar to that of Derrida's. Schmitt's texts reveal a manner of understanding that he considers to be both juridical and different from the technological rationality, insofar as it is open to the exceptional, to the meaning of the situation and to the other.

Two Kinds of Understanding

As is the case with most of the subjects Schmitt addresses, there is no specific treatment of the question of technology expressed in a single work. His thoughts about technology must be sought in numerous passages spread throughout his books, articles, and notes from various periods.[66] Usually, when Schmitt deals with technology, he does so in connection with the law, theology, politics, the elements (earth, sea, air, fire), or art. However, a more expansive study of his texts discloses a pertinent reflection on technological rationality. To be sure, Schmitt's reflection on technology has many features in common with those of some of his contemporaries.[67] Nonetheless, his remarks are original to a certain extent. Early on, he observes that technology is not only a mechanical artifact or device—mere machinery—but fundamentally a kind "of human understanding."[68] This kind of understanding determines existence in a specific way. Moreover, there is an operating motive at its basis. As we shall see, technology determines existence in an objective, calculating, and manipulating manner. Its base motive is prediction and control. Schmitt calls the mechanical aspect of technology a "soulless mechanism [*seelenlose Mechanismus*]"[69] or "the machine."[70] He names technology as a kind of "human understanding" the "spirit" of technology, "spirit of technicity [*Geist der Technizität*]," or the "rationalism of . . . technology."[71]

Herein Schmitt distances himself from Max Weber. He thinks the latter's work is not equipped with the theoretical tools to adequately address the issue of technology. Weber opposes the "spirit" to the "irresistible power of technology [*unwiderstehliche Macht der Technik*],"[72] thus dividing what for Schmitt are distinguishable but not separable aspects of one reality. By placing on one side the mechanical and on the other the spiritual, "spirit" becomes "powerless [*ohnmächtig*]" before the power of the machine.[73] On the contrary, by revealing the "spirit" behind the machine, Schmitt is in position to criticize the very ground of technology: to discover its limits as a manner of understanding, its unquestioned premises, and thus to compare it with other kinds of understanding.[74]

In this section, I expound Schmitt's treatment of technology. In studying Schmitt's treatment, I compare the technological and the juridical rationality, with a view not only to grasp Schmitt's conception of the technological rationality, but also of the juridical.

It is possible to discern four relevant differences between the juridical and the technological rationality in Schmitt's texts. First, the technological rationality is closed to the exception, whereas the juridical understanding is open to it. Second, the technological rationality neutralizes what Schmitt calls "the order of meaning" in existence, but the juridical rationality actually takes it into account. Third, the technological rationality does not regard the otherness or nonphenomenal character of individuals, whereas the juridical rationality attends to this aspect. Fourth and finally, the technological rationality does not thematize its own premises as a kind of understanding, while juridical thought does thematize them.

Closedness versus Openness to the Exceptional

Technology is a generalizing kind of rationality. It aims at identifying relations or constant sequences between sense-perceptible phenomena that allow themselves to be understood under a general rule. Its goal is to reach what is calculable and predictable in reality.[75] For the "rationalism of . . . technology," says Schmitt, "everything is calculable."[76] It certainly takes reality into account, and this is what the experiment is set out to do. The emphasis, however, is not on the concrete peculiarity of the case, but on the possibility of obtaining a general rule, one that is apt to be applied to a whole kind of cases. The case is reduced to an instantiation of rules: to an instantiation that is observable through the senses, exposed or manifest, determined, and generalizable.[77] By means of this procedure, rules are obtained that enable the prediction of cases and processes. It may be that new observations invalidate a certain rule. If so, the technological understanding hypothetically formulates a new rule, which is then tested against new experiments. Yet the relation of subjection between the rule and what is given is not altered. The kind of rule and the kind of case are already defined. The case is deprived of interiority. The rules fix empirical, exposed cases. Considerations regarding the cases—their interiority, their "depth"—cannot consequently modify the meaning of the rule. Such "depth" or interiority of the cases, any dynamism foreign to their phenomenality and in virtue of which a case may acquire a new meaning for the one experiencing it—all that is discarded beforehand.[78]

Generalization and predictability are parts of a broader process in which reality is understood in such a way that it may even become the object of "manipulations and domination."[79] In calculating and predicting, the point is ultimately to provide "formulae for the manipulation of matter."[80] The disciplined exclusion of the exceptionality, the depth, and the alterity of existence by means of formalizations make reality suitable for the subsequent execution of technological control. The distinction between generalization, calculation, control, and manipulation enables to discern two aspects of what Schmitt calls technology—namely, a scientific one, related to generalizing prediction, as well as an aspect specifically concerned with manipulation and control.[81] Both sides, however, may be seen as forming a unitary process. Therefore, they may be distinguished, but not separated. Each requires the other. Without calculation and prediction, technical disposition and control are impossible;[82] without technique, modern science cannot operate as device.[83] And, as we shall see, they are animated by the same intention.[84]

Because of its method, technology, at the same time that it gains in possibilities for calculation and prediction, dominion, and control, also diminishes in capacity for understanding. To regulate the cases and turn them into nothing but instantiations of a rule within a series of cases, one must consider them only according to their generalizable marks, that is, as determined phenomena.[85] Insofar as their depth or existential meaning is put out of play,[86] they become superficial: exposed objects, fixed as appearances.[87]

If the case is regarded in its existential import, as a singular event, and not only in what it shares with other regulated cases, then it may happen that the case varies as it continues to be the same. It is not unusual in juridical experience for the situations described in general terms to arise in an exceptional manner. That is to say, it is not unusual for them to be the same and yet different.[88] Some action is described in the law taken only in its general aspects. But every judge knows that each real case, notwithstanding its similarity with others of its kind, is different from all the others. The same appears as an other.[89] Existence has a depth that makes it exceptional. The situations we experience let themselves be described according to general marks. But it would be reductionist to try to consider them as no more than instantiations of a rule, lacking the existential significance that makes of each of them a particular and specific case.[90] This is why in human experience concepts should not be considered as determinant or fixing rules, but as notions that remain open to the irruption of the new.[91]

Schmitt claims that juridical thought in a broad sense or as "philosophy of concrete life" "must not withdraw from the exception," "but must be interested in it to the highest degree."[92] In *Political Theology*, he also writes: "The rule proves nothing; the exception proves everything: It confirms not only the rule but also its existence, which derives only from the exception. In the exception, the power of real life breaks through the crust of a mechanism that becomes torpid by repetition."[93] Schmitt highlights the exceptionality of human existence and the precariousness of the normality on which science and technology, as well as the technical-juridical understanding, are set to work. Normality is based on a background of indetermination, on a nothingness of normality, from which normality arises and to which it is always related.

The human being is affected by the exception in two senses. First, it comes into existence, but without the ability to be aware of the event of coming to be. It is not capable of achieving a full understanding of its existence and ground (which is, therefore, rather a "non-ground"). To exist is, in a way, the inability to understand how it is that one exists—to be irrevocably and persistently remitted to an abyss. Its own existence is, finally, a mystery, an "unfathomable" fact, an "open question."[94] Existence as a whole emerges from that exceptionality and is affected by the exceptional and its eventual irruption. Insofar as the human mind is finite and is thrown into existence without knowledge of its own foundations, it is impossible for it to rule out the emergence of the exceptional.[95] If normality means the validity of general rules, and the exception is the interruption of those rules by a case that trespasses them, then the recognition of the exception implies the relativization of generalities. Every generality is affected by the exception. What is general, therefore, is only properly understood if the exception is taken into account. Our awareness of the exception is what allows us to understand the meaning, the limits, and the scope of the general.[96] There are facts that can be glimpsed in previous facts and from the normal conditions of existence. Here, one proceeds by means of "clear generalizations inferred from what ordinarily repeats itself."[97] Nonetheless, these generalizations are insufficient to grasp the exceptional, the depth—the alterity betrayed by concrete existence and by each situation taking place in concrete reality. The case then arises as something different from a mere instantiation of a rule.[98] At the basis of existence and affecting every part of it is "an ineluctable reality that no human mind has conceived,"[99] capable of breaking "through the crust" of normality and its rules. Not only the juridical rules or those established by human beings, but also the rules identified with the usual conditions according to which human existence operates, can be affected by the event. This is what takes place when, from the concrete depth of a situation, there emerges a new meaning that dramatically alters everything we understood about it; when a new historical era irrupts;[100] when a fundamentally new state of existence advenes.[101]

The exceptional plays a second role in human experience. Schmitt speaks of a "distance"[102] of the individual with regard to others, the beings of the world, even regarding herself.[103] He follows Helmuth Plessner's thesis that the human being is "primarily a being capable of creating distance."[104] That distance is a condition for consciousness. Thinking requires distance between the one who is thinking and that which is being thought. The distance concerns not only one particular being, but all beings (other human beings, things, the thinker herself as being). It concerns the whole ontic sphere, which, once the individual begins to be conscious, is split from the individual. The possibility of such a distance can be explained only by the individual's position beyond the ontic sphere, in what Schmitt calls "transcendence [*Transzendenz*]." "Pure immanence"—writes Schmitt—would mean "the elimination of all distance [*Abstand*]," including that which is necessary for the emergence and operation of "intelligence [*Intelligenz*]."[105] Were the subject not removed from the immanent sphere, she could not perform the act of understanding; she would be in close contact with beings, totally immersed in her facticity, which would ultimately imply that she is not conscious. In "pure identity," consciousness would disappear.[106] That transcendence from which the human being realizes the act of understanding is inaccessible through the way in which determined beings are accessed. It is exceptional. The exceptional, then, is also transcendence as the stage of indeterminacy wherein human beings distance themselves from everything, so to speak, to be able to understand. Plessner discusses the activity that distances itself in the following terms: "The human being is not in the *here and now*, but rather *behind* it, behind itself, in no specific place, in nothingness . . . its existence is truly located in nothingness."[107]

Regarding the abysmal background from which existence and understanding emerge, Mika Ojakangas writes: "The transcendence in question is not to be understood as a substantial foundation of order."[108] Transcendence is not affirmed based on a "metaphysics of substance," as Renato Cristi argues.[109] Transcendence is the openness through which the human being exists and understands; it is that without which human existence would not take place in the way that it does, as an intelligible yet unfathomable existence.

Schmitt's postulate that "the rule proves nothing; the exception proves everything," means that immanence, while suspended above the exception, cannot be self-explanatory.[110] Reaching an understanding of the human condition requires being aware of human transcendence and exception. The awareness that human life is affected by the exceptional is "deeper,"[111] in at least three senses, than the habitual awareness dominated by what is seen in normality. First, because one thereby knows that the subject's existence is not completely bound to the ontic dimension, but emerges from the exceptional. Second, because it notices the contingency and historicity of existence, its unpredictable character. Third, because, as we shall see shortly, that awareness realizes that human understanding requires a step from the idealities toward the concrete; it requires going beyond the generality of the rules and concepts to reach, in dealing with a particular situation, interpretive decisions that are adequate to that situation.[112]

The exception cannot be subjected to the technical criteria of "mediation and calculability."[113] It does not allow itself to be controlled nor understood according to the "method for the contemplation of nature."[114] It is excluded from this kind of rationality from the start.[115] This exclusion is not circumstantial. Technology's way of proceeding, grounded on the intention to calculate and control, is what excludes the incontrollable and the exception from the beginning.[116] Nevertheless, technological rationality presupposes the exception. Technology as a kind of understanding can only proceed from a transcendence without which the distance required for understanding would not emerge.[117] Technology is based on an exceptionality which that understanding, due to its own way of working, avoids. Technology ignores the condition of its very possibility.[118]

Excluding versus Attending the Manner in Which Existence Is Revealed

Technology's exclusion goes even further. At the basis of the "methodology of the natural-technical sciences" operates an economy of knowledge, in virtue of which existence's manner of revealing itself is ignored. Schmitt affirms that human understanding is possible only if existence is revealed prior to the operations of the subject—if it is already intelligible. There is a prior disclosure of the situation before any conscious articulation. From its unfathomable and exceptional bottom, existence emerges elucidated to a certain extent; it does not remain completely hidden; it is neither a whole, closed in itself, nor a chaos.[119] If the concepts and rules with which human beings understand reality are to have any point of contact with reality and be valid, then the situations must already lie revealed in typical ways.[120]

In such revelation, existence arises bestowed with "meaning."[121] For Schmitt there is no such thing as a primordial separation between bare facts and pure values.[122] Existence and meaning form a unity.[123] That meaning is a condition for all human actions, a condition even for the scientific-technical understanding of existence.[124] Meaning operates in all thinking and knowing at the basis of the intention to think and to know.[125] The situations and the others,[126] the earth,[127] space,[128] existence as such,[129] do not initially emerge neutrally. The discernment of possible ways for interpretive decision before a given situation presupposes that existence is not totally neutral but meaningful. Only by connecting decisions to the existential meaning is it possible to explain such decisions taking place.[130]

On the contrary, just as technology ignores the exceptional due to its emphasis on the rule, so it ignores the revelation of existence and the meaning with which it emerges. Technology admits neutral objects alone. The meaning of existence does not let itself be determined in a precise, objective, calculable, and controllable manner. It arises in distinct ways in different situations; it is modified as history moves on. It resists an understanding defined as calculating and controlling. The exclusion of the existential meaning produced by technology may be explained, then, by recourse to its methodological restrictions.

Schmitt shows that these methodological restrictions, and the consequent exclusion or "neutralization" technology carries out, are not only due to epistemological requirements. They depend on a peculiar kind of intention to understand. Given that technology excludes the meaning of existence, it is impossible for it to thematize that intention. Behind the normalizing and dominating effort of technology there operates a double motive: On one hand is the overcoming of "anxiety [*Angst*]" before the unknown.[131] The motive for the anxiety is at the basis of technology's closedness both to the exceptional and to the meaning that stems from it. On the other, behind the intention of the scientific-technical rationality there lies what Schmitt calls a "will to power [*Wille zur Macht*]."[132] He adds: "causality = calculability = will to power."[133] By reducing existence to its sense-perceptible and quantifiable features, the scientific-technical rationality is able to calculate and control nature, thus escaping from anxiety and giving way to the "will to power."[134] Anxiety and will to power are then seen as two sides of the same basic impulse.[135]

The effort to control reality as an expression of anxiety and of the will to power is accomplished by means of "Utopia," which Schmitt defines as "organization for overcoming anxiety,"[136] and as "the product of a rationalist intellect that attempts to conquer life from the outside, with a mechanistic scheme."[137] Utopian is every intent of disciplining and controlling reality with the aim of shutting down the exceptional. The utopian attempt to rationalize existence is nevertheless condemned to failure, since the "exception" is unavoidable.[138] "What is ultimate and decisive cannot be fabricated."[139]

Technology, in its search for control, dispenses with the exceptional and the meaning of existence, for these do not fit with technology's standards of calculability and controllability. By dispensing with them, technology loses reference to any criterion that allows it, on one hand, to assess whether its understanding is adequate or fair to that meaning, and on the other, to thematize and criticize the eventual manipulation. Thus, its motivated operation can be carried out unimpeded. That is, technology itself closes the possibility of reflecting on its motivation as neutralizing understanding, and on the consequences of its motivation. Its intention is the intention of not considering intention. In the way in which it closes itself to the exceptional and to the meaning of existence, technology reveals itself as "activist."[140] It unfolds as a "process-progress (*Prozeß-Progreß*)" of increasing calculation and control.[141] This "process-progress," in its execution, hides the questions about the meaning and the exceptional. That execution is moved in a nonreflective fashion by an eagerness or *intention* of calculation and control, and is also realized in a nonreflective way by means of the *distance* made possible by the exceptional. In other words, it is an activity whose peculiar standpoint regarding existence makes it ignore its own conditions of possibility.

In contrast to the technological rationality, juridical thought does not leave aside the exceptional and the revelation of existence. It is precisely in reflecting on these issues that the "jurist" becomes aware of the limited character of the technological rationality, on one hand, and of the impossibility of explaining the law, as well as human experience, without attending to the ways in which existence is unveiled, on the other. Juridical thought is thus in the position to thematize the intention behind the other kinds of understanding, even to thematize its own.

CLOSEDNESS VERSUS OPENNESS TO THE OTHER, AND TECHNOLOGICAL CONTROL

The technological rationality, says Schmitt, has a "goal-oriented interest that is essentially objective [*sachlich*] and impersonal."[142] Its controlling and calculating interest, as well as its generalizations of phenomenal relations, prevent it from considering the depth and the existential meaning of the concrete and the otherness of human beings. It extrinsically determines human existence. It turns it into something superficial—into an exposed and available phenomenon.[143] This reduction operating in technology bears important practical consequences.

Modern science and technology increase the possibilities of prediction and manipulation of empirical phenomena. Human beings, then, have at their disposal more efficient mechanisms of domination.[144] Insofar as human beings themselves are also empirical phenomena, such an increase in control implies an increasing control of humans over humans.[145] As increasing control is imposed, "the dangerous questions about which men are to concentrate the immense power men have over men, and about the implications of said increase of technical power, cannot be formulated."[146] A grave omission takes place, analogous to the one stemming from the controlling intention that motivates technology, namely, the intention to calculate and control exercises its power without being questioned, precisely because it omits and hides itself.

With the development of technology, humans become progressively immersed in highly rationalized social contexts. Together with the increase of the possibilities to control humans by humans, existence is modified. Insofar as the technological organization unfolds and the exceptionality, depth, and meaning are left aside, human existence tends to become superficial.[147] The artifact, the machinery, is determined by the producer, and the possibilities of use offered by it are predictable and limited. Acting in an increasingly artificial world entails, therefore, acting on an increasingly fabricated, planned reality. Mystery and indetermination are apparently eliminated therein, and existence turns into an unending series of calculable moves. The "intensity" of life becomes a flat succession of trivialities, "comfortable superficiality."[148] Action is reduced to procedure, to a step in a series of steps thought out in advance and sequentially arranged. The plethora of life gives way to a thoroughly exposed and available object.[149] In this context of availability and calculability, individuals "are interested in everything, but are not inspired by anything."[150]

The rationalization and control of technology are facilitated by the fact that—as we have seen—technology is closed to the question of meaning. Thus, there is no criterion according to which one can question the adequacy, pertinence, or fairness of this understanding of existence, and so to reveal what is banal as banal.

The consideration of the exceptional and of meaning allows juridical thought to grasp the human being in its different aspects. "Philosophy of concrete life offers an even more subtle form of rationality than that represented by abstract rationalism."[151] Juridical thought notices that the human being appears to a certain extent without appearing. It emerges as a depth, as an alterity, which is "indeterminable," in the sense that it is inapprehensible in the way positive phenomena can be determined.[152] Human activity is performed from beyond the phenomenal sphere of presence and cannot be reduced to an object.[153]

The relation with the other is a condition to reach consciousness. For Schmitt, as we shall see, the subject has a prereflective or direct access to herself,[154] but actual consciousness requires alterity. The "relation [of the subject] *ad se ipsum* is not possible without a relation *ad alterum*. To be in the world means to be with others."[155] This relation with the other in the world is linguistic. The linguistic relation refers the subject to a given "community."[156] When a human being speaks, it speaks with another and "is no longer alone in the world,"[157] and so can determine itself and become aware of itself.

In that relation, the other emerges not only as a phenomenon, but also as another interiority, manifest in a certain way, but ultimately "unfathomable."[158] The other is homogeneous with the subject in the linguistic relation, but also heterogeneous with her. Because of the distance and interiority the human being recognizes in itself, which allows us to speak of an "insurmountable loneliness,"[159] it can become aware of an equivalent alterity in the other, one that transcends the limits of the phenomenal and emerges as indeterminable.[160]

Juridical thought recognizes, further, that the individual does not arise, either for herself or for another, as a neutral object. For herself, the individual emerges as a search for meaning.[161] The other, in turn, arises as meaningful otherness, with which she enters into relations that unfold in diverse degrees and modes of intensity.[162] Non-neutral indeterminacy—such is the outline of the human, as opposed to technology's neutralized and determined beings.

The recognition of the alterity and indeterminacy of the human being allows the juridical understanding to have a criterion warning it of reductionisms performed by theoretical and practical rationalizations. Schmitt states that the law is *ad alterum*, that is, it seeks to consider the other without circumscribing it to a mere object of representation and manipulation. Unlike technology, which is inclined toward functionalism, and according to which what is given in existence is constrained within the confines of an object and ultimately reduced to manipulable matter,[163] juridical understanding is "human in the deepest sense."[164] Consideration of the other manifests in the juridical search for social conformations capable of safeguarding and giving expression to the singularity of individuals, and of suspending and limiting violence among individuals and among states.[165] As a form of understanding open to the existential depth and meaning of the concrete, the law makes it possible to reveal the most alienating results of the technological rationality, and to aspire (not in a detached, but in a juridical and responsible manner) to more authentic ways of life. Herein lies a revealing and emancipating potential of juridical thought: insofar as it considers technology not just as machinery, but first and foremost as a kind of understanding, it is in position to exhibit the motives behind it and the reductions it undertakes based on those motives. The law can thus carry out the critical task of opening a path for less manipulative, less alienating and superficializing, forms of dealing with the other.

UNDERSTANDING

Juridical understanding differs significantly from technological rationality. The latter, as we have seen, operates by subsuming cases under rules, focusing on their generalizable aspect, thus repressing their depth and their meaning. The way in which technological rationality is self-enclosed is due to the methodical postulate of calculability and control. Insofar as it ignores the exceptional and the meaning of existence, the technological rationality cannot adequately consider the other. The other and the situations are reduced to instantiations of rules. The rule is defined as inalterable in regard to the cases. It might happen that the rule is false and should be replaced by a new one, but no adjustment will make the new rule able to accommodate the singularity and meaning of the case, which are ignored beforehand.[166] Technological rationality is activist: by blocking consideration of the meaning of existence and of the exceptional, it closes the path for thematizing its own presuppositions as a kind of understanding, as well as the criteria for judging its adequacy to the other and the situation. Technology, then, can display an unlimited process of reduction and manipulation of existence.

By contrast, the law's thematization of the presuppositions of human understanding makes it hermeneutically superior to technology. The juridical understanding recognizes the exceptionality of existence, the depth and meaning of the situations, and of the others in them. It realizes, in a reflective turn, that the exceptional and meaning are conditions for the possibility of understanding. Meaning is a condition for the intention to understand. The exceptional is a condition for the distance required for the emergence of consciousness. Insofar as the law attends to the depth and meaning of existence, the problem of human understanding is posed as that of the tension between the rule and the situation, between the ideal and the real—between the norm and the case. Understanding is always carried out by means of concepts and rules, but the existential depth of the situations and the others makes them resistant to these confines.[167]

The case, which "intelligence" and "jurisprudence" face, is typical but also always partially different from concepts and rules.[168] The case betrays concreteness, alterity, exceptionality, and a meaning irreducible to the limits of a being predetermined by thought. Mere thought is incapable of neutralizing and controlling these aspects. Every situation, every other, may reveal itself in new ways, making an other of what was the same.

Insofar as they are general, rules, concepts, and norms are, in themselves, inadequate for defining the cases by means of mere subsumption. Understanding via subsumption is reductivist.[169] Nonreductivist understanding is that which considers the fundamental heterogeneity between the terms of understanding. This heterogeneity determines that in every rule or concept there is what Schmitt calls a "moment of indeterminacy of content"[170] or "ambiguity."[171] That is, the meaning of the rule or concept is no more than a preliminary hermeneutical guide.[172] Given this indeterminacy, those who understand face the requirement of going beyond mere calculation in the sphere of rules and the consequent idealizing subjection of the cases. Before adopting the interpretive decision, those who understand must go to a diverse field—namely, that of the concrete and the other.[173] Only by considering concrete existence can such a decision—of jurisprudence and of intelligence in general—be adequate regarding the situation and the others in it. Thus, there emerges an understanding that is no longer abstract, but "existential"[174]—or "existentially correct [*seinsgerecht*]."[175]

Understanding, then, is not a speculation that leaves concepts and cases unscathed. If understanding is not to be reductivist, it demands not only grasping the case based on the rule, but also *the rule based on the case*.[176] From the rules and concepts brought forth by tradition, those who understand should direct themselves to the cases, and by considering their depth and alterity, reappropriate the meaning of rules and concepts and (eventually) bestow them with new meaning. Insofar as the concrete situation is considered, the "content" of the rules and concepts is affected to the point that Schmitt indicates that it "becomes immediately another."[177] The contents of words are tied to the different contexts from which they are derived and in which they have already been applied, as well as to the new contexts in which they will be applied and from which new meanings shall emerge. A pertinent understanding must be aware of this dynamism of concepts: interpretive decisions—insofar as they recognize the novel unveiling of existence and are affected by the displacements of meaning—produce a change in the hermeneutical framework.

Jacques Derrida and Schmitt's Juridical Thought

Having expounded the distinction between the technical and the juridical understanding in Schmitt's texts, and the scope this author attributes to the juridical understanding, I am now in position to return to Derrida's reading of Schmitt's thought and, in particular, to the inclination the philosopher believes he detects in such thought toward a rationality of control. We have seen that, for Derrida, Schmitt's thought approaches a rationality in which the exceptional and the alterity of the other are set aside due to a calculating and manipulative perspective. For Derrida, in Schmitt's theory the subject of understanding and decision presents itself as someone doubly invulnerable and active. First, it is assumed to be a spontaneous and inquisitive identity, which puts an epistemically controlled other in front of her. Second, control over the alterity of the other is intensified, who is differentiated as an enemy through the device of the state of exception. In the law already established, there is a primary tension between the generality of the norm and the singularity of the individuals and situations subject to it. However, here Derrida recognizes that two possibilities confront the agent: either she subsumes the case under the rule, thus manipulating the former, or she decides to recognize its singularity and thus eventually reinterprets or modifies the meaning of the norm. Reductions—both in the state of exception and in the state of relative normality—presuppose an inquisitive, objectifying subject. For Derrida, that conception of the subject is untenable, since prior to her activities the individual must emerge from within a linguistic context, in which two important factors are already implicated, namely, the alterity of the other, and a certain acquiescence on the part of the individual regarding language and the alterity coexisting with that language. Language, from within which one always enters into contact with another, allows itself to be described as a differential play of signs. Language refers the identity of the subject back to the movement, which Derrida—given the impossibility of positively determining that movement—calls "*différance*." He argues that Schmittian thought is oriented toward concepts first, rather than alterity, novelty, and the exceptional. Schmitt would be affected by a "dread" before what is to come. Because of that dread, he allegedly tries to find refuge in fixed conceptual distinctions, such as that of friend and enemy, which Derrida attempts to show as more unstable than they appear to be in Schmitt's work.

In Schmitt's thought, however, the juridical and technical rationalities are importantly different. Juridical understanding does not dispense with constitutive aspects of existence that technology does in fact ignore, and it is in position to thematize the presuppositions of human understanding. In light of these considerations, it is possible to answer, on Schmitt's behalf, Derrida's criticisms, thus qualifying the latter and showing the relation between the stances of both philosophers more precisely. If Schmitt's reflections on the juridical and the technological rationality are taken into account, it becomes difficult to affirm that we are presented with a discourse motivated by dread, a discourse aimed at defending and fending itself off from "what is to come"[178]—from "the *event.*"[179] Neither does it seem correct to say that we are faced with a markedly objectifying, ultimately manipulative discourse, either in the state of exception or in the state of normality. Schmitt's conception of the subject does not fit with that of a "classic, free, and willful subject . . . to whom nothing can happen."[180] The Schmittian subject is existentially and linguistically related to a heteronomy, to which she is vulnerable.

The Exception

A preliminary indication of Schmitt's attitude toward the event or the exceptional is apparent from the texts in which he articulates his theory of the state of exception. Closely examined, his theory does not seem to be motivated by a fervent dread before the exception. In *Political Theology*, the exception is actually valued: It is "more interesting than the rule. . . . In the exception the power of real life breaks through the crust of a mechanism that has become torpid by repetition."[181] An authentic existence is one that has the exceptional in view; in turn, the exception appears to be an opportunity for existential intensification and renovation.[182] In the exception, as Ojakangas says, "life itself" emerges as "the source of new meaning."[183]

In order to determine the scope—as seen by Schmitt—of the exception and of the sovereign device of the state of emergency, we must attend to the fact that, in his texts, the exception is understood in two ways: On one hand, it is understood as juridical-political exception, in which the juridical norms lose their validity and efficacy, but which eventually allows itself to be controlled by the technical-juridical device of the state of emergency. On the other hand, it is understood as what we may call "existential" exception, that is, the fact that human existence in its entirety, not just the juridical positive legislation, is vulnerable to the irruption of the exceptional.[184] The exceptional, therefore, may mean not only the loss of validity and efficacy of the juridical norms for normality—which is an exception that allows itself to be dominated by the technical device—but the alteration of the conditions for existence, as well. This is what takes place through the modification of the situation by the emergence of the new from its existential depth, of a meaning that brings forth a new historical age or the advent of an unanticipated state of existence. This second kind of exception forms the basis of the first, since the loss of normative meaning (validity) of the juridical positive norms may be due to the irruption of a new meaning from the situation, in virtue of which the situation, which was governable by a given set of rules, is no longer thus governable—but also because the existential exception affects human existence in its entirety.

Schmitt's conception of the existential exception is found in works from various periods of his career. In *Political Theology*, in the passage alluded to above, he states: "The rule proves nothing; the exception proves everything: It confirms not only the rule but also its existence, which derives only from the exception."[185] In *The Concept of the Political*, human existence arises from an abyss over which it lies suspended, and that may turn out to be the source of an incontrollable dynamism. Human existence is "undetermined, unfathomable, and remains 'an open question.' "[186] In *Hamlet or Hecuba*, Schmitt writes of "an ineluctable reality that no human mind has conceived—a reality externally given, imposed and unavoidable," a reality so abysmal that it transcends all "invention," all "construction," such that "no mortal can invent it."[187] In these passages, cited as examples, Schmitt stresses the exceptionality of human existence and the precariousness of the normality on which technology and the technical-juridical understanding aim to operate. This normality is based on a background of indetermination, from which that normality arises and to which it is inevitably related. The exception can always break through the normality and radically alter the usual conditions. In the quoted passages, then, there emerges a tension between the human mind's capacity for knowing and controlling objects in a normalized way, on the one hand, and the fundamental indetermination of existence, on the other. This tension is resolved in favor of the second. The exception is insurmountable.

The texts evince that the juridical kind of understanding endorsed by Schmitt is a broader form of understanding, which, unlike that of the technological rationality, aims at including the exceptional—a dimension of existence that, as Schmitt claims, the technological rationality ignores. This broader scope of the juridical understanding enables it to unveil the relativity of all technical-juridical attempts to limit the exception—even the sovereign device of the state of exception.[188] The broader scope allows it to recognize the pretense to abolish the exception in a definitive way by means of technical devices as utopian.[189] For Schmitt, only the Utopian could believe in the sufficiency of technical mechanisms to control the "infinite possibilities of the human being"[190] and the undetermined and unfathomable character of existence.[191]

The Subject

Schmitt's and Derrida's conceptions of the subject differ significantly, though Schmitt's does not necessarily coincide with the one attributed to him by Derrida. For Schmitt, as we have seen, the subject exists in a context already affected by the exception. The exceptional is a condition of the subject in diverse ways. That is, the subject is a spontaneity that is also passive, not a "free and sovereign creative power."[192] The exceptional is the unfathomable "ground" of existence, from which the subject and existence in its entirety emerge.

For Schmitt, the exception works, as we have seen, as the factor of indetermination that removes the subject from the immanent sphere. The activity of "creating distance" is accomplished from this position. The exceptional is the "ground" from which the spontaneity of the subject is displayed. In understanding, the subject does not only distance herself from one or more beings in particular, but from the whole ontic sphere. Human understanding is performed from "transcendence," without which, Schmitt claims, there would be no consciousness.[193]

Furthermore, the Schmittian subject is tied to a heteronomy, since her understanding also depends on the way in which existence reveals itself. Existence emerges bestowed with discernibility and meaning. The unveiling occurs even before any activity of a spontaneous conscious subject, in the form of an "unintentional development,"[194] over which the subject lacks control.[195]

Actual consciousness, for Schmitt, requires, moreover, an alterity with which to relate. We have seen that for Schmitt the "relation [of the subject] *ad se ipsum* is not possible without a relation *ad alterum*. To be in the world means to be with others."[196] This relation is linguistic.[197] Language, Schmitt thinks, points to meanings that are autonomous from the eventual control of the subject. The meanings of words are dynamic. Words enter into a process of transference from one context to another, and of interaction with new revelations of meaning, in virtue of which their meaning varies.[198]

The subject encounters, not only "outside" but already "within" herself, an alterity that lies outside of her control. Schmitt writes: "I am not sovereign [*Herr*] of that which bursts [*dringt*] into my consciousness [*Bewußtsein*], nor of that which remains unconscious [*unbewußt*] for me. My consciousness is not in my power . . . Every power is transcendent. Transcendence is power."[199] The Schmittian subject is not to be understood, therefore, as "invulnerable," nor as purely "active," nor as an "identity" closed to the other beforehand.

Schmitt and Derrida part ways, however, when Schmitt claims that the subject has direct access to herself. For Schmitt, consciousness presupposes that the subject has that kind of access to herself. In every act of thought and knowledge, the conscious subject already knows herself as subject. Insofar as the subject, as conscious subject, is a "concrete individuality,"[200] this knowledge of herself is not attainable by way of general concepts. A general concept—"in the sense of the analytical concept of a rational logic—"[201] would not allow the subject to identify herself as a concrete and unique individuality, nor to differentiate herself from the other. Such knowledge of herself, then, must have a direct or nonconceptual character.[202]

Schmitt's subject is a kind of manifold unity. This should be understood within the extremes he identifies as functionalism and substantialism. There the extreme consists in the construction of the object from consciousness. Here consciousness is dissolved into the plethoric diversity of the nonsubjective.[203] Instead, Schmitt conceives the subject as a relative unity.[204] With this conception of the subject, Schmitt distinguishes himself partially from Derrida, for whom, as we have seen, consciousness emerges from a play of differences, where the differences explain the identities, but not vice versa. The subject is a "function of language," and language is the expression of a play of differences that refers to the *différance*. Schmitt's position may be considered as intermediate. It lies *between* the extreme of dispersion and the functional conception of an absolute subject. Derrida tilts toward the pole of dispersion. For him, differentiality would be the foundation of the unity of consciousness.

This conception runs into difficulties noted by various authors.[205] Consciousness requires an identity. The subject must already know herself as subject in every act of knowledge. Such identity is not explainable from a play of differences.[206] Related elements in a system of signs evince the *relation* between them, but not their *identity* nor their *knowing themselves* as being parts of such identity. One may certainly think that between the elements of a given structure there are relations, but not necessarily also identity and consciousness of relations. Regarding this problem, Manfred Frank says: "Two or more elements related to each other reveal a great deal, but they do not reveal that they are identical to each other and, furthermore, that they are aware of this. . . . The mere reference between two marks could never in all eternity produce their sameness, and it certainly could never lead to a *consciousness* of this sameness."[207] Some underlying spontaneity is required, which must be able to identify the different elements and know about itself in the act of identification. There must be a spontaneity that has an immediate moment previous to the differential play.[208] To operate as such, the subject needs to know herself, even before she can identify and discern herself regarding others.[209] Such knowledge of the subject is not attainable by way of general concepts and cannot have the character of a reflective operation. A general concept is unable to identify and discern the subject as a "concrete individuality."[210] A reflective thematization is unable to access the subject precisely as the activity that performs the thematization.[211] It must be a direct knowledge, prior to the differential play. Without such previous and direct self-knowledge, there would be no identification criterion of any of them, namely, of the subject as a "concrete individuality" and of the elements of the system of signs that are parts of conscious relations.[212]

The Schmittian subject is spontaneous, but not a "free and sovereign creative power." Schmitt conceives the act of understanding as formed from a differentiation. On the one side, there is an alterity, discernible and exceptional at once. On the other, there is a relative autonomy, a "concrete individuality" that emerges from the exception as the "place" in which the subject's self-access, and the distancing from the reality, happens; and as the "place" from which the discernment through words and rules of that which is unveiled may occur (including the reflective relation of the subject with another and with herself). Both aspects of the differentiation appear against a background of exceptionality that affects the whole of existence: exceptionality always exposes the individual to alterity.

Further, the Schmittian subject is not necessarily closed to the other, to the new, to the exceptional, because, as I observe in the next subsection, objectivization is only one form of understanding—one from which Schmitt critically distances himself. In dealing with the other, in reflecting on the depth surfacing from each side of existence, on the tension between the rule and the case, between the norm and the exceptional, the "jurist" is required to attend to the meaning revealed by the situation. The "jurist," therefore, must take a step from the sphere of general concepts toward that of the concrete. Experience unveils an existential depth in virtue of which the meaning of concepts cannot always remain unaltered, if our understanding is to be adequate, correct, or just. The generality of concepts is, to a certain extent, necessary (a completely singular concept would be an event, not a concept) but variable. If the step toward that existential depth is taken, concepts will mutate their meaning in the different acts of understanding. Reflection on the discontinuity between concrete existence and the generality of concepts allows for opening the path to a manner of understanding that is less abstract—for concepts that emerge, as Schmitt thinks, considering the novel dynamic of the concrete.[213]

UNDERSTANDING

For Schmitt, the heterogeneity between the generality of the rules and the existential depth and meaning of concrete cases requires that, in order to understand, the step from the dimension of the rules toward that of the cases be taken. The point is to illumine the situation from a context of rules and concepts by attending to the situation's meaning, exceptionality, and alterity. Rules and concepts should not simply be overstepped, since that would imply the elimination of the cultural and juridical context that makes understanding possible.[214] But, given the meaning and novelty emerging from the situation, those who understand may be faced with the requirement to make an interpretive decision that modifies the meaning of the rules and concepts.[215] Schmitt also notes that the meanings of words are linked to traditional and new contexts, in such a way that words enter into a dynamic process of changing meanings. She who understands, if she is to do it correctly, without falling prey to the words, has to notice these displacements when making interpretive decisions.[216]

This juridical kind of understanding, exposed in Schmitt's texts, is similar in many important respects to the way in which Derrida sees juridical understanding and understanding in general. In "Force of Law," like Schmitt, Derrida inquires into that which makes a decision "just." As in Schmitt's work, the problem for the juridical understanding emerges together with the tension between the rules and the cases. If rules are general, cases are unique and individuals singular.[217] Before this tension, paths are open for Derrida similar to those considered by Schmitt:[218] mechanical subsumption,[219] decisionist caprice,[220] detachment,[221] just decision.[222]

For Derrida, as for Schmitt, justice cannot be reached by means of mechanical subsumption. "If I were content to apply a just rule . . . I might be protected by law [*droit*], my action corresponding to objective law, but I would not be just."[223] The judge as "a calculating machine" is inadmissible.[224] Nor is admissible, as in Schmitt, the attitude of the one who "doesn't refer to any law, to any rule."[225] Here we end up with another way of manipulating the singular. The anti-institutional discourse approaches the "worst" and the decisionism of the enemy.[226] Nor is the attitude of the one who "suspends his decision, stops short before the undecidable," just.[227] For both Schmitt and Derrida, "passivism" is improper. To leave justice to itself because of its incalculability is to leave it at the mercy of the calculators.[228] "That justice exceeds law and calculation . . . cannot and should not serve as an alibi for staying out of juridico-political battles, within an institution or a state or between one institution or state and others. Left to itself, the incalculable and giving (*donatrice*) idea of justice is always very close to the bad, even to the worst, for it can always be reappropriated by the most perverse calculation. It's always possible. And so incalculable justice requires us to calculate."[229]

The just, nonsubsumptive decision demands a step from the ideality of the rules toward the concrete reality of the cases and the singularity and alterity emerging from them. "Each case is other, each decision is different and requires absolutely unique interpretation, which no existing, coded rule can or ought to guarantee absolutely."[230] Derrida, like Schmitt, emphasizes the role of the decision, for the point is not to subsume the case, but to adequately understand it. This demands an interpretive decision that is adapted to the case in its "singularity."[231] The decision must, in this sense, "conserve the law and also . . . destroy it." The content of the rule must be altered. The understanding of the case needs to be "both regulated and without regulation."[232] A decision always involves a moment of discontinuity with regard to the previous rule,[233] and this discontinuity is where the difference between the technical and the juridical rationality lies.[234]

The Juridical Nature of Existence

It is also possible to find a similarity between Derrida and Schmitt on a more basic level, related to the juridical character of human existence.

In Derrida, existence appears to be seen as initially juridical. Both language and law emerge, for him, as inaugural performative occurrences. In Schmitt's terms, it could be said that, from the exceptional, existence bursts as a tension between rule and case, concept and reality, normality and exception.

"The very emergence of justice and law, the founding and justifying moment that institutes law," says Derrida, "implies a performative force, which is always an interpretative force."[235] The law is established by means of "self-authorization,"[236] which alludes to an origin without origin—to the fact that the law arises from a vacuum of justification. Its establishment is the condition for the juridical kind of understanding, but the establishment itself lacks all possible justification insofar as it is the condition for every justification and interpretation. This establishment cannot be the subject for historical research; it is not someone's work, but "an absolutely emergent order, absolute and detached from any origin," which makes every law possible—the "being-law" of the laws.[237]

Something similar takes place in language. Before its establishment, there is properly speaking no individual, identity, or consciousness. However, the institution of language coincides with an "originary violence of language;" it comprises the incorporation of an individual into a "system."[238] The singular individual is placed within a context of classifications; she is put under signs, graphemes, and phonemes by means of which her singularity is subjected to generalizations. Language is a context of remissions within which something becomes identifiable or mentionable *as* something. This determination involves an obliteration. The constitution of identity resulting from language as a system that understands through signs implies an insurmountable violence.

Language seems to operate in the same manner as the law. It emerges as an establishment in virtue of which the manifold is ruled (in the "as" of linguistic articulation). A certain legality is thus established, a binding law, not just theoretical, but practical: the individual is bound to the meanings of the signs. This "law of language" would not be different to the law of which Derrida speaks in "Force of Law"—original ruling of the concrete and singular.[239]

The bond between law and language is manifest in Derrida's allusion to John L. Austin's classification of speech acts as constative and as performative.[240] Those that are constative are under a criterion of "*justesse,*" or theoretical adequacy, not of "justice." Those that are performative, on the other hand, can only be just—in the sense of "justice"—if they are well-grounded on conventions—that is, on prior performative acts, which ultimately refer back to an inaugural performative act. Now, "since every constative utterance itself relies, at least implicitly, on a performative structure ('I tell you that, I speak to you, I address myself to you to tell you that this is true, that things are like this, I promise you or renew my promise to you to make a sentence and to sign what I say when I say that, tell you, or try to tell you the truth,' and so forth), the dimension of *justesse* or truth of the theoretical-constative utterances . . . always thus presupposes the dimension of justice of the performative utterances, that is to say their essential precipitation, which never proceeds without dissymmetry and some quality of violence."[241] There are no purely theoretical-constative acts; every constative act is grounded on a performative one. Those that are performative, in turn, are already found in a context determined by the performative establishment of the law. This act of instituting law—Derrida appears to suggest—comes to coincide with the performative act that establishes language.[242]

In Schmitt's case, as in Derrida's, existence has a juridical character. Thought can emerge only if there is a "distance," given the subject's positioning in the "transcendence." Such positioning comprises a reference to an "unconscious" background, outside the "power" of consciousness.[243] But it also imposes a separation and violence. In emerging from transcendence, the subject finds an unveiled reality, which she tries to understand by means of conceptual articulations and rules, pertaining both to language and the law.[244] Herein appears the tension. For the concepts and rules are general; the unveiled reality is singular, deep, dynamic. The generality of concepts and rules involves an obliterating potential, which is expressed, in its extreme form, as technological calculation and manipulation.

For both Derrida and Schmitt,[245] the only way out from the violence involved in the generality of the rules, of language and of the law—though it is only a partial way out, since there is no understanding without words and rules—is to make interpretive decisions that go beyond subsumption. The agent must take the step toward the cases, their alterity, and, when necessary, modify the meaning of the words and rules. This is ultimately a juridical kind of understanding—one in which the aim is to preserve and destroy the law and the law of language, in order to do justice to the singular and the other.[246] There is no escape from the establishment of language and the law,[247] but it is possible to be conscious of them and of the ability to reinterpret the concepts of language and juridical norms, in order to reach (unreachable) justice—in Schmitt's case, an "existentially correct (*seinsgerecht*)" decision.[248]

Juridico-Political Exception

In the first part of "Force of Law," the text in which Derrida deals with juridical understanding, there are no references to Schmitt. But there are in the second part. Yet Derrida does not refer to *Law and Judgment*, the early work in which Schmitt addresses the juridical kind of understanding in the normal situation. The omission is noteworthy given the striking similarities between the two texts, and is also of relevance in relation to Derrida's interpretation of Schmitt.[249] The latter's theory of juridical understanding, first sketched in *Law and Judgment*, advocates for a manner of understanding which, heedful to the normative context, is open to considering the case, its existential depth and alterity, thus clearly distancing himself from the technological rationality and decisionism.[250] Moreover, insofar as it becomes manifest that the situation is partly exceptional, even within normality, and that it is still possible to make a decision in that exceptionality that distances itself from a controlling disposition, *Law and Judgment* may offer indications regarding the question of the decision in the political exceptional situation. Given the possibilities facing the juridical agent in normality, namely, normalizing, decisionist, and just, which are treated by Schmitt in *Law and Judgment*, one may approach the decision in the state of exception and think of a just manner of deciding and understanding in that state as well. Whoever makes the decision must take the step toward the real and reappropriate the meaning of the law from that new position, eventually modifying its meaning according to what is newly revealed from the concreteness of the case. Likewise, it is possible to think, within the framework of Schmitt's thought, of a decision which, before a juridico-political exceptional situation, takes into account both the law—defied by the situation—and the alterity of the case, including the groups of individuals affected by the exception.[251] A "degenerate" and manipulating decisionism would not be the only option.[252] Additionally, there emerges the possibility of a just or legitimate decision—exposed to and moved by the alterity and depth of the concrete.[253] The extension of the criteria of normality to the exceptional situation is valid, since the possibility/impossibility of justice in the exceptional and the normal situation does not vary in its nature. In the exceptional situation, it is necessarily about groups; in the normal situation, it may be about groups. However, in both cases the situation is exceptional, in the sense that although there are general rules and concepts, they enter into crisis.[254] Precisely because of the crisis undergone by the rules and concepts due to the depth of the case, Schmitt argues that, before the decision is made, rules and concepts have an "indeterminacy of content"[255]—that their content must be eventually modified by the different acts of understanding. The need to decide is always the expression of a crisis.

This criterion, which may be obtained from Schmitt's theory of juridical understanding, is compatible with what Schmitt asserts about the decision in the state of exception. The tension between the generality of the rule and the singularity of the situation and the individuals involved in it undoubtedly acquires a greater intensity in the state of exception, that is, when the normal situation in general becomes altered as a whole and the sovereign has to decide. Nonetheless, it is still possible to find bases to ground a nonmanipulative, not purely decisionist decision.

In *Dictatorship*, a text antedating *Political Theology*, Schmitt distinguishes two kinds of dictatorship: on one hand, a juridical or commissarial, and on the other, a sovereign one. The juridical notion of dictatorship attends to, and seeks justification in, a previous crisis of the juridical order that is to be overcome. Sovereign dictatorship, by contrast, pretends to produce a radically new order. Schmitt distances himself from such a productive dictatorship. Dictatorship in general is ultimately justified as an intent to overcome a critical situation, with the purpose of restoring the situation in which the juridical norms can be valid again. Due to this character, from a juridical standpoint, dictatorship can never be anything but "commisarial."[256]

In *Political Theology*, despite the different emphasis in his manner of expression, Schmitt does not necessarily abandon his previous position. The declaration of the state of exception presupposes the "case of exception [*Ausnahmefall*]," which brings a whole juridico-political order into crisis, and before which the task for the juridico-political sovereign is to restore an order. The point is not to bring about any "situation," but one "in which legal prescriptions can be valid."[257] That is, although in the state of exception the sovereign unbinds herself from particular juridico-positive norms, she does so because there is a prior crisis, in virtue of which the efficacy and validity of those norms are no longer in place. Her action is still juridical, insofar as it is under the requirement to restore a qualitatively ordered situation. The sovereign's decision is, therefore, a *response*.[258] Her "decisionism" is not absolute, but related to the situation as well as to previous juridical concepts. The sovereign must "implement the good law of the correctly recognized political situation."[259] Even in this situation there is "order in the juridical sense," despite the norms' lack of validity.[260] Existence does not lose completely its juridical character, nor do the requirements of a correct understanding disappear. Inasmuch as what is to be restored is a normal *juridical* situation, the sovereign decision should be discerned from mere manipulation.²⁶¹

In the same text, Schmitt characterizes the law as a form of understanding that has the other in view. "The juridical form is . . . not the form of technical precision because the latter has a goal-directed interest that is essentially objective [*sachlich*] and impersonal."²⁶² If the law distances itself from technical objectivization and its closedness to the personal, it is because and insofar as it recognizes the other as "unfathomable," as an alterity that transcends the limits of an object to be controlled. The law must take the step from the ideal toward the real, heeding, in the instauration of order, the others who are affected by the crisis. The situation to be understood is still comparable to the situation to be understood in normality. Moreover, the attention to the other involved in the exceptional situation separates the decision in such a case from a purely conservative operation.²⁶³

FRIEND AND ENEMY

I have said that, for Derrida, Schmitt's inclination toward a controlling rationality and clear conceptualizations is expressed in the friend-enemy distinction. However, this distinction, as fixed as Schmitt wants to hold it (for on it depends, according to Derrida, the existence of the political),²⁶⁴ betrays instabilities. For Derrida, the tension of enmity may mean that in it there is a more attentive regard of the other and her individuality, a more authentic dealing with her than in a friendship where the friend is seen through conventions; the tension allows for a greater intensity than the superficiality of the general.²⁶⁵ Such instability rests on a prior impossibility. The alterity of the other impedes her determination. The fixing of an other as a friend or enemy is the product of an act carried out by an inquisitive subject, who aims at determining what is ultimately undeterminable, since that which is defined by its resistance to the phenomenal order cannot, in the end, be exposed in a definite form.²⁶⁶

I have already indicated that Derrida's reading of Schmitt's thought, as being closed to the exceptional and alterity, must be qualified. As we have seen, Schmitt's thought is open to the exceptional, to the unfathomableness of the other, to the depth of existence, and to the variable meaning of language. The juridical understanding is characterized, in the strict sense and as understanding in general, not by trying to remain in self-contained idealities, but by taking the step toward the concrete dimension of the real, where the other is found. The experience in attending to reality and the other in concrete contexts demands from the subject to recognize the insufficiency of her conceptual tools.

Friend and enemy, writes Schmitt, are "existential" concepts, different from "abstractions" or "normative ideals."[267] One must transit from the ideal sphere to that of the "existential reality [*seinsmässige Wirklichkeit*],"[268] in order to understand its "concrete and existential sense."[269] In such an understanding, the other is not reduced to the phenomenal field. She appears precisely without appearing, she appears as an other—"wholly other [*Ganz Andere*]," ultimately "unfathomable," "indeterminable," and "dynamic."[270] Human existence emerges bestowed with meaning. Neutrality is the product of neutralization; it is not original. That is, the other arises in relations of affective intensity, of proximity or distance.

The other is for Schmitt certainly inscribed within language.[271] "Language and the address to the other" allow, says Derrida, to "cross lightly," "with the lightness of unawareness," the difference with the other.[272] And yet, despite it all, Derrida himself cannot help admitting that the other never ceases to be an alterity. "*Every other (one) is every (bit) other* [*tout autre est tout autre*]," he says in *Politics of Friendship*, and: "the other appears as a being whose appearance appears without appearing."[273] In *The Beast and the Sovereign*, he claims that "we are overcome with the feeling that between a given other . . . and ourselves" we are "separated . . . by an abyss," by an "uncrossable difference."[274] The other, writes Derrida in *Violence and Metaphysics*, arises "as originary non-presence . . . [as] the phenomenon of a non-phenomenality."[275] The unfathomable character—the manner of appearing without appearing, the feeling, to which Derrida alludes—can be explained only if one attends to the heterogeneity between the immediate experience the human being has of itself and the experience it has of the other, who always and irreducibly appears to it as alien.[276] Along with the possibility "of being-together in allocution" with the other, in understanding there is—as originally as the possibility just mentioned—an irreducible distance between the subject and what is understood. Given this difference, in encountering the others there is an incalculable risk, insofar as the other is not mere phenomenon but also an alien interiority. The others are indeterminable interiorites, capable of acting, affected by the same uncertainty each individual has regarding the other. As Plessner indicates, the other—to which Schmitt refers—appears as "the foreign [*das Fremde*]"—that is, as "the proper, the trusted, the secret in the other." For me, the other is an inaccessible interiority. The greater the interiority of the other, the greater its being "uncanny [*das Unheimliche*]."[277] The mere presence of the other is, then, in itself a putting myself in question. And this takes place even before any explicit questioning, either from my side or hers: *the lucidity of awareness suffices*. Herein lies an irrepressible basis of the dynamism of human relationships.

The order of language is also a basis of the tensional dynamism of human relationships. The linguistic openness to the irreducible otherness of the other occurs within a context of legal and linguistic rules and concepts, which are already affected by previous interpretations. The demand to do justice to the other in her singularity is thus always determined by the context in which understanding takes place. Schmitt is clearly aware of the potential for conflict posed by concepts and rules. In many cases, these conflicts are influenced by "self-interested" interpretations,[278] such that a tension between manipulators (or a manipulating party) and those manipulated (or the party deciding to make a less manipulative decision) can emerge. But even in the case of an interpretive decision that tries to fit the meaning of the rules to the situation, such as by expanding the sphere of recognition to others formerly excluded, the tension does not disappear. For the interpretive decision is necessarily referred to a previous context of rules and prior interpretive decisions that will usually have adherents. Whether the decision is conservative, thus favoring the previous meaning of rules; whether it is nonconservative, thus favoring a reinterpretation of the rules in order to recognize what is new; whether it seeks to abolish the previous situation for the sake of the new; or, finally, whether there is rather an abstention to make a decision—in all these cases, the possibility of conflict and controversy remains intact due to the insuppressible tension between the previous rules and the novelty of the cases.[279]

Chapter 2

Law and Theology

Heinrich Meier's Interpretation

In *Political Theology*, Schmitt writes: "All significant concepts of the modern theory of the state are secularized theological concepts."[1] In a letter to Jacob Taubes of 1977, he acknowledges: "All that still concerns me today, is for me a question of political theology."[2] Two of Schmitt's books contain the phrase "political theology" in their titles. References to theological dogmas or allusions to the Bible are also interspersed throughout Schmitt's works. From a meticulous compilation of texts, Heinrich Meier was able to reach the decisive conclusion that Schmitt's thought is grounded on faith in revelation. "The center of Schmitt's thought is his faith in revelation,"[3] in such a way that it can be called political theology. "'Political Theology' is the apt and solely appropriate characterization of Schmitt's *doctrine*."[4]

Meier characterizes political theology, including the political theology of Carl Schmitt, according to three principal marks. These features differentiate political theology from political philosophy.[5] The first mark is the assumption that "divine revelation" is the "supreme authority and the ultimate ground."[6] "Human wisdom"[7] and "reason"[8] do not provide definitive legitimacy or "foundation."[9] Political theology postulates a dichotomy between the separate paths of faith and reason. Before this dichotomy, theology considers itself as following the path of religious faith. Theology is "grounded" on, not just motived by, the "faith in divine revelation,"[10] thus rejecting the path of "reason," of "human wisdom," of philosophy. Thought is therefore conditioned by, and subordinated to, faith; and in cases where thought is employed at all, it is for the sake of faith.[11]

A second mark of political theology is that, contrary to political philosophy, "it cannot prescribe any particular taking of sides"[12] and is "unable to provide historical action with any 'concrete' orientation."[13] This second mark depends on the first. Faith orders obedience to the call of God. The order to obey, since it is referred to an omnipotent being, cannot be countered or restricted by any principle that human beings may be able to discover based on their cognitive capacities and rational critique.[14] "The paths of Providence are unfathomable."[15] Political theology cannot, therefore, be tied to a specific content.[16] When the command takes place, the call is an authentic event, inaccessible through the analysis of its preconditions, as it breaks into the situation and radically modifies it.

Finally, the third mark, according to Meier, is that philosophy is linked with immanence and theology with transcendence. Reflection on transcendence is properly theological, whereas philosophy is limited to immanence. This distinction appears in several passages where Meier relates theology to metaphysics and ontology.[17] According to this third characteristic, the definition of a science or intellectual discipline as theological or metaphysical depends, consequently, less upon the way in which it operates than on the kind of matter it studies—in this case, transcendence. Meier links all thought that is open to the "*Ereignis* (appropriating event)"[18] with theology. For him, philosophers such as Martin Heidegger, Jean-François Lyotard, and Jacques Derrida are, insofar as they go beyond the limits of immanence (towards the *Ereignis*, death, the alterity of the other), closely related to theology.[19]

In the second edition of his book on Leo Strauss and Carl Schmitt, Meier provides three additional clarifications regarding Schmitt's political theology and his attitude as a political theologian. First, he states that in facing the political theologian, we primarily face "an existential position."[20] In this sense, the political theologian is distinguished from what Meier refers to as the "mere doctrinaire." While the former "joins the postulates of his theory with his existence as a theoretician," the latter avoids directly considering the question of historical action. The doctrinarian "seeks, by referring to firm traditions or higher institutions, to relieve himself of problems that the commandment of obedience poses for 'historical action' in general and for the 'historical action' of the theoretician in particular."[21] The political theologian is independent of such intermediary traditions and institutions; rather, she seeks to act in history by answering directly to the divine mandate. This mandate determines the theologian's whole vital activity, including her role as theoretician.[22]

The second clarification added by Meier in 1998 is that political theology is "the center and the context"[23] of Schmitt's thought, and that the politico-theological nature of his thought does not affect every one of its details. One should not confuse "the scholar with the thinker" and thus short-circuit the more scientific parts of his work with its center.[24]

Meier offers a third clarification. He states that the effort to determine Schmitt's thought "does not mean to reduce the activity of the theoretician to the doctrinal contents he relays."[25] The task that Meier imposes on himself does not consist simply in investigating the data before him—namely, the different texts written by Schmitt, but in going beyond that world of appearances toward an essentially mysterious center of Schmitt's thought. Meier carries out this hazardous task by way of inferences supported by certain manifestations—the "results or sediments of his activity"[26]—on the basis of which it would be possible to reveal Schmitt's hidden ideas.[27]

I must now address the three marks of political theology advanced by Meier, which are problematic even before trying to apply them to Schmitt's thought. According to the first mark, political theology, insofar as it is grounded on faith and determined by it, must be separated from philosophy, rational critique, and human wisdom. Without additional clarifications, this separation is highly questionable. It might be that in Schmitt's case, or in that of some particular theologian, theology or political theology should be identified with a certain faith that excludes the path of reason and philosophy. As for Schmitt, this is a matter we shall confront later on. But such a characterization of theology is by no means necessarily correct.

Theology, as *logos* of the *theos*, aims at being the thought of the divine. Such thought is distinguished, in principle, from religious experience or faith, which are parts of the subject matter of theology. If they are called "theology," they are that in an improper sense. There must be a reflective abstraction separating an experience and its thematization. That is, theology as a discipline requires some degree of reflection. In principle, therefore, it is compatible with human wisdom and critique.

The thought of the divine may be undertaken, of course, from a movement arising from religious faith. But it may also arise from the disposition to counter religious faith, or even from a disposition that is independent of it. In case the thought of the divine arises from religious faith, faith may still fulfill two roles: either simply be the *motivation* for such thought of the divine, or instead end up *determining* or *conditioning* that thought. Of these two cases, only in the second does an incompatibility between religious faith and the path of philosophy, rational critique, and human wisdom properly come about. In this second case, theology would be a thought emerging from the faith, which thus ends up being conditioned by it, to the point of either becoming diluted or operative, but under the orders of faith. In this latter case, we should be in the presence of a theology as Meier defines it: some positive religious beliefs are assumed, and thought is subordinated to them.[28] If thought is employed in this context, it is not with the aim of developing autonomous critique and reflection, but for the purpose of strategically validating those religious beliefs.[29] Insofar as there is no autonomous, reflective, and eventually critical thought regarding religious beliefs, but one subordinated to them, the logos plays no determining, but only a determined, role.

Thus, one should ask oneself about the pertinence of excluding from theology, as Meier does in his first note, all studies and thinking of the divine that are not conditioned—although perhaps motivated—by religious faith. When the thought of the divine distances itself from faith's conditioning, it can, as is the case with any other discipline, regard its object of study (or its nonobject, in case one holds the impossibility of objectifying transcendence) by means of observation, analysis, and critique. Examples of this kind of theology are found in the works of Anselm,[30] Aquinas,[31] Meister Eckhart,[32] and Descartes.[33] Theological thought can also be found in the work of Paul Tillich and of Clayton Crockett, who understand theology as dealing with matters "of ultimate concern," a dealing, namely, that distances itself from a metaphysical consideration of God.[34] To define theology, with no further qualifications, as conditioned by faith and excluding autonomous, critical thought of divinity and transcendence, is to excessively restrict the term.

Regarding the second mark proposed by Meier, it must be said that, as with the first mark, and leaving aside for the moment its applicability to Schmitt's thought, it lacks the required necessity concerning theology. Indeed, theology's ability to guide concrete action depends on the kind of theology in question. Needless to say, the theology of a theologian who is waiting for a direct order from God in history is unlikely to orient human praxis intersubjectively. But insofar as theology is considered as a discipline that thinks and reflects about the divine, or even about transcendence, it becomes possible for it to provide guidelines for action that are in principle apt to intersubjective validation. One might think here of Aquinas's moral theology, which is set within a traditional metaphysical framework. One might also think of the practical implications of the reflections of an existentialist philosophy about the exceptional, or regarding the manipulative character of the generalizing rationality of technology.[35]

Meier's third mark is that philosophy restricts itself to immanence, while theology considers transcendence. This gives rise to three problems. First, Meier's distinction between philosophy and theology depends on a strict separation between an immanent and a transcendent sphere. Only under this separation does it make sense to understand philosophy and theology as parallel disciplines, and to classify as nonphilosophical the attempts to show the relations between immanence and transcendence—even if such attempts are executed in a critical or reflective manner. According to this mark, what defines philosophy and theology as distinct from each other would be the matter of their respective studies, not the way in which their studies are conducted. However, if the strict separation between the immanent and the transcendent is questioned, the separation between philosophy and theology postulated by Meier starts to crumble. What if transcendence is considered not just on the basis of faith, but also as a necessary condition for the elucidation of immanence?[36] As we have seen, by reflecting on the different ways in which human understanding may be carried out, Schmitt notes that the scientific-technological "methodology" is incapable of thematizing some implicit assumptions which are required for this kind of understanding. For Schmitt, transcendence is a condition for the elucidation of immanence in at least two senses: as the unfathomable ground from which existence emerges, and as the basis of the distance needed for understanding to take place. If we affirm that immanence depends on transcendence for its elucidation, the separation between both spheres collapses, and so does the strict separation between philosophy and theology. At this point, that is, the study of transcendence for the elucidation of immanence, theology, and philosophy coincide. Nevertheless, the theology involved in this elucidation does not need to be based on, or conditioned by, faith.

We have seen that Meier understands Heidegger's, Derrida's, and Lyotard's philosophies as close to theology, inasmuch as they are open to transcendence—the *Ereignis*, the other, death. Philosophy, on the contrary, would merely occupy itself with what is immanent. According to Meier, Socrates embodies this way of philosophizing, "of whom it is said was the first to call philosophy down from heaven."[37] Meier states: "Plato and Xenophon placed" his life "before our eyes as the philosophical life simply. Montaigne says of him that he regarded dying as a natural and morally indifferent event."[38] A nonreductionist understanding of human life, however, seems hardly compatible with the omission of the fact that it arises from an exception that conditions it in the two stated senses: as the place for its emergence, and for the distance needed for consciousness. Coming into existence or dying, insofar as they are referred to transcendence, cannot be considered as purely natural phenomena. The omission of the question of transcendence can be seen as the avoidance of thinking about the human condition. I have shown that Schmitt, like other existentialist philosophers, understands that, behind the inclination to escape thinking of the exceptional, there is an interest in ultimately overcoming the "anxiety" before the uncertain[39]—an interest in reaching some alleged "security."[40] By reducing existence to its immanent features, human understanding is then able to procure for itself a self-contained and controllable sphere. The abyss of exception affects and perturbs the human being so profoundly that it tries to obviate it. As we have seen, this anxiety before the uncontrollable is for Schmitt the counterpart of a desire for predictability, calculation, and control.[41]

Meier's third mark presents a third problem. In defining political theology by his first and third mark, he incurs an internal conflict and eventual contradiction. If, according to the third mark, theology addresses transcendence, while, according to the first mark, theology is conditioned by faith in revelation, some odd consequences result. Indeed, the third mark leads to the conclusion that Heidegger, Derrida, and Lyotard, along with those who "revolve around the *Ereignis*,"[42] should be called "theologians." But if we now focus on the first mark, it follows that the theories proposed by these authors are conditioned by faith in divine revelation—certainly a rather curious way of viewing such theories.

Differences between Law and Theology

For Schmitt, the law as a form of understanding occupies an intermediate place between theology and technology.[43] As is the case with technology, his reflections on theology contribute to make the scope and boundaries of his juridical thought more distinct. As with technology, in the case of theology Schmitt's treatment is not exhaustive in any of the texts in which he touches upon it. But in scattered passages it is possible to identify a thematization of theology where the latter is characterized and distinguished from technology and the law. One can discern four distinctive marks of theology in Schmitt's texts. First, it opens up transcendence, something that is not achieved by technology, but which is in fact accomplished by the law. However, in theology, as opposed to the law, such opening-up is done either without, or at least without sufficient, epistemological control. Second, theology recognizes a meaning emanating from that transcendence, again either without, or at least without sufficient, epistemological control. Third, theology is inclined toward privileging the end, thus marginalizing the question regarding the means, the concern about normality and its conditions, and the care for the other. Fourth, theology doesn't thematize enough the conditions for understanding.

SUBSTANTIALISM AND JURIDICAL EPISTEMOLOGICAL CONTROL

"Theology," writes Schmitt, is situated at the pole of a "total substantialism;" it "is necessarily totalitarian regarding the substance and the result." It privileges the "result" over "method," "substance" over "function."[44] It is found, therefore, at the antipodes of technology. We have seen that the functionalism of technology is a generalizing and controlling rationality that focuses on immanence and on the effectiveness of the means. For Schmitt, the functionalist ideal points to something like a whole epistemological domain of an object that completely answers to cognition, and to a technical capacity for producing and manipulating physical reality. Conceptualization comes to play an active role in the constitution of reality. The scientific-technical method tends to discard the aspects of reality that offer resistance to the functional control of the concept.[45] At the other extreme, the substantialism of theology works in the opposite direction, inclined toward the pole of the real. In theology, privilege is given to the experience of that reality regarding which epistemological controls tend to play an attenuated or a marginal role. Reality is conceived as already constituted, and conceptualization is understood, explicitly or not, as an ascertaining of reality, without considering—or without doing so sufficiently—the functional or spontaneous role of the subject in the conformation of it.

If the total activity of the functionalist ideal is impossible to reach, so is the purely passive attitude of total substantialism. Complete activity is impossible for a finite subject, who is always referred to an uncontrollable existence.[46] On the other hand, the complete absence of subjective activity, a mere surrendering to the other, a pure receptivity with no spontaneous activity on the part of the subject, pure "substance" with no "function"— that would mean going even beyond the "intoxication of the dream" and falling unconscious.[47] Regardless of how much one moves toward the pole of reality, a minimum of subjective spontaneity must always be involved. Neither the reduction of the manifold of the real to the unity of the subject (or of passivity to functionality), nor the scattering of the unity across the manifold (or of activity in passivity), allow for an explanation of consciousness. The latter is always placed *between* both poles as the unity of the manifold, as an activity necessarily related to the real.[48]

Depending on how close or how far they are to the poles—namely, the pole of the substance and result, and the pole of the function and the method—different kinds of "theology" may be distinguished. A first kind is that which admits the real in the way of a naked faith (T1). Here one may speak of an absence of method or epistemological control.[49]

Religious experience may also present itself accompanied by the exercise of thought. Here one could think of two kinds of approaches to transcendence and divinity. The first is a theology in which some religious beliefs are assumed through faith, and thought is used for many different purposes, but not for an autonomous reflection aimed at justifying and questioning the religious beliefs. Human thought is thus conditioned by faith (T2). Schmitt cannot be a "theologian" in this sense. On one hand, he explicitly distances himself from this kind of theology.[50] Further, his openness to transcendence is not the product of a faith that subordinates thought; his theories are not grounded on faith in the revelation. Instead, those theories and that openness are justified by means of observation and critique; more specifically, and as we saw in the previous chapter, they are justified by means of a strict reflection on the conditions for understanding.

Second, one may also think of a rational theology (T3). Here faith is also accompanied by thought. Thought is not conditioned by faith to the extent that a reflective, justifying, and critical exercise of thought is no longer possible. In this theology, however, the "result" still predominates over the "method." There is no careful examination of the conditions for understanding and of the roles played by the mind and reality. Although thought is present, it is not exercised with sufficient epistemological control, whereby one could notice the insurmountable character of the tension between the reality that is exceptional and the concepts, and in virtue of which epistemological control or awareness the exceptional—though recognized as a source of revelation—is considered precisely as exceptional regarding concepts.[51] Due to this lack of sufficient epistemological control, the focus on "substance" prevails over considerations of the role of the "function." The spontaneous conceptualizing activity of the subject inadvertently determines transcendence as a substantial being. By not sufficiently thematizing the tension between the poles of understanding and the active or functional role of the subject, the conceptualization of transcendence performed by this kind of theology dogmatically attributes certain properties to it, to the point of thinking of it as a reified being.[52] The lack of sufficient reflective attention to the conditions for understanding leads to the mere aggregation of concept and reality, instead of being considered in their relation and tension. That is why Schmitt cannot be a theologian in this sense, either, inasmuch as he has explicitly thematized the problem of the tension and the relation between the ideal and the real. In juridical thought, the mere aggregation is overcome by a consideration of the specific roles of concepts and reality as the irreducible and related conditions for understanding: on one hand, concepts as products in which the spontaneous activity of the subject intervenes,[53] and on the other, an unveiled yet exceptional reality to which understanding is always referred.[54] In this consideration, the functional is not reduced to receptivity, nor is the exceptional surreptitiously laden by the products of the conceptualizing activity of the subject. Both are recognized in their specific status. It is admitted, moreover, that for experience to take place, the tension cannot lead to a complete separation; the poles must be related in a certain way beforehand: there is no understanding without distance and conceptualization;[55] there is no understanding without a pole of the real, which, besides being exceptional, also emerges unveiled in typical ways.[56]

SURRENDERING TO MEANING WITHOUT, OR WITHOUT
SUFFICIENT, EPISTEMOLOGICAL CONTROL

In its openness to transcendence, theology finds a meaning to which it surrenders without, or without sufficient, epistemological control. This openness, as is the case with the openness to transcendence, admits several variants. One may think of a sort of permanence in "the relation of intoxication or the dream," or in mystical abandonment (T1).[57] It is also possible to think of religious positions that are capable of defining courses of action, grounded on faith, where thought plays a rather instrumental and subordinated role (T2)—for example, in the form of a "revolutionary" "social criticism,"[58] or of a reactionary decisionism.[59] The orientations for action may acquire, finally, the form of a moral-theological articulation grounded on higher degrees of reflection on the revelation (T3).[60] In all these cases, however, what characterizes theology is its surrendering to a meaning, a surrender done without sufficient epistemological control, and that does not adequately recognize the poles of human understanding, the conceptualizing activity of the subject, and the tension between that activity and the pole of the real.

The juridical understanding is similar to the theological understanding, where it distances itself from technology, because it recognizes a meaning in existence.[61] In chapter 1 we have seen that this meaning is a condition for human action, even for the operation of neutralization carried out by technology.[62] That meaning, which the law justifies, arises from an existence that is considered as fundamentally exceptional and unfathomable. It emerges from a background of indeterminacy and mystery that is not directly accessible. In light of this consideration of the conditions for understanding, the law must separate itself from a surrender to that meaning without, or without sufficient, epistemological control. Insofar as the transcendent is regarded precisely as transcendent, it is not possible for the law as a discipline to access the direct mandates of a positively determined God. For that same reason, the indications one may obtain from a revealed God, even if mediated by a moral theology, are not a matter that should concern the jurist as such.[63] Despite this recognition, the law, as we saw in the previous chapter, can in fact obtain orientations for action, insofar as the human being, in understanding, is interpellated by the meaning with which existence unveils itself.[64] From the consideration of the meaning of situations and of transcendence as a mysterious source of meaning, it is possible, for example, to notice the shallow or manipulative character of the technological rationality, and to identify a less manipulative, juridical, kind of rationality. To this I now turn my attention.

INSTITUTIONALIZATION AND RECOGNITION OF THE OTHER

Juridical thought reflectively recognizes a meaning in existence and thematizes the relation between reality—its meaning, exceptionality, and alterity—and the rules and concepts through which it understands that reality. In this context, the other emerges as an unavoidable aspect of that reality, as irreducible as reality itself to rules and concepts. The other is "unfathomable," and every other is "wholly other [*ganz andere*]."[65] That recognition and thematization place the law under the demand to institutionalize the situation,[66] to conform it as a realized normality that must express the meaning of existence, recognize the other, and constitute itself into a lawful and meaningful order.⁶⁷ For Schmitt, human existence is determined by the poles of understanding, and, consequently, there cannot be such an existence without conceptualizations and institutionality. Within a context in which different types of decision and of institutional conformations are possible, detachment matters as an evasion: to ignore the question of the fairness, the correctness, the justice of the institutional conformation, and the decisions within it. Schmitt points out here that such evasion, such renunciation of the exercise of understanding, leaves free the way to capricious or manipulative decisions or institutions, in which the other is neglected.⁶⁸

Juridical understanding distances itself from a substantialist theology that ignores the institutional question, or does not attend to it sufficiently.⁶⁹ The substantialist inclination of theology may lead it to privilege the result, to marginalize the existential significance of the institutional aspect, which might be discarded as mere machinery.⁷⁰ In a substantialist theology, especially in its less sophisticated versions, the question of the legitimacy of the means loses its importance.⁷¹ The absolute significance and divine character of the end tends to lead to the conclusion that "the just side" can "use any and all means of violence" in order to achieve it.⁷² Thus, it may happen that the "religious claim to always have the truth [*konfessionelle Rechtshaberei*]"⁷³ triggers "brutality,"⁷⁴ and that the other ends up being seen "as something that must be destroyed."⁷⁵ If juridical understanding is "*ad alterum*," in the extreme, "for theologians, the *altera pars* is the enemy, the devil."⁷⁶

Juridical understanding aims at the "recognition" of the other, "of the individual [*Person*] based on mutual respect even in a situation of conflict," and at the fulfillment of the conditions for "a reasonable human existence."⁷⁷ It realizes the recognition of the other through the juridical order, the state, and its diverse organs, which face the task of expressing the situation and the other by means of adequate rules and decisions.⁷⁸ Examples of juridical institutions include (1) the political unity;⁷⁹ (2) the judicial institution,⁸⁰ and the judicial process, "an orderly procedure, due process, without which there can be no law,"⁸¹ a mechanism that relativizes the claims of the parties, giving equal possibilities to present themselves before a third party who will then weigh the claims involved;⁸² (3) the "institutional guarantees," "constitutional provisions" designed to ensure "special protection" to "particular institutions;"⁸³ and (4) the assurance of peace and the limitation of war.⁸⁴ Tension arises in the case of the juridico-political exception, but even there, as we have seen in the previous chapter, Schmitt considers the device of the state of emergency as one that should only be activated in reaction to a previous challenge; to establish a qualitative non-impersonal, juridical order.[85]

Broader Scope of Understanding

When distinguishing the law from theology, Schmitt assumes—as when he distinguishes the law from technology—a much broader notion of the law than is usual. The law extends over the entire sphere of human existence and is defined by the manner of understanding it brings forth, rather than by its object of study. We have seen that the law, as a form of understanding, emerges insofar as it thematizes the tension and the relation between the situation and the rules and concepts, a tension and relation that constitute the basis of human understanding in general. Between the poles of understanding—the concepts and rules and the concrete situation, unveiled and exceptional—a certain dynamic takes place. In this dynamic, the cases are elucidated by means of a subjective activity. The elucidation may operate as a mere subsumption of the case to the rule (technology); as an openness to the case without, or without sufficient, control (theology); or in accordance with a simultaneous consideration of reality and the rules, eventually altering the meaning of the rules and concepts to adequate it to the meaning of the real. By holding in view the rules and concepts, and the activity of the subject elaborating them, such a juridical elucidation heeds also the dimension of the real and its existential depth.

Schmitt's attitude regarding theology is anchored in his hermeneutical theory. His thematization of the tension and relation between the function and the substance, conceptuality and reality, prevents him from stepping into the sphere of the real emphasizing the "result" or ignoring "method." Rather, his hermeneutical thought calls for reflection on the possibility and limits of human access into reality. Schmitt notices the scope of the rules and concepts, as well as the role of the subject in their production. He considers that with those rules and concepts no self-sufficient knowledge and no completely determined object can come about, since the real is irreducible—but also, that those rules and concepts are necessary conditions for a lucid understanding. They do not suffice, however, for determinately identifying a transcendent being. In noting concepts and the intellectual activity as conditions for a lucid understanding of existence, he distances himself from the mystical or less rational forms of theology. In noting the impossibility of objectively determining the exceptional, he also distances himself from the more rationalized forms of the substantialist theology.

For Schmitt, theology is distinguished from the law because of its substantialism. Nonetheless, just as the law, albeit with differences, is near to technology, insofar as it addresses the question of the means and aims at exercising epistemological controls, the law is also near to theology. Of course, the law distances itself from theology as thought conditioned by faith, even from theology as rational theology. However, in thematizing the relation and tension between the ideal and the real, the law must recognize the exceptional: both as abysmal bottom from which existence emerges and unveils itself, and as condition for the distance required for consciousness. Insofar as every discipline that recognizes the transcendent may be called theology, in a broad sense, juridical thought may also be called, with the necessary qualifications, theological.[86] The law operates once the question of transcendence is in place. The law's contribution consists in explicitly thematizing the relation and tension between the concept and "the intangible (*das Ungreifbare*);"[87] the rule and the case; the abstract and the concrete; the norm and the exception. Insofar as the exceptional is brought to the fore as a condition for existence, that effort can be considered as theology, but only in the sense that it is a thought that thematizes transcendence and the exceptional and its relation with normality and immanence. The exception, the other, God, the meaning of existence, escape conceptual determinations.[88] And it is through the recognition of such overabundance of the real, and of the contrast between it and the concept, that juridical thought emerges, in the broad sense in which Schmitt considers it, as "a philosophy of concrete life."

The law's proximity to theology seems nonetheless on par with Schmitt's assertion that "all significant concepts of the modern theory of the state are secularized theological concepts."[89] He illustrates the idea of the secularization of theological concepts into the political realm with various cases: for example, the transmutation of the notion of sin into the political concept of the problematic nature of the human being,[90] and that of the "transcendence [of God] vis-à-vis the world" into "the transcendence of the sovereign vis-à-vis the state."[91] The relation between juridical and theological concepts, says Schmitt, takes place not only because of the "historical development" of the theory of the state from theology, "but also because of their systematic structure."[92] Schmitt appears to claim that theology grounds the law. It might be argued, therefore, that Schmitt's statements on the difference between law and theology that I have presented ultimately lose their validity.

In establishing this relation, however, Schmitt does not actually admit that the law, as a form of understanding, is a discipline grounded on dogma and religious faith. In the passages referenced above, he explicitly writes from the perspective of what he calls a "sociology of juridical concepts."[93] It is important to determine Schmitt's understanding of this discipline, in order to discern the meaning of his claims and to identify what we may call an improper use of the term "theology."

Schmitt writes: "The sociology of concepts, which is advanced here . . . aims to discover the basic, radically systematic structure [of the philosophical conceptualization of an era] and to compare this conceptual structure with the conceptually represented social structure of a certain epoch."[94] This sociology does not ground or justify the law by means of theology and faith in the Christian revelation. Instead, the Schmittian "sociology of concepts" tries to elucidate and identify, first, the fact of the theological or metaphysical conceptualization of a given epoch; second, the fact of the juridical conceptualization of that epoch; and finally, the character of the relation between these two.[95]

Schmitt continues: "Metaphysics is the most intensive and the clearest expression of an epoch."[96] Within this context, neither metaphysics nor theology (both terms are used improperly and interchangeably) is considered in the sense of a discipline conditioned by faith or of what I have called a "rational theology." Instead, Schmitt views here theology or "metaphysics" as "the image of the world created by a certain epoch."[97] They are the fundamental manner of conceptualization of existence current to a given historical period.[98] Taken in this broad sense, "metaphysics" admits within it some theological and metaphysical conceptions in the more traditional sense of the terms, but also that which Schmitt calls "scientific thinking," "scientism," or the "conceptions of immanence."[99] Thus, for example, Schmitt understands that "at the foundation of" the "identification" claimed by Hans Kelsen "of state and legal order rests a metaphysics that identifies the lawfulness of nature and normative lawfulness;" a "pattern of thinking . . . characteristic of the natural sciences."[100] Given the unusual broadening of the term "metaphysics" within the context of the sociology of concepts, it is not the case that metaphysics is the "most intensive" and "clearest expression of an epoch" because it is bound to a theology based on religious faith. It is rather the reverse: Schmitt calls "metaphysics" the conceptual elaboration determining an epoch, its "image of the world," regardless of the philosophical position embodied in that image or elaboration.

Within the context of the Schmittian "sociology of juridical concepts," the theory of the state, in turn, is the fundamental conceptualization of the institutions of a given epoch. This theory of the state is considered, in its different stages, as a fact, without first attending to its merits in each one of those stages.

Schmitt suggests that the fundamental conceptualization of the institutions current in a given epoch depends on the fundamental conceptualization of existence of the epoch in question. That is, there is a correlation between the "metaphysical" or "theological" conception of a historical period and its juridical-political conception. Thus, for example, the sociology of the "concept of sovereignty" notes that the monarchy during the seventeenth century corresponded "to the general state of consciousness" of Europe of the time. A "juridical construction of the historical-political reality can find a concept whose structure is in accord with the structure of metaphysical concepts." Thanks to that coincidence, "monarchy thus becomes as self-evident in the consciousness of that period as democracy does in a later epoch," the latter being dominated by a different "metaphysics," namely, that of "scientific thinking" or the "conceptions of immanence."[101]

The kind of study realized by the sociology of juridical concepts—although not primarily aimed at justification and critique, but, prior to that, at identifying conceptions already given and at comparing and analyzing the dependency relations between those conceptions—may nevertheless serve as a basis for justification and critique, but in a way that is very different from that of dogmatic theology. The exposition and study of the diverse conceptions of existence (the different "metaphysics" or "theologies") allow one to thematize and subject them to evaluation and critical scrutiny. Once such fundamental conceptions are presented, one may inquire into the pertinence with which they understand existence.

There is, for Schmitt, a "metaphysical" import in every fundamental conception of existence, because every such conception, as an understanding of existence, operates within a context that is unavoidably referred to something beyond immanence.[102] All understanding presupposes "transcendence" or the exceptional as the unfathomable source from which the subject emerges and from which that subject is able to distance herself from reality and achieve consciousness.[103] In this precise sense, it becomes plausible Schmitt's assertion that "metaphysics is . . . unavoidable," or that, even in immanent conceptions of existence, the "metaphysical attitude" remains.[104]

The juridical understanding, as "philosophy of concrete life," evaluates the different conceptions of existence on the basis of the inquiries and observations of the "sociology of juridical concepts." In that evaluation, and from the standpoint of the conditions for understanding, it can bring into relief the deficient consideration of those conditions on the part of purely immanent conceptions. More precisely, it brings into relief the fact that purely immanent conceptions ignore the exceptional or transcendent aspect of existence, without which understanding is impossible.

For Schmitt, ignoring the transcendent and exceptional is not only untenable from a theoretical viewpoint.[105] Immanentism—what we may call the denial of the "metaphysical" import, or reference to transcendence of understanding—also has negative practical consequences. Immanentism implies a loss or undermining of practical consciousness. According to what I noted in the previous chapter, the immanentism of the technological rationality is an extreme that impedes an adequate consideration of the concrete and exceptional of existence, of its alterity and meaning.[106]

Heinrich Meier on Schmitt's Thought

OMISSIONS

Heinrich Meier's interpretation, according to which Schmitt's thought is determined by his faith in revelation, is based on a procedure consisting, first, in the separation of philosophy, or autonomous thought, from theology (taken as Meier defines it), and second, in attending to Schmitt's religious or theological allusions, and in gathering them as documentary evidence. However, Meier omits tasks that are necessary to validate his interpretation. If his interpretation is to acquire scientific value, it should be tested against its alternative—namely, that Schmitt's writings harbor a thought that is not conditioned by his faith in revelation. Nonetheless, Meier neglects to make a serious inquiry into whether Schmitt's work may be read in light of that alternative. Further, in expounding upon his own reading, Meier omits a proper explanation. He limits himself to stating *that* Schmitt's thought is theologically determined, without clarifying *how* theology actually determines Schmitt's work. In Meier's view, Schmitt's faith compromises the very ground of his theories (at least the ground of those theories lying at the center of his thought or connected to it). As "grounded in faith in divine revelation,"[107] these theories are affected by recourse to divine revelation as their foundation.[108] The task Meier should carry out, then, is that of showing, with regard to Schmitt's main doctrines, how they are intrinsically determined by dogma—in what way their organization and exposition, their argumentative structure, are determined by faith.

These two omissions—that of neglecting to seriously consider an alternative interpretation and that of neglecting to explain how faith determines Schmitt's main doctrines—become manifest the moment two facts are brought into view. On one hand, Schmitt's thought consists preponderantly of juridical and political reflections: on the modern state; on the different kinds of states according to their predominant function; on the liberal and democratic rule of law; on the crisis and eventual overcoming of the state; on great spaces (*Großräume*); on the evolution of the conceptions of space; on judicial interpretation; on juridical normativism and positivism; on the law as concrete order; on parliamentarism; on dictatorship; on the crisis of the Weimar Republic; on the political theory of liberalism and the different versions of socialism; on the partisan, from its origins until Schmitt's time; on the concepts of the constitution and the evolution of constitutionalism; on basic rights and institutional guarantees; on political representation; on the notion of values and its implications for the juridical and political field; on war and its different conceptions; on international law; and so on.[109] On the other hand, the preponderantly juridical and political character of Schmitt's work is manifest in its massive reception from the beginning. Regardless of whether this reception shares or rejects Schmitt's justifications, the fact is that it attends to the theoretical significance of Schmitt's oeuvre, instead of merely regarding it as an expression of Schmitt's faith.[110] Those juridical and political reflections, which constitute the vast majority of Schmitt's work, along with the reception of his thought, make the demands on Meier's interpretation even more pressing—namely, the demand to consider the alternative reading and to explain in what way faith operates as a determinant foundation of Schmitt's thought, including his most important juridical and political reflections. Instead, Meier seems to rest content with the gathering of Schmitt's religious or theological remarks and with affirming, based on these remarks, that Schmitt's thought is theologically determined.

Meier's approach may be illustrated by two striking examples. First, he states that Schmitt's critique of normativism has a moral sense and is ultimately theological. Meier understands that, for Schmitt, normativism avoids the "demanding moral decision" before the call of God, "with respect to which only a 'concrete historical decision' can be of concern."[111] Meier's point neglects the notorious fact that Schmitt's critique of normativism is justified by the theoretical insufficiencies of that position, which he clearly identifies. Schmitt attends to how normativism ignores that the norm presupposes an ordered situation, both as a condition for its efficacy and its validity (its normative meaning or obligatory sense). In a chaotic situation, where there are no typical recognizable aspects, the concepts of the norm have no applicability to reality. The norm, therefore, loses its bindingness.[112] A second example of Meier's approach is his reading of Schmitt's grounding of the political. In *The Concept of the Political*, Schmitt justifies the possibility of conflict and of the political as a sphere determined by that possibility. (Here I must refer back to chapter 1, and to what I shall say on the matter after this section.) Instead of reading the Schmittian argument in its theoretical import and value, Meier, even in the face of the evident fact—which he acknowledges[113]—that the argument is independent of faith, is unhesitant: that argument has but a bizarrely theological purpose, which is "to bring the doctrine of original sin into play."[114] Of course, Meier could take refuge in the idea that these and other doctrines and reflections are not part of "the center and the context" of Schmitt's thought. But that claim would be far-fetched, since the center and context of Schmitt's thought would then be reduced to a few remarks or to those texts where he is explicitly addressing a Christian audience.

Finally, and above all, a third omission should be called into attention, one of the utmost importance: Meier ignores, in his documentary search and in his interpretation, the reflections on human understanding that Schmitt persistently puts forth throughout his writings. As we have seen in this and the previous chapter, at the basis of Schmitt's works is a thought that emerges and is articulated from an analysis of the conditions for human understanding: of the tension and the relation between the rules and concepts, on one hand, and the cases, on the other. Based on this thematization, Schmitt is able to identify and to distance himself from the two manners of understanding that emphasize either one of these poles: the conceptual pole, in the case of technology, and the pole of the real, in the case of theological substantialism.

The Applicability of Meier's Criteria and Clarifications to Schmitt

In what follows, I seek to determine to what extent Schmitt may be classified as a theologian and his work as "theology," by taking into account Meier's conception of political theology; more specifically, its three constitutive marks and three further clarifications on Schmitt's thought later added by Meier.

There are, certainly, as I have already mentioned, many allusions to religion, faith in revelation, as well as to theology, dispersed throughout Schmitt's work. In some cases, they express Schmitt's motivation—when, for example, he defines himself as a "Catholic."[115] In other cases, he makes reference to religion in the context of analyzing problems proper to Christianity, such as in "The Visibility of the Church," or when he writes about the *Katechon* or the Christian view of history.[116] There are also passages where he speaks of himself and relates his thought to Catholicism as a form of rationality,[117] or to political theology.[118] Dogmas appear as illustrations of political and legal problems, or they arise in order to emphasize the importance of a given subject. For example, he mentions Babylon when writing about what he considers as inadequate forms of political existence; he also refers to a religion of technicity as the belief that identifies technical progress with human progress; he even says that the concepts of the theory of the state are "secularized theological concepts," and that the notions of the intellectual sphere generally have dogmatic implications.[119] These texts corroborate a religious motivation in Schmitt—that he has high esteem for the efforts at systematization in theology as a discipline, and that he considers it relevant to inquire into the theological and metaphysical (in a wide or improper sense) roots of juridical, political, or (in general) "spiritual" concepts. However, there is a fundamental discontinuity between his religious motivation and his treatment of philosophical, theoretico-juridical, and theoretico-political problems. That discontinuity is determined by his juridical manner of understanding, which impedes him from grounding his arguments on faith in divine revelation.[120]

The Three Marks

If we analyze the marks proposed by Meier to depict political theology, and Schmitt's in particular, the third mark—namely, that theology is an inquiry open to transcendence, and that philosophy is the inquiry into immanence—is the least inadequate to characterize Schmitt's thought. Schmitt could be viewed as an existentialist thinker, near to the tradition of authors such as Kierkegaard, Heidegger, or Derrida. This is a point that Michael Marder,[121] Hasso Hofmann,[122] and Mika Ojakangas,[123] among others, have emphasized. Nonetheless, the following questions should be raised again regarding Meier's third mark: first, whether it is appropriate, as he does, to restrict philosophy to the sphere of the immanent and to exclude from it any inquiry into the exceptional and the transcendent, and second, whether it is pertinent to bind to theology any thought that, as is the case with Schmitt's, attends to the insufficiency of the attempts to explain existence in a purely immanent way, *and* to link, without further elucidation, theology understood according to this third mark with theology understood according to the first mark, that is, as a thought conditioned by faith in revelation.

Regarding the second mark—that Schmitt's thought, as theological, cannot provide concrete orientation to praxis—it should be remembered that, in Schmitt's works, there are orientations for action that are in principle intersubjectively valid. Here I must return to issues already addressed, namely, Schmitt's conception of the technological rationality as a manipulative manner of understanding and operating, which leaves human beings exposed to increasing levels of control and makes their lives progressively superficial; his consideration of the excesses to which the theological dogmatism leads; his rejection of normativism, decisionism, detachment; his remarks on the judicial manner of understanding and the right or just decision; and his observations on the conditions for a "reasonable human existence."[124] It is hard to attend to all the passages where Schmitt touches on these subjects and to still be able to deny the capacity of his thought to orient human praxis, or to still attribute to him the attitude of a theologian decisively bound by his faith in revelation and determined by his desire to answer the direct call of the divinity. Those positions of Schmitt are, moreover, parts of "the center and the context" of his thought;[125] they form the very trunk of his conception of existence, which means they cannot be set aside as annexed, secondary, or added pieces of his stance.[126]

The second mark depends, to a certain extent, on the first—namely, that Schmitt is a theologian because the determining ground of his thought is his faith in revelation. However, if we attend to the main aspects of his thought, we can establish that they evince a specific theoretical value independent of the author's faith. That we find in Schmitt's work a massive body of texts arranged for intersubjective discussion, and nothing like the application of a theology foreign to the path of reason, becomes clear in the three main parts of his thought, namely, in his conception of understanding in general (A); in his theory of juridical understanding (in the more restricted sense of the term) (B); and in the basis of his political understanding (C).

(A) In Schmitt's theory of understanding, the exceptional character of existence is philosophically, not theologically (in the sense of Meier's first mark) justified. The thought of a finite subject is incapable of completely determining an existence of whose emergence and limits it has no insight.[127] Schmitt's justified stance implies that any eventual reference to God must be located within the initial recognition of the tension between the human mind and reality. Inasmuch as it is inexhaustible by the mind, the real remains exceptional. That is why Meier in some sense is correct when he says that, in Schmitt's thought, God is found in the sphere of "the incomprehensible."[128] The consequence of this recognition, adds Meier, is that the human being must maintain an attitude of "humility."[129] However, such an approach to God, insofar as it considers the latter as "the incomprehensible," cannot regard God as knowable in the manner of a determined being who dictates orders that are also knowable, as Meier maintains that Schmitt does. Humility—if anything of the sort is attributable to Schmitt's thought—is but a consequence of the acknowledgment, based on the consideration of the very conditions for human understanding, of thought's inability to fully understand reality.

Meier criticizes that Schmitt refers to himself as a jurist.[130] For Meier "jurist" is a specific-scientific role, whereas for Schmitt the jurist is, in a fundamental sense, the one who attends to the tension between the mind and the real, the "concept" and the "intangible," and thematizes this tension.[131] The recognition of that tension marks the division between a substantialist theology and Schmitt's position as a jurist. I have already stated that although both are open to transcendence, the jurist is so with greater epistemological guard, heeding to the "method," not just to the "result"; the jurist is open to transcendence as the exceptional. Schmitt is, *as* a jurist, a thinker who is conscious of the exceptionality of existence; he is, therefore, faced by the theoretical and practical requirement to moderate, from a juridical or epistemological standpoint, any references to a determined and knowable divinity. Meier affirms that for Schmitt's God, no natural order, nor any logical or natural law can be a limit.[132] If this is so—and it is insofar as God is found in the sphere of the exceptional—there cannot be, for Schmitt, an "end to uncertainty," as Meier concludes.[133] On the contrary, there is only space for a faith inseparable from the recognition of the unfathomable, the correlate of the limitation of cognition. This admission of the exceptionality of existence and of the tension between rule and reality, though not incompatible with a nondogmatic faith, is nevertheless justified by means of juridical thought. Faith may have motivated or illustrated, but not conditioned, the author of an argument that is sustained independently of faith. The question then arises: how can this attitude coexist with the dogmatism and certainty of such religious faith, that Meier believes pollutes the very basis of Schmitt's thought? A thought so radical as to be able to become conscious of the conditions, scope, and limits of human understanding may be classified as theology, insofar as it attends to the exceptional—but not as dogmatic theology, neither as a theology of mere faith, nor as a theology of a faith that conditions thought, nor even as what I have called "rational theology." The dogmatic side rather appears in Meier himself, where he criticizes some direct consequences of Schmitt's explicit thematization of the conditions, scope, and limits of understanding, without Meier himself thematizing those conditions, scope, and limits. Thus, he ends up expressing, without further questioning, his trust in a "knowledge of what is always valid [*Erkenntnis dessen, was immer gilt*]."[134]

We have also seen that the Schmittian admission of a dynamism of existence is grounded on the recognition of the exceptional. This admission leads to a certain "historicism" in Schmitt's thought, which is noted by Meier and linked by him—once again—to theology.[135] That historicism, however, is, like the recognition of the exceptional, not the expression of faith's conditioning of Schmitt's thought, but the justified result of his critical reflection on the scope and limits of understanding. If the exceptional is at the basis of historical facts, history is and remains an "event."[136] Schmitt's claim about the insufficiency of general criteria to determine history, derives from this reflection. It is not the case that God alone is unfathomable; existence is exceptional and, consequently, event—and so the other and a possible God are also events.[137]

The attention to the poles of understanding, to the exceptional, to the meaning with which existence unveils itself, allows Schmitt to critique the technological rationality and its consequences. But it also allows him to critique the decisionism that does not adequately consider the rules and the situational contexts,[138] as well as the detachment of an aestheticizing attitude.¹³⁹ All these stances are justified in Schmitt's thought, and one need not focus on a certain religious faith to be able to understand the justifications.

(B) We have also seen that, from a *specifically* juridical standpoint, Schmitt's thought attends to the tension between the rule and the case, between the generality of the juridical norms and the particularity of the situations—their variability and meaning. In virtue of this tension, the juridical decision, if it is to be correct or just, cannot remain in the sphere of norms, but can be made only by previously stepping into the concrete dimension of reality.¹⁴⁰ Based on Schmitt's consideration of the limits of normativism, one can obtain a criterion warning against the controlling inclination behind the logic of subsumption.¹⁴¹ From a specifically juridical standpoint, Schmitt also criticizes decisionism, because it ignores both the rules (which implies renouncing the principle of juridical certainty and the fall into arbitrariness¹⁴²) and the typical aspects and meaning of the situation.¹⁴³ Finally, one can also see a critical approach to juridical detachment, which is not, as Meier suggests, determined by dogmatic theology, but justified by arguments. For Schmitt, juridical detachment entails abandoning the demand to decide and assuming a certain complicity with those who manipulate.¹⁴⁴

(C) Meier argues that Schmitt's distinction between friend and enemy, as well as his conception of the political community, evince the theology lying at the basis of his thought. Further, these notions could not but be theological: "The 'fundamental theological dogma of the *sinfulness* of the world and of man' cannot be 'substituted' with any insight nor with any result of anthropology."¹⁴⁵ Meier determines that for Schmitt the basic human sin must consist in the "disdain for the sovereignty of God" and in "man's endeavor to live his life based on his own resources, following natural reason and his own judgment alone."¹⁴⁶ That is to say, original sin is nothing but philosophy. Consequently, the pretense to elucidate the true (theological) meaning of original sin by means of sinful philosophy is impossible.¹⁴⁷

In Schmitt's texts, however, there is in fact a justification of the problematic character of the human being and of conflict that is clearly independent of dogma. The justification has two strands, as we saw in chapter 1. On one hand, there is the strand of what may be called the order of experience, and on the other, the strand of the dispute of interpretations.

In the order of experience, the capacity "of creating distance"¹⁴⁸ defines the way in which the human being relates with others.¹⁴⁹ The other appears as "wholly other [*Ganz Andere*]"—as ultimately "unfathomable" and "dynamic."[150] Moreover, experience emerges bestowed with meaning. Neutrality is the product of neutralization.[151] The other is placed in a context of relations of affective intensity, of proximity and distance, in which appreciation and rejection, and hence peace and conflict, are possible.

In his justification of the problematic character of the human being, Schmitt resorts to diverse authors. He mentions, among others, Machiavelli, Hobbes, Spinoza, Pufendorf, Bossuet, Fichte, de Maistre, Hegel, Donoso Cortés, and Plessner.[152] He especially attends to Plessner, Hobbes, and Machiavelli. In *The Concept of the Political*, Schmitt quotes Dilthey on Machiavelli: "What Machiavelli wants to express everywhere is that man, if not checked, has an irresistible inclination to slide from passion to evil: animality, drives, passions are the kernels of human nature—above all: love and fear. Machiavelli is inexhaustible in his psychological observations of the play of passions. . . . From this principal feature of human nature, he derives the fundamental law of all political life."[153] Machiavelli's exposition and argumentation regarding political life—to which Schmitt alludes via Dilthey—operate from a consideration of anthropological dynamism, and not from a resort to theological positions. Schmitt also pays heed to Thomas Hobbes's anthropological argument for the political. "For Hobbes," says Schmitt, "the pessimistic conception of man is the elementary presupposition of a specific system of political thought."[154] For Hobbes, the roots of conflict are already found within the individual. The individual is home to a series of drives and inclinations that are not in harmony. There is, instead, "a perpetual and restless desire of power after power, that ceaseth only in death."[155] Human beings "are stirred by their drives (hunger, greediness, fear, jealousy)."[156] Due to this inner tension, the human being's relation to others can always give rise to conflict. It becomes necessary, then, to overcome the "state of nature" and the "condition of continual danger" given within that state. It is before this situation that the figure of the *Leviathan* acquires plausibility. Years later, in *Ex Captivitate Salus*, Schmitt returns to the idea of the inner tension constitutive of human beings.[157] I have already addressed, in chapter 1, Plessner's conception of the other as someone who does not emerge as something indifferent. The other is "the alien," an indeterminable interiority. This interiority is "the proper, the trusted, the secret in the other." The greater the interiority of the other, the greater her being "uncanny,"[158] and the greater the risk to which the individual is subject in her relation with her.[159]

The strand that I have called concurrent interpretations notes the fact that the relation with the other is inscribed in a context of rules and concepts, and is bound to the ways in which, based on those rules and concepts, the human being interprets reality. The interpretations differ.[160] They may be inclined toward either of the two poles of existence. Insofar as any act of understanding operates within the tension between the generality of the rules and the peculiarity and meaning of the situations, it is always possible for an interpretive decision to conflict with other interpretive decisions.[161]

Meier indicates that, for Schmitt, the problematic character of the human being is ultimately determined by means of dogma, and that there would be no proper justification "derived from other sources."[162] We have seen, however, that Schmitt does enter the "sinful" road of justifications through reason and reflection. Meier himself paradoxically ends up recognizing that Schmitt does provide a justification of the political. "He . . . presents its truth in a formulation that is immediately plausible to common sense."[163] But, how is it possible to advance a formulation of the problematic character of the human being that is "immediately plausible to common sense," if it is not grounded on a consideration of the human being that may be intersubjectively valid? Meier persists in overlooking the presence of an argument in Schmitt's texts, when he writes that Schmitt "uses the anthropological quarrel to bring the doctrine of original sin into play."[164] In other words, even where Schmitt argues, and eventually persuades, he is not actually arguing, but playing something like a game of theological exhibition.[165]

Three Additional Clarifications

I have stated that, in the second edition of his book on Strauss and Schmitt, Meier makes three additional clarifications regarding his determination of political theology and the political theologian. According to the first clarification, the political theologian is characterized by an existentially committed attitude, one of answering the divine call.[166] In making this clarification, Meier is operating on the basis of a sharp separation between a reflective philosophy and an existential position of the activist, faith-conditioned kind. The political theologian "joins the postulates of his theory with his existence as a theoretician."[167] There is in some sense an accentuation of the contrast between philosophy and theology. The theologian is completely determined by her faith. Morality cannot be thematized, for the theologian's attitude—that of Schmitt as a theologian—is entirely and directly moral.[168] Regarding this clarification, I must refer back to what I stated about the first and second marks proposed by Meier: Schmitt does in fact reflectively thematize existence and praxis.

As for the second clarification—namely, that political theology is "the center and the context" of Schmitt's thought,[169] and that the politico-theological character of that thought does not affect every one of its details[170]—it is worth asking, how many parts are concerned here? Meier's attempt to qualify his characterization of Schmitt as a political theologian in this uncertain manner ends up appearing much like a confession of the weakness of his interpretation. The weakness comes into view as soon as one considers both the already-mentioned large mass of juridical and political doctrines included in Schmitt's work, and his persistent reflections on the conditions for human understanding. Moreover, the distinction proposed is questionable if it is related to the first additional clarification. If we follow Meier, Schmitt would appear to be a theologian at certain times, and to be a scholar or theoretician at others. But if to be a political theologian amounts to being existentially determined by theology even as a theoretician, it is certainly problematic to see Schmitt sometimes as a scholar who is not a theologian. Meier would need to demonstrate how the activities of the scholar producing scientific results are compatible with the pathos and the existential attitude of a genuine political theologian operating *as a theoretician*.[171]

Meier's third clarification indicates that the theological core of Schmitt's thought is hidden in his texts. Therefore, one should not focus exclusively on "the doctrinal content he relays."[172] Meier provides examples of his strategy for unveiling the intention behind Schmitt's assertions. He attempts to refer Schmitt's critique of normativism, or his justification of the political, or his sociology of concepts, to positions conditioned by faith in revelation.[173] Beyond the implausibility of trying to find a religious conditioning behind the arguments of Schmitt in each of these cases,[174] there is still an explanation pending, on the part of Meier, of how it is possible to make assertions based on, and conditioned by, faith—while hiding that basis and conditioning. We should seriously think about the meaning of an assertion being not just religiously motivated, but determined or conditioned by faith. In principle, such determination should deprive the assertion of any validity outside the circle of believers or of inattentive readers.

This third additional clarification, in spite of its serious intrinsic difficulty, eases Meier's task to a certain extent. For although the evidence speaks largely against him, Meier can still strain Schmitt's texts alleging that their true and covert basis is theological, and thus claim that those texts are theologically determined. He is able to do this—and actually does—even with regard to texts that are wholly unrelated to religious beliefs. Meier thus reserves for himself the right to carry out the task of discovering hidden theological determinations, even when faced with immediate opposing evidence. Such a procedure is justified, according to Meier, because Schmitt plays a game of strategic cover-up. When Schmitt does address a topic as remote from theology as the "proclamation of a 'pure politics,'" for example, Meier asks himself, before even trying to explain the organization of the arguments in the texts themselves, whether perhaps this is not "the expression of a rhetoric" or "part of a strategy" to bring theology into play.[175]

Chapter 3

Juridical Thought

The hermeneutical problem appears early on in Schmitt's thought as a topic of explicit consideration, revealing a broad scope from the very beginning. Although there is no single monograph on the subject in his work, multiple passages from various writings, when jointly interpreted, demonstrate that Schmitt takes a justified step both in relating understanding as such with juridical understanding, and in considering juridical thought as philosophy of concrete life, as a fundamental manner of understanding existence. For Schmitt, what defines juridical thought, and bestows it with a fundamental character, is the explicit thematization of the hermeneutical conditions. Juridical thought is different in this from other forms of understanding, and in this lies the reason for calling a fundamental form of understanding *juridical*—namely, it has in view and thematizes the relation and tension between rule and case, the general and the particular, norm and exception. All human understanding operates within the context set by those poles. Moreover, every understanding is faced with the task of resolving difficulties generated by this polarity. Thus, for example, new rules are invented and tried that better account for a series of phenomena, or new uses of language are tested that allow for a more proper expression of the meaning of an experience. Yet it is not the case that in every understanding the relation and tension between its poles is *elevated to a subject of reflection*. When this actually takes place, we are, following Schmitt, in the presence of juridical thought as fundamental understanding, or what he calls "a philosophy of concrete life."

Schmitt's hermeneutical thought and his consideration of the general scope of juridical understanding regarding human existence are important contributions to legal hermeneutics and to hermeneutics in general. Decades later, and in the context of his hermeneutical theory, Hans-Georg Gadamer will note "the exemplary significance of legal hermeneutics:"[1] "*Legal hermeneutics is no special case* [of hermeneutics] *but is, on the contrary, capable of restoring the hermeneutical problem to its full breadth.*"[2] Gadamer stresses the significance of legal hermeneutics for the theory of understanding based on the consideration that in every understanding there is the same "tension" that exists in juridical understanding, the tension namely "between the universal and the particular," between prior rules and concepts, a text, and the "situation" in which the one who understands finds herself.[3] Insofar as the situation is concrete and bestowed with meaning,[4] understanding cannot be realized through a "subsumption" of the situation under universal rules and concepts whose content remains untouched; instead, it requires attending to the meaning of the rules and concepts also in light of the meaning of the situation.[5]

In *Law and Judgment* (1912), Schmitt warns about the error of viewing understanding as if there were first a universal endowed with a "meaning established prior (both temporally and logically) to the decision," and then a case that must be submitted in the mode of a "subsumption."[6] Instead, the situation emerges with a meaning, and such meaning is a defining part of the meaning of the rule.[7] Rules and concepts are not properly understood prior to knowing the situation in which they should be applied. Before application, rules and concepts are only preliminary indications, whose content is still indeterminate.[8] For that reason, in understanding, the correct decision cannot be legitimized in advance, but its legitimation is "something yet to be produced."[9] The one who understands must take a step from the order of rules into a "completely different sphere"—the dimension of the real and the concrete—and by considering the meaning of the situation and the meaning of the rule, adopt the decision.[10]

In terms similar to those used by Schmitt in *Law and Judgment*, Gadamer indicates: understanding "does not mean first understanding a given universal in itself and then afterwards applying it to a concrete case" in the form of "a subsumption;"[11] "understanding always involves something like applying the text [, the rules, the concepts] to be understood to the interpreter's present situation."[12] The application of rules, concepts, of the text to the cases and the consideration, in such application, of the meaning of the situation, are constitutive parts of understanding.[13] Similar to Schmitt, Gadamer demands to take the step from the abstract to the concrete, and an activity of "mediation" between both, in the form of an interpretive decision.[14] Application is not subsumption. The conception of the hermeneutical act as "a mere act of subsumption, is untenable," because only in the application of the concepts and rules, of the text to be understood to the concrete situation, can the abstract and indeterminate meaning of rules and concepts—of the text—acquire a determined and concrete meaning.[15] "The meaning to be understood is concretized and fully realized" only thanks to this application.[16] The hermeneutical situation "codetermines" the meaning of the respective text.[17]

Karl Larenz, who takes up Gadamer's remarks, says that the juridical manner of understanding acquires validity not just "in a juridical-philosophical sense," but, more broadly, "in the whole field of the human sciences [*Geisteswissenschaften*]."[18] Such broadening is justified because, in juridical hermeneutics, the "content of the meaning" of the rule "must always be illumined anew" by considering the situation one is trying to understand.[19] And this is precisely what happens when understanding takes place in the field of the human sciences. "The understanding of works of the spirit," of a text, of rules and concepts, does not happen in the way in which a "subsistent object 'in itself' is represented before the knowing consciousness." Such works, texts or concepts are not immune to the "interpretive process," but they are dependent on it. Each interpretive act is referred to the situation to which those concepts, texts or works are applied. That situation is not static but dynamic: it can emerge in new ways, according to new meanings that are not predictable by means of calculation with ideal meanings. By virtue of these novelty and dynamism, in each act of understanding, the text, the work or the concept in question "can acquire new outlines."[20]

Derrida also thinks in these matters in a manner similar to Schmitt. I have mentioned, that "Force of Law" is a text whose argument has a striking resemblance to *Law and Judgment*. In it, Derrida relates juridical understanding to understanding in general based on the recognition of a similarity between the tension of rules and cases in the juridical situation and that same tension in any other context of understanding. Like Schmitt, Derrida thinks that a nonreductionist understanding must take the step toward the situation, consider the meaning of it, and, if necessary, alter the meaning of the rules—the rules of law and the rules of language—in order to do justice to the singular and the other.[21]

In the first part of this chapter, I attempt to expose what we might call the genesis of Schmitt's hermeneutical theory, how it arises in his different works until it reaches definite bounds. A second part will be dedicated to the systematic exposition of the fundamental aspects of Schmitt's theory of understanding. Finally, in the third part of this chapter, I demonstrate how each of Schmitt's main texts may be read as expressions of that hermeneutical conception.

Juridical Thought as Philosophy of Concrete Life

The law as a discipline has preponderantly in view, as its problem, the relation and tension between rule and case. In the judicial decision, the judge is faced with the tension between general and abstract norms, on one hand, and a singular and concrete case, on the other. The case is a situation that emerges from a real background, heterogeneous from that of idealities,[22] revealed in typical forms[23] and bestowed with meaning.[24] Its depth, constitution, and meaning place the judge before the requirement of not simply submitting the situation, but of also adequating herself to it in her decision.[25] There will be situations that will eventually pass effortlessly through the rule's concepts. But others will not.[26] The judge is exposed to the duty of justification.[27] She must adopt a "correct [*richtige*]" decision.[28] In order to reach it, she cannot remain in the self-contained sphere of norms and their corresponding meanings, and merely subject the cases to those prior normative meanings in her decision.[29] Such an operation involves a subsumption of the cases that disregards their meaning. If the decision is to be just, the judge must take a step "towards another sphere"—that of "real life,"[30] of "plethoric life"[31]—and consider the "specific particularities"[32] of the situation. The tension between rule and case leaves her confronted with the demand—which she may not, and in many instances in fact will not, fulfill—of reflecting on how to orient them to each other in a manner that is full of meaning. She will have to render a verdict through acts of imagination and reflection, which may eventually change the meaning of the rule.[33] This presupposes, at least rudimentarily, an acknowledgment of the distinct character of the ideal and the real, of the way in which they relate to each other, and of the fact that there always persists a tension and heterogeneity between them.[34] Schmitt begins his intellectual path, in *Law and Judgment*, by paying heed to this problem, which is specifically juridical in the traditional sense of the term.[35] The topic of juridical understanding, however, betrays from the beginning a broader scope than one limited to judicial decisions.

William Rasch has plausibly shown that the "judgment" through which Schmitt tries to solve the problem of the tension between rule and case in the judicial situation "bears . . . a striking resemblance to aspects of Kantian aesthetic judgment."[36] Before the problem set by the heterogeneity of rules and cases, and the meaning with which the latter arises, the path of determining subsumption appears inadequate. Schmitt rejects the view that the correction of the judicial decision could be defined by its "conformity to the law [*Gesetzmäßigkeit*]," where the law is thought of as "norm" with a "meaning established prior (both temporally and logically) to the decision."[37] If understanding is to be adequate or correct, it must take a step from the order of rules to the real dimension of the concrete through a "reflective judgment."[38] The judge, says Schmitt, must reach a "general decision for the concrete case."[39] In that decision she must consider both the "meaning" of the rules and the concrete meaning that emerges with the situation.[40] Rasch notes that, as with Kant's aesthetic judgment, where the one who judges expects to produce and demands the approval of others, the judge expects that the "grounds of her decision" "produce a general persuasion"—that is, the recognition of the correctness of the verdict by a community.[41] Such pretension is justifiable given the circumstance that the judge's decision must be correct by having in view also how others would decide by considering the meaning of the rules and of the situation. The juridical decision for Schmitt is "correct, when one can assume that another judge would have decided in the same way [*ebenso entschieden hätte*]."[42]

With these considerations, Schmitt's hermeneutical thought attains a broader scope, apt not only for the juridical field strictly speaking. Juridical understanding, insofar as it thematizes the tension and relation between rule and case, without neglecting the case's concreteness and meaning, proves its capacity to heed the way in which one must address all those situations where it is not admissible to preclude the depth, indetermination, and meaning affecting them by reducing each of them to a case-of-the-rule.

Four years after *Law and Judgment*, in *Theodor Däublers "Nordlicht,"* Schmitt explicitly moves from the specifically juridical field toward existence in a broader sense. He once again addresses the problem of the relation and tension between rule and case, but now as a hermeneutical question in general. This text is a commentary on an epic poem, in which Schmitt notes that human existence emerges from a background of unfathomableness and mystery, on the side of both reality and of the subject.[43] Existence rises from "the depths of the world and of the soul."[44] The act of understanding is articulated in an "intuition that becomes word."[45] Human understanding unfolds between two poles: that of existence, which is both revealed and unfathomable, and that of "words" and "formulations" with which the subject brings existence into thought.[46] This polarity may be conceived as a "dualism"[47] of the ideal and the real, from which Schmitt distances himself. Instead, he sees the poles of the ideal and the real as parts of a relation—as a unity of opposites in tension.[48]

The recognition of the relation and tension of the ideal and the real open different paths for understanding. At the extremes, we find "inactive negation"[49] or detachment, and technological manipulation or the "clever technique of the mechanistic age."[50] Between these extremes, Schmitt allows for an understanding that seeks to provide an adequate mental articulation of existence. This kind of understanding tries to capture the existential depth of the real.[51] Language can become "the container [*Gefäß*]" of that existential depth, "intuition" can be carried into "words" and "formulations," the subject can "discover the knowledge" they "embrace," and this knowledge can then be articulated even in a philosophical thought.[52]

The consideration of the tension and relation of the poles of understanding, and of technology as a rationality inclined toward functionalism, allows Schmitt to develop an early critique—foreshadowing that of his later "The Age of Neutralizations"—of the position advanced by Max Weber and his generation, who admit an "opposition of mechanics and soul."[53] They overlooked, however, that technology is not mere "mechanics"—that behind mechanics there lies a "spirit [*Geist*];"[54] that is, mechanics is the expression of a manner of understanding inclined toward the functional pole. Schmitt does remark upon what one might call the background animating the machine: the "spirit of the mechanistic age," that is, a form of rationality wherein "understanding is freed from all the shackles and continues its rationalism unimpeded; its end is to know the earth in order to dominate it."[55]

A few years later, in *Political Romanticism*, Schmitt again addresses the problem of the relation and tension between rule and case as the question of juridical understanding and of understanding in general. With modernity there appears a dualism, distinctly expressed in philosophical terms by the Cartesian separation of thought and reality. "Modern philosophy is governed by a schism between thought and being, concept and reality, subject and object."[56] This separation makes the mind's access to a "real being" problematic, which then becomes irrational and inexplicable.[57] Thus arises the philosophical-hermeneutical question—namely, how can the rules (causal, juridical, or moral), our concepts, thoughts, the thinking mind, determine what is in principle heterogeneous with respect to them, that is, being, reality, cases?

Schmitt views romanticism as a movement that, reacting to rationalism, is inclined toward the pole of the real.[58] The turn toward the real ends in "a world without . . . functional cohesion, without a fixed direction, without consistency and definition."[59] In the romantic attitude, there is a surrendering to the real, done either without or without sufficient epistemological control. In this surrendering, reality loses its contours, its consistence, and dilutes. After leaning toward the pole of the real and distancing itself from the conceptual one, romanticism gives, however, a second step. An aspect of such diluted reality is taken as the occasional starting point of a "fanciful construction,"[60] of the "playful sorcery of the imagination."[61] "Concrete reality . . . serves as an incidental occasion" for "romantic productivity."[62] Such productivity sees reality as a "point of departure," from which it distances itself.[63] For the romantic operation, the real events are mere occasions for the unfolding of a rootless creative activity. They end up being considered as "intrinsically indifferent" by that productivity.[64] In this second moment, one can speak of a " 'manipulation of the universe.' Forms without substance can be related to any content."[65] The external events—"even the greatest external event"—become the mere material—the neutral and malleable material—of the imaginative caprice.[66]

Schmitt notes the insufficiencies of the romantic stance by attending to the conditions for understanding. With its initial emphasis on the real and disregard of the conceptual; with its subsequent productive game mounted on the previous surrendering to the real; as well as with its inattention to the connection, at the basis of the tension, between the conceptual and the real, romanticism ultimately renounces an "adequate relationship to the visible, external world,"[67] to "concrete reality."[68] The lack of reflective and rational distance makes it impossible for romanticism to consider reality beyond the statement of occasional or arbitrary enunciations.[69]

Schmitt also distances himself, however, from what he sees as a functionalist solution to dualism, couched in the theoretical philosophy of Immanuel Kant. Schmitt argues, that Kant fails in his attempt to supersede dualism because he ends up isolating thought from existence. In Kant's theoretical philosophy, existence is ultimately replaced by "objectivity," which "consists in thought's moving in objectively valid forms."[70] We have, then, thought and its objectivity on one hand, and on the other an existential situation which, due to its depth and meaning, is not objectifiable and is hence unattainable by means of objective thought. The concrete meaning of the situations, the otherness of the other, and the dynamic ways in which they are unveiled, prevent them from being determined, without violence, by means of universal forms of objectivity. Regarding the dualism of Kant's theoretical philosophy, it is also always possible to pose a previous question: namely, how is it that universal concepts and rules can determine a contingent and dynamic reality, in principle foreign and heterogeneous from the "objectively valid forms" of the thinking mind?[71]

In *Political Theology*, Schmitt returns once more to the juridical problem of the tension and relation between rule and case. It is again a question of both juridical and philosophical scope, which is now inscribed within the relation and tension of "the general" and "the exception."[72] The exception affects both "jurisprudence" and philosophical hermeneutics. As with the "positive theory of the state," and the Kantian and Neokantian theory of law, theoretical rationalism excludes the exception beforehand. "It would be consequent rationalism to say that the exception proves nothing and that only the normal can be the object of scientific interest. The exception confounds the unity and order of the rationalist scheme."[73] On the contrary, for a "jurisprudence" that goes beyond the limits of normativism and rationalism, "the exception remains, nevertheless, accessible."[74] So too for a general (juridical) understanding, or "philosophy of concrete life," which "must not withdraw from the exception . . . but must be interested in it to the highest degree."[75] In Schmitt's view, only an understanding that considers the exception can arrive at a consciousness of the tension between the ideal and the real, the rules and the exception, and of the scope and limits of understanding. We have seen that Schmitt argues, in *Political Romanticism*, that Kantian theoretical rationalism fails in its explanation of the way to supersede the dualism between the ideal and the real. This insufficiency, in Schmitt's view, is ultimately due to something that appears more clearly in *Political Theology*'s thought of the exception. By emphasizing the constructions of the mind, Kantian theoretical rationalism neglects the pole opposite to that of constructions: the exception—the hidden and uncontrollable background from which existence emerges.[76] The philosophy of concrete life thematizes existence as exceptional and, while hidden, as also unveiled.[77] This thought keeps both poles in view: the exceptional-existential and the conceptual, thus aiming at an understanding that, without abandoning itself to the pole of the real, attends to it in its ultimately unfathomable character.[78] Notwithstanding the abysmal character of existence, of its exceptionality, it emerges revealed in certain ways, which can be discerned. The disclosure is the basis for any understanding.[79] Existence is both exceptional *and* unveiled.

In *The Concept of the Political*, Schmitt again views the question of the tension and relation between rule and case as a general hermeneutical problem. If understanding is to be correct, it must take a step from the sphere of the ideal toward that of the real. Only by means of that step can we "correctly recognize, understand and judge the concrete situation."[80] The result of this understanding could therefore be "existential," expressed in concepts and rules nourished with the meaning and depth of the real. The neglect of this requirement to step into "existential reality"[81] results in a self-contained thought that persists in "abstractions" and "normative ideals."[82]

In the second part of *The Concept of the Political*, "The Age of Neutralizations and Depolitizations," Schmitt affirms: "all concepts of the spiritual sphere"—that is, not only juridical notions in the strict sense, but all practical and theoretical concepts—"are pluralistic in themselves."[83] He also states: "We recognize the pluralism of spiritual life."[84] Immediately following the first passage he adds: "All the essential concepts are not normative but existential."[85] He asserts, further, that in "every concept and word" there exists an irreducible "ambiguity."[86] Together, these statements thematize, from a broadly speaking juridical or philosophical standpoint, human understanding, its conditions, and the tension and relation between concepts and concrete existence. Before being applied, the concept is still undetermined. It is thus ambiguous, able to serve as the ground for various interpretive decisions. In being applied, its content changes; it is determined, insofar as it must be reinterpreted in light of the meaning to which one gains access in concrete existence. The "pluralistic" character of concepts to which Schmitt alludes is, therefore, insurmountable, since, if the meaning of concrete existence is taken into account, the concept acquires a new significance in every hermeneutical act. Understanding is persistently required to heed the situation and its existential depth. "All the essential concepts are not normative but existential" means that—if concepts are to be distinguished from abstract formulae used to merely subject reality—understanding must proceed from the formulae to concrete existence, and from it reinterpret the rules and concepts. Schmitt calls this kind of understanding—attentive to concrete existence—"an integral understanding," that is, one that does not emphasize only the rules, but considers *all* the aspects involved in the situation.[87]

In *On the Three Types of Juristic Thought*, Schmitt stresses the similarity between "intelligence [*Intelligenz*]" and "jurisprudence,"[88] which operate in a likewise manner. All understanding takes place based in traditionary concepts and rules.[89] The subject tries to illumine the cases by means of rules and concepts. Any adequate understanding of the cases demands that one be attentive to the situational contexts and to the meaning present in them, which, again, leads Schmitt to warn against efforts to simply reduce the situations to the rules.[90] Schmitt thus criticizes "functionalism,"[91] which, due to its emphasis on the conceptual and the rules, lacks the ability to understand concrete existence—its "order" and eventual "disorder."[92] Moreover, it does not take into account that the revelation of existence as "order" is the condition for the validity of the rules, as well as for understanding in general. Neither the rules of "jurisprudence" nor those of "intelligence" could be applicable to a situation, unless the situation reveals itself in typical ways and is bestowed with a discernible meaning, not too heterogeneous from the meanings of the rules.[93]

In a comment appended in 1958 to the article "The Plight of European Jurisprudence," Schmitt writes: "Philosophy of law is not for me a vocabulary contained in an existing philosophical system and then set upon juridical questions, but the development of concrete concepts emerging from the immanence of a concrete juridical and social order." Such "juridical thought," he adds, "freed from the alleys with no way out of general concepts," is "superior to every philosophy."[94] The law, in this broad sense, is the fundamental manner of understanding. It can, however, tend toward functionalism, enter "the alleys with no way out of general concepts," or instead rise up, in a properly juridical gesture, to a lucid consideration of the tension and relation between rule and case. That lucidity requires that the understanding take into account the dimension of the concrete and its existential meaning, to then draw it into the concept.[95] This concrete dimension cannot be chaotic or compact; it must emerge beforehand as discernible.[96]

The Tyranny of Values contains, in Schmitt's words, "the reflections of a jurist upon the philosophy of values."[97] He refers, as a jurist, to a philosophical matter. His "juridical" reflection claims to coincide with that of Martin Heidegger.[98] A "juridical" consideration can be philosophical, if, as Schmitt clarifies—repeating an idea that he has pointed out in "The Plight of European Jurisprudence"[99]—the notions of philosophy and law are not restricted according to the usual division of the sciences.[100] The philosophy of values is a reaction to the existential situation in which "natural scientism [*Naturwissenschaftlichkeit*]" puts human beings and the "human sciences [*Geisteswissenschaften*]." The emphasis placed on a neutralized object by scientific rationality resulted in a search on the side of the cultural sciences for a "substitute"—namely, values—to the neglected meaning of existence.[101] The philosophy of values, however, obstructs the correct or nonabusive understanding of the situation. It tends toward a consideration of the meaning of the pole of the ideal while ignoring the meaning of the real.[102] The "position [*Setzung*]" of a value implies—due to the "specific logic" of the "value"—the devaluation of its opposite.[103] "The urge to make values prevail becomes a coercion to enact values directly."[104] An attentive pondering of the ideal meaning of concepts along with the real meaning of concrete situations, the juridical mediation between the meaning of the ideal and that of an existence that emerges bestowed with meaning, is replaced in the philosophy of values by a dispute of positions (*Setzungen*) regarding values that push for the immediate execution of the respective ideal: the concrete reality being submitted.

Systematic Exposition of the Fundamental Aspects of Juridical Understanding as the Manner of Understanding of the Philosophy of Concrete Life

Based on the observations of the previous section and chapters, I turn now to an exposition of the fundamental aspects of Schmitt's thought regarding juridical understanding in the broad sense.

THE POLES OF UNDERSTANDING

For Schmitt, understanding takes place between two poles, those of the ideal and the real. The pole of the *real* is that of given existence, which finds itself revealed, emerging in typical ways and according to a certain meaning. Yet it appears against a background of exceptionality—from an abyss of indeterminacy and mystery.[105]

The realization concerning this background of exceptionality from which existence emerges allows the human being to be aware of its condition, as well as of the scope and limits of thought and knowledge. The articulations of the mind—the words, concepts, and rules—discern existence. They are, however, heterogeneous with respect to the exceptional, the depth, the alterity betrayed by concrete reality and the particular situations within it. In virtue of this indetermination and depth, the situations, the cases before the human mind, differ from mere examples-of-a-rule, and cannot fully be reduced to the articulations of the mind.[106] The situations possess a depth from which they arise, a depth that makes each of them to be also a specific and peculiar case. Insofar as at the basis of existence there is "an ineluctable reality that no human mind has conceived,"[107] it is always possible that it emerges in a way that breaks "through the crust" of normality and the articulations and determinations of the mind.[108]

From the unfathomable and exceptional, existence appears, however, unveiled to a certain extent. It is not wholly closed in itself, completely hidden or totally chaotic. The unveiling prior to the operations of the subject is a condition for the intelligibility of existence and for human understanding.[109] Understanding is grounded in an uncovered reality, "in the manifestness of the thing encountered," in "the reality that comes to meet us,"[110] in a "given order."[111] Without such manifestness, the mental articulations through which existence is understood would lack contact with reality. "A general rule," affirms Schmitt, is valid regarding a situation "only in so far as the situation has not become completely abnormal and so long as the normal presupposed concrete type has not disappeared."[112] "The norm or rule does not create the order; on the contrary, only on the basis and in the framework of a given order does it have . . . validity."[113] This claim has a general scope for human understanding: "There does not exist a 'free-floating' jurisprudence any more than there exists a 'free-floating' intelligence."[114] There must be a certain relation between the poles of the real and the ideal, if the articulation of the real in words and statements is to become possible. There exist no concepts or rules that are "applicable to a chaos."[115]

We have already seen that, for Schmitt, existence and meaning are not separate, as if they were nude facts and pure values, but, rather, form a unity.[116] The meaning of existence is a condition for all thought and action. It operates at the basis of the intention of thinking and knowing.[117] Only with reference to this existential meaning can the possibility of discerning options to adopt interpretive decisions be explained, and that such decisions are, in fact, adopted. "Only in connection to a historical, concrete, total order," an order distinct from a situation in which there is a simple opposition of neutral facts and abstract rules or values;[118] only with regard to a meaningful existence,[119] an "order of meaning [*Sinnreich*],"[120] are decision and action explainable. It can be said, then, that a meaning emerges in the situation and that it is only then that the situation is constituted, because only from a previous revelation of meaning is it possible to explain the decision and any action, including the action of valuing. "A meaningful order lies at the basis of reality [*Wirklichkeit*]."[121] Such order "arises as unintentional development," and is only later "brought into consciousness in understanding."[122] Schmitt also shows, as we have seen, that a meaning operates even in the attempt of technological rationality to prescind from the meaning of existence. Behind its generalizing and controlling mode of understanding there is an "anxiety" regarding the unknown[123] and a desire to discard it by means of a control that expresses a "will to power."[124] Behind the technological rationality is a "spirit" that animates it as a reductionist form of understanding.[125]

Despite the typical and meaningful character of existence, we must insist, however, in its heterogeneity vis-à-vis the articulations of the mind through which existence is understood. Existence remains exceptional. It is irreducible to the boundaries of a predetermined being.[126] Each historical situation, each individual or group of individuals, have their own depth due to the abyss from which they arise, and to their alterity with regard to the phenomenal horizon, such that they may unveil themselves in new ways.[127]

Understanding is realized through an activity of the mind that brings the diversity of the real to the unity of consciousness. The pole of the ideal is that of the mental elaborations by which the subject brings to such unity that multiplicity.

Schmitt maintains, as we have seen, that thought and knowledge require a "distance" between the thinker and what is thought, between the knower and the known.[128] Such distance takes place in relation to each and every being and to the ontic sphere as a whole. That radicality is only possible if the subject is placed beyond the ontic sphere, that is, in a "transcendence." "Pure immanence," on the contrary, would amount to the "elimination of all distance."[129] In such a situation, the subject would find herself as fused with things, thus resulting in the disappearance of consciousness.[130] The transcendence from which the human being realizes the act of understanding[131] is not accessible in the same way as beings are.[132] It is exceptional. The exceptional appears here, then, as the "place" of indeterminacy in which the subject gains the necessary distance to reach consciousness. Consciousness presupposes, furthermore, that the subject have self-knowledge as subject. We have seen, in chapter 1, that for Schmitt the subject cannot achieve this self-knowledge by conceptually thematizing herself. General concepts are necessary but not sufficient condition of consciousness. The subject's knowledge of herself is not attainable by way of such concepts. The subject is a "concrete individuality."[133] A general concept is unsuitable to discern a concrete individual among others.[134] A thematization of the subject through general concepts would not enable her to identify herself as a singular individual and thus to differentiate herself from the other. Such knowledge of herself, then, must have a direct or nonconceptual character.[135] The conscious thematization of the subject rests on that previous direct access of such subject to her subjective singularity. In addition to the subject's location beyond the ontic sphere and her self-knowledge, actual self-consciousness, however, still requires the mediation of the articulations of the mind, namely, of "rules" and "concepts."[136] The complete absence of mental articulation of experience would also amount to a lack of the distance required by consciousness.[137] These articulations, insofar as they depend on a distancing of the mind from reality, cannot but keep the distance regarding the peculiarity of the situations. The generality of the concepts and rules expresses precisely that distance between intelligence and reality, which makes consciousness possible. Singularity is also immediacy, such that an understanding that becomes possible from transcendence will always also be generalizing to a certain extent. Yet mental articulations can be more or less distant or close regarding the real, its depth and meaning, more or less adequate or inadequate.

The Hermeneutical Dialectic

The mental articulations through which reality is understood are general. The cases or situations, on the contrary, are particular and concrete; they refer to the exceptional, to an existential depth, to an alterity that makes them resistant to words, concepts, rules, and norms.[138] This antagonism or tension between the ideal and the real results in a hermeneutical dialectic in general and legal in particular. A nonreductionist understanding cannot leave aside the fundamental heterogeneity between the terms of understanding.

The heterogeneity between the terms of understanding becomes manifest to consciousness insofar as, on one hand, it is aware of its general articulations, and on the other, it has access to a revealed, yet also hidden and dynamic existence, and to a meaning with which that existence is unveiled. There is an awareness of existence—also of the subject's own existence—that is independent of words, of "generalizations," of the "talk about the general."[139] In that exposition and access of the subject to concrete existence, she can notice the heterogeneity of that existence with regard to words and general rules.[140] The subject can notice, then, that there is not a perfect fit between the concrete meaning of the real and the generality of the rules and concepts. In view of that tension, and faced with the hermeneutical task, she can notice, moreover, that the heterogeneity between the generality of the rules and concepts and the peculiarity of the case leaves rules and concepts in a situation of "indeterminacy."[141] Their general content, if contrasted to the peculiar meaning of the case, betrays what Schmitt calls "ambiguity."[142] The rules and concepts are, taken abstractly, preliminary indications for understanding. If their meanings are grasped as fixed and univocal, independent of the concrete cases, the real is consequently reduced, when understood according to such concepts.[143]

In front of the meaning, the depth, and alterity of the case, the subject must adopt an interpretive decision that differs from a simple subsumption of the cases under the meanings of concepts and rules taken as fixed.[144] The subject must adjust or make adequate the traditional meaning of the rules, words, and concepts to the concrete meaning of the case. This implies that the subject must both *remain* in the sphere of words, rules, and concepts, and *step outside* of it to consider the pole of the real, to gather it in the hermeneutical act.

It is necessary that the interpretive decision *remains* in the sphere of general mental articulations. We have seen that without transcendence as a source of distance or without the mental articulations that arise from it, there is no possibility for understanding. A complete absence of subjective conceptualizing activity, the complete lack of "functionalism," a total receptivity, would imply a fall into the unconscious.[145] The subject acquires the capacity to elucidate reality from her distance with regard to it. Rules and concepts allow her to fix experiences, keeping an epistemic determination of what is known.[146] The typical character with which existence is revealed is received actively in conceptualizations that make it possible for the subject to have a reality bestowed with "cohesion [*Bindung*],"[147] and to have a world in common with others.[148] To disregard those rules and concepts in order to tend toward the pole of the real implies a neglect of that common world, of the typical character with which existence is revealed,[149] and ultimately leads for Schmitt, as I have noted above, to a "renunciation of an adequate relationship" with it.[150] The lack of consideration of the rules and concepts can give way to a purely random or arbitrary enunciation.[151] The absence of attention to the capacity for determination held by concepts and rules, and of their usual and traditional meanings, can lead—via occasionalism—to a loss of "certainty," without which human communal existence becomes arbitrary or subject to manipulative decisions against others.[152] Reality can also be interpreted according to non-thematized results of conceptual formulations that become surreptitiously added to it.[153]

The interpretive decision, however, must in a certain way *surpass* the sphere of rules and concepts. Understanding requires going beyond the calculus of rules and concepts: it is about considering existence. No rule can as such, taken separately, provide the knowledge of the concrete reached in experience. Further, no rule is sufficient to indicate how to realize the interpretive decision beforehand.[154] The interpretive decision is related to concrete experience heterogeneous from the rules. Any rule about how to realize the interpretive decision still remains in the ideal dimension of the rules.[155] Insofar as it is a general representation, whose contents are prior to and independent from the corresponding newly arising situation, any rule containing indications about the "application" of other rules will remain distant from the concrete field of reality and its existential depth. Without a step toward the concrete, its indication shall always be, compared to the content or meaning of the concrete, irreducibly ambiguous or indeterminate.[156] Thus, despite all the preliminary indications, understanding operates in a discontinuity between the abstract and the concrete, which can be saved only by way of a decision.

All concepts, as we have seen, have some level of generality. A singular concept would not be a concept, but rather an event. Yet insofar as they are more or less related to the pole of the real, they may be considered either as abstract and "normative,"[157] or instead as "existential" concepts.[158] Abstract or normative concepts are those that result from a mental activity that remains tied to the pole of the ideal or of the functional and attempts to bring the real to the ideal, keeping the rules unaltered. The one trying to understand operates as if the concept or rule had a "meaning established prior (both temporally and logically) to the decision." She does not notice that, given the concreteness and meaning of the situation, the concept can solely receive its specific content by being applied to the situation in question, by means of a decision that regards the meaning of the concept in the light of the situation.[159] The determination of real cases through those ideal concepts[160] amounts to a reduction of the cases to the rule and its prior meanings.[161] The case is made superficial, inasmuch as it is subjected to the previous meanings of a general rule.[162] The case is thus decided in the form of a subjection. The rule shows the case in such a way that what is relevant and significant in it—namely, that which is to be decided, the meaning requiring an interpretive decision—is neglected.[163]

If the one trying to understand notes the heterogeneity between the situations and the concepts, and the reduction of the cases produced by their subjection to the abstract meaning of the rules and concepts, she is faced with a *demand*. If she is to understand and not to detach herself or merely calculate by means of concepts and subsume reality, she must reach the dimension of the concrete and the other, in order to heed the way in which the concrete and the other lie unveiled, and to their meaning.[164] Thus alone is she in her condition to "correctly recognize, understand and judge the concrete situation."[165] Only by stepping outside the sphere of concepts and rules can concrete reality be articulated by means of concepts and rules whose content, though general, is modifiable in the hermeneutical act according to the meaning revealed in it.[166] The certainty of the traditionary, without which understanding and the hermeneutical community disappear, must partially give way to the meaning of the concrete.[167] The ideal meaning of the rules and concepts has to be reflectively adjusted to the meaning of the situation.

If the understanding takes that step toward reality and is open to its concrete meaning, then it is possible to reach an order of concepts other than those of the abstract and the ideal. These concepts may be called "existential" or "concrete," insofar as they emerge from a consideration of concrete existence.[168] The concept here grasps and is nourished by the meaning and existential depth of the real. The interpretive decision can thus become "existentially correct."[169]

Understanding implies a creative activity that includes the attention to the real and the adoption of interpretive decisions. From a context of prior rules and concepts, the subject takes a step into the dimension of "existential reality."[170] By considering its depth and alterity, she reappropriates the meaning of the rules and concepts, and eventually endows them with a new meaning. Given that the case and its meaning are here a defining part of the meaning whereby the rules and concepts are determined in the decision, understanding as creative activity establishes that these rules and concepts ever acquire "a new content."[171] Insofar as the meaning of the rules in interpretive decisions is adjusted to the meaning of the cases, the meaning of both is modified in the hermeneutical act.[172]

The difference between abstract concepts and concrete concepts results from divergent means of understanding. The abstract concepts are the product of an understanding that considers the concept and its meaning as a finished result, which must be followed as unchanging in the successive hermeneutical acts. The concrete concepts, instead, are the result of an understanding that attends to the emergence of meaning, which is renewedly recognized in the successive hermeneutical acts. If the first means of understanding (that of abstract concepts) begins with the consideration of an already determined or objectified and self-contained meaning, the second means of understanding (that of concrete concepts) begins with "the lived experience in which meaning comes into being as the happening of understanding."[173] In the first mode of understanding the unity of the concept is fixed and closed to the multiplicity of the real. The determination of the real in the concept excludes other possibilities of emergence of the real. In the second means of understanding, the multiplicity of the real is brought to the unity of the concept, but heeding the manifold within the unity, as well as the unfathomable and dynamic character of the source from which the manifold emerges. Here there is no determinant closure, because in this understanding reality is recognized as novel and ultimately uncontrollable.

Juridical understanding—and concrete concepts as its products—is thus evinced as an activity whose whole content cannot be defined or fixed beforehand. We have seen that, for Schmitt, "All concepts of the spiritual sphere . . . are pluralistic in themselves," and that "all essential concepts are not normative but existential" because the concrete meaning of the situation is a constitutive element of the meaning of the understanding and of its product, namely, the concrete concept.[174] There is a mutual influence between the concept and the situation. The consideration of the situation makes the situation enrich the concept and the concept become adequate to the situation. "The general concept meant by the word is enriched by any given intuition of the situation, so that what emerges is a new, more specific definition which does more justice to the particularity of that situation."[175] For Schmitt, given that the definition of the content of the concept still requires endowing it with a meaning that is accessed by stepping into the concrete dimension of the real, such definition is always "something yet to be produced [*erst zu bewirken*]."[176]

The evaluation of an interpretive decision requires having had the case in view as it emerges, from its depth, along with the new meaning that the concept thereby acquires in the hermeneutical act. The effort to determine what the correct decisions are before stepping into the concrete existential dimension amounts to remaining tied to the ideal dimension of the rules and of the preconceived possible cases, but without understanding.[177]

If this is correct, then, in its fundamental sense, understanding cannot be seen as a speculative activity, which, starting from norms and concepts that remain unchanged, subjects the cases and exposes them to the limits of an object. Rather, it is an activity that, given the concrete character of the cases and their meaning, also and always involves *praxis*.[178] The subject realizing this activity is in a certain way always a juridical agent, someone who decides and produces interpretations that may eventually modify the meaning of the cases and of the rules and concepts.[179] The modification of the meaning of the rules and concepts that occurs through stepping into the real dimension of the concrete, and in virtue of which the individual notes its existential depth and alterity, produces that the different acts of understanding leave a mark in the hermeneutical activity.[180] Hermeneutical consciousness is not, then, something immutable, fixed once and for all, but is altered and determined by the new acts of understanding.

In the first section of this chapter, I noted an eventual proximity between juridical and aesthetic understanding. Aesthetic and philosophical understanding coincide when their articulations achieve the capacity to give expression in a reflective way to the existential meaning. Schmitt alludes to that capacity in his commentary on Theodor Däubler's poem *Das Nordlicht*: "the depths of the world and the soul reveal themselves in . . . words, in a language that has abandoned all mediacy [*Mittelbarkeit*] to become the container [*Gefäß*] of wonderful images and thoughts." The existential depth, grasped by the "intuition, is brought to the word, and the word discovers whatever knowledge resides in it." These pieces of knowledge permit themselves to be expressed in "philosophical formulations."[181] In *Hamlet or Hecuba* (1956), Schmitt also notes the link between artistic and juridical understanding. The understanding realized in tragedy is, for Schmitt, analogous to juridical understanding in the broad sense, because it has the same fundamental structure. Schmitt addresses the relation and tension between the rule and the case apropos the dramatic work and considers how they determine the difference between the "play"—be it "comic [*Lustpiel*]" or "tragic [*Trauerspiel*]"—and "tragedy."[182] The play (whether comic or tragic) is a "fiction" that freely develops as "a completely self-contained, internally self-sufficient process."[183] In the play, the author's imaginative ideation—her "free and sovereign creative power"[184]—can accrue more weight than reality by its "fundamental negation of the serious situation [*Ernstfalles*]."[185] By contrast, *tragedy*, while still an artistic form, is characterized by its decisive consideration of the real. "All participants are conscious of an ineluctable reality that no human mind has conceived—a reality externally given, imposed and unavoidable."[186] If the play can rest on the free play of invention and the constructions of the mind, tragedy is defined by its reference to "living experience."[187] The play resembles technological understanding, inasmuch as concrete existence and its depth are neglected for the sake of rules and concepts. Schmitt describes the play as a self-contained product, a "rigorous . . . construction" according to certain "rules," in which the concrete situation and its depth are set aside.[188] Instead, tragedy is a means of understanding similar to that of the juridical. Juridical understanding steps from the ideal to the real, allowing the real to be expressed in an interpretive decision. Analogously, tragedy also emerges when that step to reality is accomplished and the story expresses the real.[189] Tragedy collects and articulates reality in such a way that reality receives an effective expression. "This unalterable reality is the silent rock on which the play is broken and from which the onslaught of the waves of the authentic tragedy emits its foam."[190] The artist's capacity to receive and respect that reality, without subjecting it to the limits of "self-contained" rules, to reflect on it without subsuming it, permits reality to emerge precisely in the way of a "living experience."[191]

The similarity between juridico-fundamental and aesthetic understanding is not merely factual. Given that Schmitt's hermeneutical thought rests on a critique of rationalism and on the affirmation of the impossibility of a determining exercise of the mind able to subsume an existence that is ultimately unfathomable, then in juridical understanding the mind encounters a situation similar to that in the aesthetic domain. If "by determining the object, science also excludes all the object's other possibilities, the work of art does not produce this kind of closure, because it reveals the world in a way which cannot be finally controlled."[192] As with artistic understanding, juridical understanding encounters a reality that is both revealed and unfathomable. Mental articulations do not grasp existence in its whole indeterminable depth. Nonetheless, they can elucidate and express existence in ways that are more or less pertinent, adequate, or correct. This correction or pertinence depends on the capacity of mental articulations to give expression in a reflexive way to the meaning of the reality. The interpretive decision is correct when it expresses the situation in a meaningful and intersubjective acceptable way.[193]

The statement of the coincidence between aesthetic and juridical understanding does not necessarily imply an attitude of surrender to the pole of the real. Instead, such statement is grounded in the admission of the unfathomable, revealed, and meaningful character of existence, which, along with being hostile to mere subsumption, requires, however, the adoption of an interpretive decision. Given the fact that existence reveals itself with meaning, the subject is faced with the demand to comprehendingly decide, avoiding the extremes of functionalism and passivity. The Schmittian thematization of existence—of the poles of understanding—prohibits the adoption of an attitude of complete surrender, preponderantly passive regarding the pole of the real. As we saw, apropos of *Hamlet or Hecuba* and the commentary on Däubler's poem, Schmitt's reflections on the work of art unfold as a juridical consideration conscious of the conditions involved in the aesthetic that allow to discern detachment and a self-contained production, and, between them, an effective articulation of the real in the work.

THE LAW AS FUNDAMENTAL FORM OF UNDERSTANDING

Understanding admits of different levels. The understanding of the judge or of a political agent when faced with a particular case differs from the consideration of a jurist or of a political scientist regarding a certain aspect of the juridical or political field (e.g., the constitution, the state, war), or of these fields themselves. And these understandings differ from the thematization of existence as a whole. There is a first-order understanding, more directly concerned with a particular case; but there is also second-order understanding, focused on a certain aspect of a field or on a certain field of existence. Finally, there is a third-order understanding, occupied with existence in all its possible aspects. In these three levels, the poles of the ideal and the real are already operative, and hence there is partial conceptualization. For example, the particular case a judge reviews is always unveiled and has some degree of linguistic articulation. The poles of the ideal and the real are also discernible within the juridical or political field and their diverse aspects. For example, the political constitution as a phenomenon includes linguistic formulations, along with a constitutional situation to which it is referred and which is also unveiled. The same could be said of existence as a whole. Conceptuality and reality, linguistic articulation and situation, are discernible but not completely separable. Given that the three levels are similarly conformed, the hermeneutical requirements are alike. If the understanding is to be correct, pertinent, or adequate, it must attend to the relation and tension between, on one hand, rules and concepts, and, on the other, the situations to be addressed. To understand always means to understand the pole of the real from that of the ideal, and vice versa. In all three levels, the one who understands must consider the meaning of the rules and concepts, and heed the requirement of reinterpreting the rules and concepts through which the situation is considered, noticing the novelty and meaning of the particular case, the juridical or political situation (or some aspect thereof), or the existential situation as such. Within particular juridical cases, and before the heterogeneity betrayed by the cases with regard to the rules, there is occasion for noting that tension between the poles of understanding. This consideration opens to a reflection on the relation of the polarities of the case and the rules. When that relation and tension are thematized, the law rises to a reflection and understanding that look explicitly at its own presuppositions as a discipline. Insofar as it is recognized that this tension affects not only understanding in the juridical field in its usual sense, but understanding in general, the law then reaches the level of what Schmitt calls the philosophy of concrete life.

Schmitt describes the result of juridical understanding, that is, the "juridical concept [*Begriff*]," as "the grabbing from the incomprehensible into the intangible [*der Griff aus dem Unbegreifbaren in das Ungreifbare*]."[194] The activity of juridical understanding is thematized as that which is realized from a field of indeterminacy (the incomprehensible), from a transcendence, which allows the subject to gain distance with regard to what is understood.[195] This understanding comes to fruition through a conceptualizing activity that is meant to consider something that is unveiled and yet ultimately "intangible [*Ungreifbare*]," which constitutes the basis of existence as a whole.[196] Here the poles clearly appear as the defining hermeneutical elements: the pole of the ideal, expressing the conceptualizing activity of the mind, and the pole of the real, as the exceptional and transcendent, from which human existence emerges. In this context, the thematization of understanding achieves awareness of the conditions, and of the scope and limits of hermeneutical activity. Juridical understanding considers, in a reflective fashion, these defining polarities as the extremes of a framework within which existence and understanding in general unfold. Thus, juridical understanding notes that the poles are indispensable as aspects of existence and as conditions of understanding in general. The poles of understanding can be seen, then, as discernible but related parts of a whole: an existence at once hidden and unveiled—that is, articulable in an understanding. The law, as a fundamental form of understanding, reflectively discerns the poles as aspects of the totality of existence. In the thematization of "abstraction" and "concreteness," of the "rule" and the "exception" made by the law, these terms are not and cannot be regarded as "binaries," where the affirmation of one excludes that of the other, such that the subject trying to understand is bound to commit herself to one pole or the other, instead of moving to an intermediate position.[197] The law considers itself precisely as an intermediate position in the sense that it reflectively justifies the status of the poles as related hermeneutical conditions, and as irreducible aspects of existence. Despite its "apparent opposition," the poles of the ideal and of the real are "intrinsically related."[198]

This reflective attitude forms the basis of Schmitt's critique of the extreme positions of technology and theology. In the extremes, one of the two poles is totally or partially neglected.

Schmitt's critique of theology (in its many forms), as we have seen in chapter 2, points to theology's surrendering to the pole of the real, either without, or at least without sufficient epistemological control. Theology does not adequately consider the activity of the subject in understanding. Thus, concept and reality tend to remain in a mere juxtaposition. I have noted that many attitudes are possible in this context, according to the level of reflection engaged. In the extreme, theology alludes to the surrender to the pole of the real—its exceptionality, meaning, and mystery—in the manner of bare faith. It is also possible to conceive a faith in which there is a disciplined use of reason and thought, yet with a strategic purpose: a thought at the service or in defense of faith. A higher engagement of thought is found in what I have called "rational theology." Here the exceptional, the meaning, the mystery, and the numinous are admitted. However, rational theology does not sufficiently consider the role of the spontaneity of the subject in understanding. Without sufficient epistemological control, that conceptualizing activity now reifies the numinous or exceptional. Although it first regards the exceptional and the meaning of the pole of the real, in a second moment that pole is (incoherently) subjected to a conceptualization (i.e., to the functional) that reduces it to the limits of a determined being—to the bounds of the "unexceptional." The exceptional is reduced in a nonreflective way by a conceptual function. The reduction is nonreflective inasmuch as there is here no critical examination regarding the legitimacy of the use of the determining function—an examination that allows juridical understanding to note the incoherence of such reduction.[199]

In the Schmittian reflection, transcendence or the exceptional betray some marks that make it compatible with the notion of the "numinous" that forms the basis of religious experience and theological thought. Transcendence or the exceptional is mysterious. As the uncontrollable, it is the source of uncertainty and angst.[200] As the depth from which the entire existence emerges, it may be called "the *tremendum*."[201] As the background of existence's unveiling and meaning, it is also "attractive and fascinating."[202] However, at this point where the juridical understanding, or the philosophy of concrete life, coincides with what may be called theological thought, Schmitt fundamentally distances himself from other theologies (T1, T2, and T3; see chapter 2), and especially from the theology that Heinrich Meier attributes to him. In other theologies, either faith plays an exclusive or subordinating role vis-à-vis thought, or thought does not exercise sufficient epistemological control. By contrast, juridical understanding legitimizes transcendence, its exceptional character, and the limits of cognition by means of a reflection on the conditions for understanding.[203]

In the case of functionalism, Schmitt directs his critique toward revealing it to be a reductionist manner of understanding.[204] Functionalism provides an unsatisfactory explanation of the relation between the real and the ideal. Insofar as it emphasizes the conceptual, functionalism is unable to properly understand the pole of the real, the exception, the meaning of the situations, the alterity of the other as another interiority that is incomprehensible if dealt with in the manner of objects.[205] Functionalism fails to heed the way in which existence emerges, and the source of mystery from which it emanates. We have seen that Schmitt includes in his critique of functionalism the theoretical philosophy of Immanuel Kant. He extends his critique also to other authors whom he situates within the functionalist field.[206] Prominent among them is Ernst Cassirer,[207] who explicitly advocates for a functionalist notion of the "concept," which he opposes to a substantialist view. The substantialist notion regards the concept as an abstraction from already existing beings. Cassirer shows that substantialism fails to sufficiently recognize the role of the subject in understanding, and especially in the production of conceptual articulations. As a worldview noncritically inclined to the real pole, substantialism is unable to account for the spontaneity through which the subject becomes self-conscious, and actively understands existence according to concepts and rules.[208] Unlike Cassirer, however, for whom in scientific understanding "the individual case is not excluded from consideration" and the scientific concept "does not disregard the peculiarities and particularities which hold under it,"[209] Schmitt argues that thinking that "universal" rules of science can define existence presupposes, in the end, a reduction of it to conceptual functions. Schmitt notes the exceptionality of that existence, its meaning, its depth, the irremovable alterity of the other. These considerations warn him against the attempt to refer that existential aspect, without any loss, to a system of determining rules.[210]

The Manner of Juridical Understanding in Schmitt's Texts

Each of Schmitt's main works can be interpreted as expression of the juridical manner of understanding. This manner of understanding extends to various domains of knowledge and aspects of human existence. Several of Schmitt's texts are concerned with theoretico-juridical problems in the narrowest sense of the term: judicial praxis; constitutional or international public law; ways of considering the law. Others attend to theoretico-political subjects: the political as a domain; political understanding; geopolitical matters; the analysis of contemporary or past political ideas. Cultural or aesthetic issues are addressed in various texts as well. Yet none of these works can be properly interpreted except as expressions of that juridical manner of understanding that persists in the author's oeuvre as its hermeneutical frame.

As we have seen, the main concern in *Law and Judgment* (1912) is judicial praxis. It is brought to the fore through a thematization of the relation and tension between the polarities of the rules and the cases.

In his next book, *The Value of the State and the Importance of the Individual* (1914), Schmitt discerns a juridico-philosophical "method" with respect to a consideration oriented to praxis.[211] Such a "method" involves the establishment of a strict distinction between facticity and ideality, in which the law as a mental construction falls on the side of the ideal.[212] In this work there is thus a functionalism that is more marked than in preceding or succeeding writings. Schmitt tends to consider reality as empirical facticity and confronted to the idealities.[213] However, he qualifies this position. In contemplating existence in an empirical way, Schmitt consciously assumes a natural-scientific conception of reality.[214] He pays heed to the partiality of this method,[215] although he does not further thematize the problem of the reduction of the real that such a method carries out, the manner in which it accomplishes the reduction, and the status of what is reduced. But the explicit mention of the partiality of this method implies that Schmitt leaves open the possibility of considering reality in a broader manner. This different way of understanding is realized, in fact, in Schmitt's own text, where he explicitly admits the validity of the standpoint of "praxis."[216] Before the conformations of power, factually considered, he states that "the liberty of the individual can be formula for concrete political requirements."[217] That is to say, even if there is an emphasis on the opposition between facts and idealities, some positions are discernible that have sense only through the recognition of meaning in the situations. From the admission of that meaning, one can also understand Schmitt's indication that "from the standpoint of praxis, one readily sees the incorrectness of the statement that the judge is the mouthpiece of the law [*Mund des Gesetzes*]." The same consideration elucidates his notice of the "incompleteness of the law" regarding the concrete case.[218] His awareness of this incompleteness can arise only if there is—as Schmitt admits—a "reality" deserving "recognition."[219] Only an acknowledgment of a meaning of the real provides an explanation of Schmitt's view that "under certain circumstances it is absolutely more important *that* [*daß*] something is actually decided than the concrete content the decision may have"[220]—or, finally, of his indication that in some situations there is a "requirement [*Bedürfnis*] for a concrete decision."[221]

I have already mentioned that in *Theodor Däublers "Nordlicht"* (1916) and in *Political Romanticism* (1919), Schmitt expands his juridical-hermeneutical reflections toward human understanding in general, noticing the relation and tension between the poles of the ideal and the real, the possible hermeneutical positions, and defending a way of understanding that attends to the meaning of both reality and ideality.

Dictatorship (1921) is a study of the theory of the state and the law, whose central issue—namely, dictatorship—is approached from the consideration of the tension between the poles of the ideal and the real. The political existence of the people is usually articulated within an institutional configuration of norms and stable practices. That articulation, however, can enter a crisis. There are three principal means of understanding the fact of the crisis: a liberal understanding, another which might be called juridical, and a revolutionary understanding. Each of these positions corresponds to one of the fundamental hermeneutical positions differentiated by Schmitt: respectively, functionalism, law, and substantialism. Liberalism is inclined to the functionalist extreme. Its embrace of a mode of understanding that emphasizes the pole of the ideal over that of the real restricts its ability to properly consider the exceptional situation, while it persists in the idea of a self-contained order of rules. Liberalism rejects the notion of dictatorship and identifies it with an arbitrary exercise of power.[222] By contrast, the revolutionary is inclined toward the extreme of substantialism. From a view of human perfection, the revolutionary develops a radical critique of the "existing order," to the point of proposing steps that lead to the overcoming of the state-juridical institutionality.[223] The dictatorship loses its "commissarial" or limited sense.[224] Juridical thought, on the other hand, advocates neither for a self-contained functionalism, nor for a revolutionary overcoming of the juridico-political order.[225] The juridical institution points to a realization of meaning that, insofar as it adequates to the situation and does not subsume it in the manner of technological rationality, makes it possible to reach a stability through means other than the mere violence of subsumption. Juridical thought remains aware, however, of the depth and dynamism of existence and the eventuality of a crisis. Given the impossibility of denying these aspects of existence, the dictatorship acquires a special relevance through juridical thought, as a dispositive that allows for the reestablishment of the conditions under which juridical rules can once again be valid.[226]

In *Political Theology* (1922), as we saw above, Schmitt explicitly puts forth the tension between the ideal and real, both in the domain of understanding in general and in that of juridical understanding in the usual sense of the term. He identifies the law in the broad sense with the philosophy of concrete life. In the usual juridical domain, Schmitt criticizes normativism because it ignores the exceptional situation; he avoids the aestheticizing detachment, incapable of making a decision; he also rejects the decisionistic arbitrariness and the attitude that uses the dispositive of the state of emergency to actively produce an exceptional situation. Instead, for Schmitt the point is to reestablish the situation where norms can achieve validity.[227] In this book, Schmitt also formulates his theory of the "sociology of juridical concepts," concerning the relation in a given epoch between the fundamental philosophical conception and the juridico-political conception. The comparison of these two kinds of conceptualization allows him to recognize that understanding in general has a "structure" similar to that of juridical understanding.[228]

In *The Crisis of Parliamentary Democracy* (1923), Schmitt distinguishes parliamentarism from democracy.[229] The first is an elaboration of liberalism that rests on the idea "that the truth can be found through an unrestrained clash of opinion and that competition will produce harmony." From this are assumed two requirements: namely, "the postulate of openness in political life and the demand for a division of powers."[230] The legislative function, carried out by the parliament, acquires special relevance. It is conceived in strict opposition to "everything concrete," whereby the concrete is reduced to "a case for the application of a general law."[231] Democracy rests, in turn, on "homogeneity," in a "substantial equality," under which alone "universal and equal suffrage," as well as the idea that the decisions of the rulers express those of the governed, may seem "quite reasonable"—insofar as there is an "identity of governed and governing."[232] There is, then, a tension between a functional principle (parliamentarism) on one hand, and a substantial principle (democracy), on the other.[233] Schmitt contends that, "because of the development of modern mass democracy," the parliamentary system is in a crisis: public deliberation becomes "empty formality," turning into a dispute of "interests," a matter of "compromises," and of parties that gain votes through "a propaganda apparatus."[234] The crisis erupts at various, perceptible moments: one that is Marxist; one that is irrationalist, expressed in the works of Proudhon and of Bakunin; and then one of mythical thought, which reaches political expression in the fascist myth of the nation. This last, the myth of the nation, comes to be "the most powerful symptom of the decline of the relative rationalism of parliamentary thought." Schmitt sees a "danger" in irrationalist tendencies, before which merely "repeating the question, 'Parliamentarism, what else?' "[235] is no longer pertinent. Although in *The Crisis* Schmitt does not develop an answer to the emergency, he lays out its direction: a politico-institutional system capable of facing the danger of the substantialist-irrationalist inclination requires compensating liberal formalism (parliamentarism) with aspects of substantialism (democracy), a homogeneity of contents that allows for the constitution of the corresponding political group as a form of common existence.[236]

In *The Concept of the Political* (1927), Schmitt notes the tense and serious character of existence. The tension is here expressed as the antagonism between friend and enemy.[237] It is a tension formed by the relation between the knowledge the subject has of herself and the unfathomableness of the pole of the real, from which the other arises.[238] We have seen that Schmitt reflects here explicitly on the question of the tension and relation between the ideal sphere of concepts and the real as a general hermeneutical problem.[239] In the second part of the book, Schmitt refers to the difference between the technological manner of understanding, and that which has the dimensions of both the ideal and the real in view: a form of understanding that can therefore note the ambiguity and pluralism of words and concepts, and that their determination requires a renewed attention to concrete existence.[240]

In *Constitutional Theory* (1928), Schmitt distinguishes the constitution in a formalist sense, according to which it is reduced to certain norms, whatever their content, that are written and whose "alteration" depends on "qualified prerequisites and procedures."[241] This formalist concept of constitution arises after the crisis of a notion, prevalent in the Enlightenment, of the constitution as "a closed system of higher and ultimate norms"[242]—a notion that depends on the "rationalistic belief" that it would be possible to achieve "a conscious and complete plan for the entire political and social life."[243] The variability and depth of concrete political existence erodes such a belief, however, and proves the enlightened project to be unviable. Schmitt contrasts the normativistic notion to a previous conception of the constitution as "the concrete manner of existence that is given with every political unity."[244] The constitution in a normative sense rests on the "constitution" in this existential sense, in a dependency that is grounded on the recognition that the "text of every constitution is dependent on the political and social situation."[245] The "validity" of the norms presupposes a politically and juridically ordered situation.[246] Schmitt inquiry into the origin of the constitution leads him to consider the "constitution-making power," which he describes in terms of a "political will, whose power or authority is capable of making the concrete, interpretive decision over the type and form of its own political existence." Such power lies at the basis of "any additional rule."[247] In a specifically political sense, the constitution-making power emerges from "the people,"[248] a collective that arises from an unfathomable background, whose irruptions are not controllable in advance.[249] The tension between the polarities of the functional and the substantial is also found in the "constitution" of the "bourgeois Rechtsstaat," a constitution "composed of a *linkage and mixture of burgeois Rechtsstaat principles and those of political form.*"[250] Those principles can be viewed as a normalizing rationalization of the state's capacity for political action.²⁵¹ They do not exhaust, however, the totality of the constitution, for there is also "the political component,"²⁵² upon which the agency of the state depends. That agency operates between the "two principles" of "identity" and "representation," neither of which is disposable "in the reality of political life."²⁵³ If identity alludes to an element that is eminently substantial (the people), representation alludes to one that is preponderantly functional. They thus assume the relation of a tension of opposites.²⁵⁴ Nevertheless, both refer, in turn, to the poles of the functional and the substantial: the people must achieve the status of a political nation to be an operative entity;²⁵⁵ representation, on the other hand, lacks efficacy unless it becomes "something *existential*."²⁵⁶

The main aspects of Schmitt's *Constitutional Theory* are understood juridically, from the consideration of the relation and tension between the poles of the ideal and the real. The constitution can be existentially or normatively understood; the constitutional-making power operates through an articulation of substantive elements; the constitution of the bourgeois Rechsstaat emerges as a relation and tension between the bourgeois component and political principles; political principles—identity and representation—are related, respectively, to the poles of the real (identity) and the ideal (representation), and they are, in turn, existential and ideal.

In *Legality and Legitimacy* (1932), Schmitt formulates a typology of political regimes, according to the way in which they produce and apply the law. He distinguishes four states: "legislative," "jurisdiction," "administrative," and "government" state.²⁵⁷ In the legislative state, a parliament dictates norms according to a certain procedure of "discussion and publicity."²⁵⁸ Norms can thus gather some "qualities": they are "impersonal, that is, general and preetablished"; they are "meant to be lasting," and "have a definable, determinable content."²⁵⁹ The legislative state presupposes a rationalist "belief" in "*idées générales*."²⁶⁰ The vitality of this belief depends on the fulfillment of the procedure of deliberation and on the qualities of the law indicated above. In the absence of these conditions, the mere form of parliamentary majority ascribes the character of the law to any decision.²⁶¹ This is what occurred in the Republic of Weimar.²⁶² Yet a parliamentary regime would still be possible even when those qualities of the law and the vitality of parliamentary procedure are lost, if there is some popular homogeneity. Without it, "the abstract, empty functionalism of pure mathematical majority determinations"²⁶³ leads to crisis. The legislative state loses its specific character, and a circumstantial majority can exclude the minority.²⁶⁴ Schmitt detects an inconsistency in the Weimar

Constitution. It affirms the principle of the legislative state, which has acquired a degraded, merely functionalist manner, but it also contemplates, however, in its text and in practice, what Schmitt calls "three extraordinary lawgivers:" the parliament, acting in certain matters whose approval needs more than a simple majority; the people, by means of plebiscite; the president in his or her capacity to issue decrees through a recognized practice regarding matters of law.[265] Because of this inconsistency, Schmitt concludes that "the Weimar Constitution is two constitutions:" one of a legislative character, which has become merely functional, and another attempting "to establish a substantive order."[266]

The typology of regimes, the analyses of the legislative state, and of the problem of Weimar parliamentarism, are brought about through a juridical (in the wide sense) manner of understanding. The difference between the regimes can be ascertained by the more or less abstract or concrete nature of their juridical production, with the legislative state tending toward the pole of the abstract, and the other three toward the concrete.[267] In the case of the legislative state, however, it is possible to distinguish a conformation where there is still a "substantive" meaning of the laws and of the law,[268] from a moment where it becomes a "functionalist view without substance"[269] of the circumstantial mathematical majorities. The crisis of the Weimar Republic depends, for Schmitt, on the tension between that functionalist vision and the attempts to recover the connection with concrete existence by strengthening popular participation and the operating capacity of the president.[270]

I have previously referred to the juridical (in the wide sense) understanding in *On the Three Types of Juristic Thought* (1934). Schmitt's critique of normativism and juridical decisionism, as well as his idea of the law as an order, are justified by a consideration of existence as a tension and relation between the ideal and the real.[271]

The Leviathan (1938) is a study on Hobbes's work that is also carried out through juridical understanding in the wide sense. Schmitt notes the symbolic nature of the *Leviathan*, both in the tradition and in the allusions made by Hobbes himself.[272] The Leviathan as a symbol is a figure that has the capacity to effectively articulate human collective existence. Schmitt then considers the "conceptual and systematic construction of Hobbes' theory of the state,"[273] with the "fear of the state of nature" as his starting-point:[274] "fear brings atomized individuals together."[275] Before the individual, the state occupies a juridically "transcendent" position.[276] The Hobbesian construction is also linked to technological rationality, insofar as it appears like a "mechanism" or "instrument" that enables to reach a "neutralization" of the religious dispute with which modernity begins. It is the "first product of the age of technology" and the condition for the possibility of subsequent technological development.[277] Hobbes is thus located at the functionalist pole of understanding.[278] His genius, which is able to provide conceptual support to a form of organization capable of overcoming the precarious condition of the human being in the state of nature, is ultimately limited by that functionalism.[279] Hobbes's emphasis on identifying the functionalist aspect of the state is the basis of an emerging tension that cannot be resolved within such a functionalist framework: the tension between the visible mechanics and the invisible interiority of the human being, which is expressed as "the distinction between private and public, faith and confession."[280] For a state conceived in a functionalist manner, an interiority that may become the source of another kind of justification, and that may even become conspiratorial in the end, is incomprehensible and ultimately unmanageable.[281]

Land and Sea (1942) is a reflection on the evolution of the conceptions of space. The starting-point of human existence is "the firmly grounded earth."[282] In modern times there is a turn toward the sea; navigating technologies are invented; a continent is discovered.[283] The struggle for the new spaces is intertwined with the struggles over religion.[284] These factors, coupled with a conceptual and scientific consolidation, result in a "planetary spatial revolution."[285] Within the arising scientific view, space is considered as "infinite" and "empty."[286] The war also changes. Armed conflicts at sea are more difficult to limit than those on the land.[287] The new scientific conception makes possible the industrial revolution,[288] and the sea then becomes an object of technological control.[289] Technology advances to conquer another element: the "*air*," control over which is achieved by means of the airplane and radio waves.[290] "Explosive motors" appear, at last, as an expression of "*fire*."[291] Due to an increase of technological activity, "space has become a force field of human energy, activity and achievement."[292] In Schmitt's considerations, the earth occupies the pole of the concrete, while the sea, the air, and fire are more elusive and abstract and require more technology in order to be controlled. In its spatiality, however, all elements come from the pole of the real. Spatial changes set the mind to the task of a new understanding, as it occurs with the "nothing"[293] opened up by "empty space" in the epoch of the first spatial revolution, and with the "void" produced by the new spaces in current times.[294]

In *The Nomos of the Earth* (1950), Schmitt calls "*nomos*" the order that emerges with an original "land-appropriation,"[295] realized by a human group and in virtue of which "order and orientation"[296] are achieved. The *nomos* contains an "inner measure." It is prior to any normativistic rationalization, since it is condition for the validity of the norms and rules.[297] The land-appropriation should not be understood as a sovereign act, as bare "establishment [*Setzung*]."[298] There is a previous revelation of space as an "order of meaning,"[299] bestowed with specific qualities.[300] Based on the consideration of the juridical and political order as resting on the spatial, Schmitt analyzes the historical movement from the juridical Middle-Ages to European international law. Medieval juridical order and thought, theological in nature, yield, due to religious conflicts and the new spatial conformation, to a specifically juridical conception of existence.[301] The "great advance" of this step lies, according to Schmitt, in the consideration of the parts in conflict as equally legitimized. The concept of war abandons the question of the "*justa causa*," and focuses on the "*justus hostes*."[302] This distinction makes it possible to eliminate the "tendency," included in the concept of *justa causa*, to "discriminate against the unjust opponent,"[303] and to avoid the deprivation of rights and the abuses that follow from discrimination.[304] The new juridical order is not a normativistic construct, but a concrete configuration of spatiality. It is composed of a set of sovereign European states, articulated in a certain unity that acquires a marked profile against the background of the new immense maritime spaces and the lands of foreign peoples, "open to land-appropriations."[305] "Firm land" and "free sea" emerge as distinct orders, with differentiated concepts of "enemy, war, booty and freedom." The contraposition allows for a "balance of land and sea."[306] Within that order, the continental potencies reach juridical stable modes of relation and, if "not the elimination," at least "the bracketing of war."[307] After centuries, the order heads into crisis, marked by the loss of spatial consciousness in juridical thought. The order turns into an "empty normativism of allegedly recognized rules."[308] The planet is homogenized under the rules of generalizing rationality.[309] European collective order is weakened, the economy becomes autonomous from the law, and new potencies arise.[310] A "League of Nations" is forged between highly heterogeneous states. They are not effectively—but just formally—equal.[311] The new situation is determined, moreover, by the decompensating appearance of the United States, a potency that vacillates between "isolation" and "intervention."[312] The normativization of the concrete order modifies once again the notion of war. The doctrine of *"justus hostes"* is abandoned, and war is increasingly moralized and criminalized.[313] The United States' conception of space and their idea of a "Western Hemisphere," abstract and virtuous, influences this moralization.[314] Schmitt ends *The Nomos of the Earth* by considering the shift from war on land to war at sea and in the air, which takes place thanks to technological advances, and the increasing abstraction and destructive power of war technologies. If the moralizing concept of war allowed one to behave more cruelly with one's enemies, the cruelty of the new technologies can be admitted only insofar as the enemy is morally discriminated and criminalized.[315]

At the beginning of this text, Schmitt locates "jurisprudence" "between theology and technology."[316] The book can be read as a study of the transition from a Christian theological order to the European juridical order, and of the dissolution of the European juridical order by the irruption of a combination of technological rationality and liberalism. The Christian order is inclined toward the pole of substantialism. Despite its distinctions and weighings, it is discriminating. In contrast, the European order of international law is developed by a juridical, nondiscriminating rationality, and rests on a concrete configuration of space. Due to conceptions unrelated to concrete space, and to certain economic and technological developments coupled with the abstract rationalities behind them, discrimination returns, though in a new, functionalist form.

In *Hamlet or Hecuba* (1956), as I have discussed at length above, Schmitt unfolds what may be described as a juridical conception (in the wide sense) of art. The difference between "play" and "tragedy"[317] is that the former is a "fiction" that freely develops as "a completely self-contained, internally self-sufficient process"[318] in which the author's "free and sovereign creative power"[319] can acquire more weight than reality, while in "tragedy" there is a decisive reference to reality.[320] Just as technological thought is, for Schmitt, a manner of understanding in which concrete existence is neglected, the play is a "rigorous . . . construction" according to certain "rules," in which the concrete situation and its meaning tend to be left out.[321] And just as juridical understanding takes the step from the ideal to the real, allowing the real to be expressed in an interpretive decision, tragedy also emerges when that step is taken and the force of the real is expressed in the story.[322]

In *Theory of the Partisan* (1963), Schmitt defines the partisan by four marks: "irregularity" (regarding the regular army, which aspires to dominate a public sphere);[323] the "intensity" of her "political engagement;"

her "increased mobility" in "combat;" and her "telluric" character.[324] These marks make the partisan a phenomenon difficult to apprehend through the usual juridical manner of understanding, and also make the conflict in which partisans are involved particularly intense.[325] Schmitt addresses the evolution of the partisan in the thought of Clausewitz, Lenin, Stalin, Mao Tse-tung, and Salan. He then considers the figure in its "last stage."[326] Conspicuous in this stage are the relation of her presence with the "destruction of social structures,"[327] and her involvement in a "global-political context," detaching herself from her telluric-defensive character.[328] Also important is her "technical-industrial aspect," which places the partisan within an emerging tension: technology, with its emphasis on the normalization of existence, loses the ability to understand a figure that technology itself makes possible, insofar as it provides her with new means for action.[329] Finally, Schmitt refers to the step from the "real" to an "absolute enemy," made possible by the loss of the telluric and defensive character of the partisan, in both revolutionary thought and praxis.[330] Schmitt conceptualizes the partisan in consideration of the tension and relation between normality and exception. The figure evolves from boundedness to the territory and its defense, to the lack of roots—from the concrete to the abstract. The road to abstraction is fueled by two factors: technological rationality and the universalistic motive of revolutionary thought.

Political Theology II (1970), Schmitt's last published book, contains a response to Erik Peterson's thesis about "the theological impossibility of any 'political theology.' "[331] For Peterson, the Christian Trinitarian dogma does not allow for the affirmation of any determined relation between theological belief and the political situation.[332] Schmitt shows the implausibility of eliminating the possibility of political theology, in the sense in which he considers it in his "sociology of concepts,"[333] through a theologico-dogmatic argument, as Peterson tries to do.[334] The strict separation between a purely political and a purely religious sphere, which operates until the "liberalism of the nineteenth century," has become untenable. Schmitt states that thereafter, any matter, including a theological one, may become political, depending only on the "intensity" it reaches.[335] Moreover, Schmitt argues that there is a polymorphism of the "realm of political theology or metaphysics,"[336] which is a field of multiple implications between worldviews and political views. When in chapter 2 I turned to *Political Theology*, we saw the possibilities admitted by the relation between "metaphysics," in the broad sense Schmitt considers it, and "politics." In this context, there emerge various ways to critique the diverse political and philosophical ("metaphysical" or "theological") conceptions. A purely theologico-dogmatic conception, such as Peterson's, is an arguably fragile stance before a positivistic "metaphysical" conception. The last can, without great difficulties, "turn a purely theological closure of political theology into a scientific closure of theology itself."[337] Without a nondogmatic awareness of the conditions of understanding, and of the relations between politics and the "metaphysics" operating at its ground, it is neither possible to notice the epistemological deficiencies of a positivistic conception, nor the difficulties of both a theological closure of political theology and a scientific closure of theology.[338]

In *Political Theology II*, Schmitt engages with a second author, Hans Blumenberg.[339] The reference to Blumenberg situates the discussion about theology and metaphysics in their relation with politics on the "horizon" of the "contemporary situation."[340] Blumenberg pursues a task that is the opposite of Peterson's: "to negate *scientifically* any political theology."[341] The immanentist position should be able to sustain itself independently from any reference to transcendence and the exception.[342] Schmitt has already observed that this negation is difficult to criticize from a theology such as Peterson's. Yet a position that is aware of the conditions for understanding can address the insufficiencies of immanentism. This is what Schmitt carries out schematically in the final pages of *Political Theology II*: a critique of the technological rationality and its theoretical and practical problems—its emphasis on the pole of the ideal and its manipulative aggressiveness.[343]

The works I have commented upon schematically, here in this closing section, can be analyzed in detail. In each case, objections could be raised against Schmitt's various positions. In this chapter, I have instead concentrated on showing how the manner of approaching each subject in the texts is juridical—in the sense that, in each, the study of the themes in question is made from the consideration of the relation and tension between the two poles of understanding: rule and case, norm and exception, function and substance, concept and reality. Both poles are always included as parts of a tension, as non-negligible aspects of what is ultimately a fundamental relation of existence.

Notes

Foreword

1. See Hugo E. Herrera, *Carl Schmitt als politischer Philosoph. Versuch einer Bestimmung seiner Stellung bezüglich der Tradition der praktischen Philosophie* (Berlin: Duncker & Humblot, 2010). Regarding this book, see, among others, Paul-Ludwig Weinacht, "Über Carl Schmitts Arbeit an Begriffen. Wort und Begriff des Staates," in *Staat—Staaträson—Staatsbürger. Studien zur Begriffgeschichte und zur politischen Theorie* (Berlin: Duncker & Humblot, 2014), 67-90; Harald Seubert, "Hugo Eduardo Herrera, Carl Schmitt als politischer Philosoph." *Zeitschrift für Geschichtswissenschaft* 59 (2011): 862-64; Montserrat Herrero López, "Carl Schmitt als politischer Philosoph." *Philosophisches Jahrbuch* 120, no. 1 (2013): 196-97; Erik Lehnert, "Maschke, Herrera, Schmitt—Blick in neue Bücher." *Sezession* 41 (June, 2011): 40-41; Redaktion, "Rezensionen." *Archiv für die Geschichte des Widerstandes und der Arbeit* 20 (2016): 799-800; Arne Arps, "Rezension zu: Hugo Eduardo Herrera: Carl Schmitt als politischer Philosoph. Berlin: 2010." *Portal für Politikwissenschaft*, April 13, 2011. pw-portal.de/rezension/33602-carl-schmitt-als-politischer-philosoph_40231.

Introduction

1. See Schmitt, *Glossarium. Aufzeichnungen aus den Jahren 1947 bis 1958* (Berlin: Duncker & Humblot, 2015), 13; Carl Schmitt, in Fulco Lanchester, "Un giurista davanti a se stesso. Intervista a Carl Schmitt." *Quaderni constituzionali* 3, no. 1 (1983): 34.

2. See Schmitt, e.g., *Political Theology. Four Chapters on the Concept of Sovereignty*, trans. Georg Schwab (Chicago and London: University of Chicago Press, 2005), 14-15; *The Concept of the Political* (German ed. Berlin: Duncker & Humblot, 1963) 15-16; *The Nomos of the Earth in the International Law of the*

Jus Publicum Europaeum, trans. Gary L. Ulmen (New York: Telos Press, 2006), 37–39, 159; *Glossarium*, 13, 18, 100, 165, 237–38; *Ex Captivitate Salus. Experiences, 1945–47*, trans. Matthew Hannah (Cambridge and Malden, MA: Polity Press, 2015), 58, 60, 71; *Die Tyrannei der Werte* (Berlin: Duncker & Humblot, 2011), 9, 32, 35; *Political Theology II. The Myth of the Closure of any Political Theology*, trans. Michael Hoelzl and Graham Ward (Cambridge and Malden, MA: Polity Press, 2008), 148 (footnote 2).

 3. See Schmitt, *The Nomos of the Earth*, 38; *Glossarium*, 18, 100, 165, 237, 238; see "The Plight of European Jurisprudence," *Telos* 83 (1990): 64–66; *Ex Captivitate Salus*, 58, 60.

 4. Schmitt, *Glossarium*, 238 (footnote); see "Das Problem der Legalität," in *Verfassungsrechtliche Aufsätze aus den Jahren 1924–1954: Materialien zu einer Verfassungslehre* (Berlin: Duncker & Humblot, 2003), 447.

 5. See Schmitt, *Glossarium*, 121; *The Leviathan in the State Theory of Thomas Hobbes. Meaning and Failure of a Political Symbol*, trans. Georg Schwab and Erna Hilfstein (Chicago and London: University of Chicago Press, 2008), 85.

 6. See Schmitt, *Glossarium*, 238.

 7. Schmitt, *Political Theology*, 15; see Agostino Carrino, "Carl Schmitt and European Juridical Science," in *The Challenge of Carl Schmitt*, ed. Chantal Mouffe (London and New York: Verso, 1999), 180, 184. Regarding his position, Schmitt points out the following: "Naturally, with the terms jurist and jurisprudence, I do not understand something like a professor, who conceives his science in accordance with the current specializing organization of teaching and evaluation." "The Plight" (German ed.: "Die Lage der europäischen Rechtswissenschaft," in Carl Schmitt, *Verfassungsrechtliche Aufsätze aus den Jahren 1924–1954: Materialien zu einer Verfassungslehre* [Berlin: Duncker & Humblot, 2003], 427).

 8. See Schmitt, *Political Theology*, 21. In "The Plight of European Jurisprudence," Schmitt says, moreover, that the first great philosophers—Socrates, Plato, and Aristotle—were "primarily jurists and not what today are called philosophers." "The Plight," 427 (German ed.).

 9. Heinrich Meier, "What is Political Theology," in *Leo Strauss and the Theologico-Political Problem* (Cambridge: Cambridge University Press, 2008), 81; *Carl Schmitt and Leo Strauss. The Hidden Dialogue* (Chicago and London: University of Chicago Press, 1995), 76.

 10. Meier, *Leo Strauss*, 84; *The Lesson of Carl Schmitt. Four Chapters on the Distinction between Political Theology and Political Philosophy* (Chicago and London: University of Chicago Press, 2011), 173; see 20–21.

 11. Meier, *Leo Strauss*, 84.

 12. Meier, *The Lesson*, 173.

 13. Meier, *Leo Strauss*, 84, 161.

 14. See Jacques Derrida, *The Politics of Friendship*, trans. George Collins (London and New York: Verso, 2005), 107 (footnote 4); see also *Rogues. Two*

Essays on Reason, trans. Pascale-Anne Brault and Michael Nass (Stanford, CA: Stanford University Press, 2005), 39.

15. John P. McCormick points out that Schmitt "reflects a dualism that he himself attributes to modern thought." Schmitt does not remain bound in dualism, but understands that, despite their "apparent opposition," the poles of the ideal and the real are "intrinsically related." J. P. McCormick, *Carl Schmitt's Critique of Liberalism. Against Politics as Technology* (Cambridge: Cambridge University Press, 1997), 16–17.

16. See Schmitt, *Gesetz und Urteil. Eine Untersuchung zum Problem der Rechtspraxis* (Munich: Beck, 1969) (2nd ed.), 8–9; *Political Theology*, 18–21.

17. Schmitt, *Political Theology*, 13–15; *On the Three Types of Juristic Thought*, trans. Joseph Bendersky (Westport, CT: Praeger, 2004), 73.

18. See Schmitt, *Gesetz und Urteil*, 59; *Political Theology*, 21.

19. Schmitt, *Political Theology*, 13–15.

20. See Schmitt, "The Plight," 427 (German ed.); *Political Theology*, 15. By focusing on the law not only in the strict and narrow sense, but also as a fundamental kind of understanding, the present investigation distances itself from such works as Mariano Croce and Andrea Salvatore's *The Legal Theory of Carl Schmitt* (Oxford: Routledge, 2013), or Volker Neumann's *Carl Schmitt als Jurist* (Tübingen: Mohr Siebeck, 2015), where Schmitt's character as *jurist* is dealt with specifically in relation to his juridical-scientific contributions strictly speaking.

21. Schmitt, *Glossarium*, 238.

22. See Schmitt, *The Concept of the Political*, trans. Georg Schwab (Chicago and London: University of Chicago Press, 2007), 62.

23. See Schmitt, *Gesetz und Urteil*, 1.

24. See Schmitt, e.g., *Political Theology*, 3; *Constitutional Theory*, trans. Jeffrey Seitzer (London and Durham, NC: Duke University Press, 2008), 60–66, 100, 135–39, 245; *The Crisis of Parliamentary Democracy*, trans. Ellen Kennedy (London and Cambridge, MA: The MIT Press, 1988), 2, 6, 9, 17, 30, 33–50, 76; *Legality and Legitimacy*, trans. Jeffrey Seitzer (London and Durham, NC: Duke University Press, 2004), 87–94.

25. See, e.g., Schmitt, *On the Three Types of Juristic Thought*, 47–57.

26. See, e.g., Schmitt, *The Crisis*, 1–17.

27. Schmitt, *The Concept of the Political*, 62.

28. See second section of chapter 1.

Chapter 1

1. Derrida, *The Politics of Friendship*, 68; see *Rogues*, 11–12.
2. Derrida, *The Politics of Friendship*, 232.
3. Derrida, *The Politics of Friendship*, 68, 232.

4. See Derrida, *The Politics of Friendship*, 18, 68; *Rogues*, 84, 87.

5. Jacques Derrida, "Violence and Metaphysics: An Essay on the Thought of Emmanuel Levinas," in: *Writing and Difference*, trans. Alan Bass (London: Routledge, 2001), 153.

6. See Derrida, *The Politics of Friendship*, 68; *Rogues*, 87, 152.

7. Derrida, *The Politics of Friendship*, 150; see 150–167.

8. Derrida, *The Politics of Friendship*, 232, see 68–69; *Rogues*, 100–101.

9. Derrida, *The Politics of Friendship*, 152; see *Of Grammatology*, trans. Gayatri Chakravorty Spivak (Baltimore, MD: John Hopkins University Press, 1997), 112; Uwe Dreisholtkamp, *Jacques Derrida* (Munich: Beck, 1999), 141–48; Christopher Johnson, *System and Writing in the Philosophy of Jacques Derrida* (Cambridge: Cambridge University Press, 1993), 64; Marian Hobson, *Jacques Derrida* (London and New York: Routledge, 1998), 30.

10. Derrida, *The Politics of Friendship*, 150. The individual's "putting in front inquisitively" is also self-directed: "The question injures me: it is a wound within myself." *The Politics of Friendship*, 150. In any human being's interior, the subject establishes an inquisitive treatment which puts it in front. "The reason for questioning is usually to call us into question—our very selves and our existence." Schmitt, *Ex Captivitate Salus*, 61, see 70–71.

11. Derrida, *The Politics of Friendship*, 232; see 87.

12. Derrida, *The Politics of Friendship*, 232; see "Violence and Metaphysics," 128, 153.

13. Derrida, *The Politics of Friendship*, 88.

14. Derrida, *The Politics of Friendship*, 68.

15. Derrida, *The Politics of Friendship*, 67, 150, 152, 162–63.

16. See Derrida, *The Politics of Friendship*, 150.

17. See Derrida, *The Politics of Friendship*, 67–68.

18. See Derrida, *The Politics of Friendship*, 68; 150–55.

19. Derrida, *The Politics of Friendship*, 68.

20. See Derrida, *The Politics of Friendship*, 67.

21. Jacques Derrida, "Force of Law: The 'Mystical Foundation of Authority.'" *Cardozo Law Review* 11 (1990): 949.

22. See Susanne Lüdemann, *Politics of Deconstruction. A New Introduction to Jacques Derrida* (Stanford, CA: Stanford University Press, 2014), 66–69.

23. See Derrida, "Force of Law," 949.

24. Derrida, "Force of Law," 961; see 949; *The Politics of Friendship*, 67.

25. See Derrida, *The Politics of Friendship*, 68, 150, 152.

26. Derrida, "Force of Law," 961; *Rogues*, 150.

27. See Derrida, *The Politics of Friendship*, 68–69, 244, 249; *Rogues*, 87, 152; *The Beast & the Sovereign I*, trans. Geoffrey Bennington (Chicago and London: University of Chicago Press, 2009), 301; François Raffoul, "Heidegger and Derrida

on Responsibility," in *A Companion to Derrida*, ed. Zeynep Dyrek and Leonard Lawlor (Oxford and Malden, MA: Wiley Blackwell, 2014), 425; John D. Caputo, *Hermeneutics. Facts and Interpretation in the Age of Information* (London: Pelican, 2018), 212.

28. Derrida, *The Politics of Friendship*, 244.
29. Derrida, *The Politics of Friendship*, 38.
30. Derrida, *The Politics of Friendship*, 244.
31. See Derrida, *The Politics of Friendship*, 244, 249.
32. Derrida, *The Politics of Friendship*, 249; see Maxime Doyon, "The Transcendental Claim of Deconstruction," in *A Companion to Derrida*, ed. Zeynep Dyrek and Leonard Lawlor (Oxford and Malden, MA: Wiley Blackwell, 2014), 141–43.
33. Derrida, *The Politics of Friendship*, 42; "Violence and Metaphysics," 117.
34. Derrida, *The Politics of Friendship*, 38.
35. See Ferdinand de Saussure, *Course in General Linguistics*, trans. Wade Baskin (New York: McGraw-Hill, 1966), 120.
36. Jacques Derrida, "Differance," in *Speech and Phenomena and Other Essays on Husserl's Theory of Signs*, trans. David B. Allison (Evanston, IL: Northwestern University Press, 1973), 140.
37. Derrida, "Differance," 140.
38. Saussure, *Course*, 116.
39. Derrida, "Differance," 139;
40. Jacques Derrida, "The Linguistic Circle of Geneva," in *Margins of Philosophy*, trans. Alan Bass (Chicago: University of Chicago Press, 1982), 138; see Rodolphe Gasché, *Inventions of Difference. On Jacques Derrida* (London and Cambridge, MA: Harvard University Press, 1995), 39–40; Christopher Johnson, *System and Writing*, 56.
41. Jacques Derrida, "Signature, Event, Context," in *Margins of Philosophy*, trans. Alan Bass (Chicago: University of Chicago Press, 1982), 318, 320–21. The signifier has a certain independence even regarding the signified aspect. It may be employed, for instance, as an example to illustrate a problem proper to a context foreign to the one in which the meaning emerged; see "Signature," 318.
42. Derrida, "Signature," 320; see Uwe Dreisholtkamp, *Jacques Derrida*, 85–86.
43. Jacques Derrida, "Positions: Interview with Jean-Louis Houdebine and Guy Scarpetta," in *Positions*, trans. Alan Bass (Chicago: University of Chicago Press, 1981), 65.
44. Derrida, "Positions," 66.
45. Jacques Derrida, "Implications: Interview with Henri Ronse," in *Positions*, trans. Alan Bass (Chicago: University of Chicago Press, 1981), 14.
46. See Derrida, "Signature," 320–21; "Differance," 139–40; "Positions," 66.
47. Jacques Derrida, "Force and Signification," in *Writing and Difference*, trans. Alan Bass (London: Routledge, 2001), 29.

48. Derrida, "Differance," 140.
49. Derrida, "Differance," 129–30, 137, 139.
50. See Jacques Derrida, "Speech and Phenomena: Introduction to the Problem of Signs in Husserl's Phenomenology," in *Speech and Phenomena and Other Essays on Husserl's Theory of Signs*, trans. David B. Allison (Evanston, IL: Northwestern University Press, 1973), 50–52, 75–76, 82; "Differance" 142, 147; Rodolphe Gasché, *The Tain of the Mirror. Derrida and the Philosophy of Reflection* (London and Cambridge, MA: Harvard University Press, 1986), 194.
51. See Gary Gutting, "The Obscurity of 'Différance,' " in *A Companion to Derrida*, ed. Zeynep Dyrek and Leonard Lawlor (Oxford and Malden, MA: Wiley Blackwell, 2014), 81–82.
52. Derrida, "Differance," 145–46.
53. "This movement of differance is not something that happens to a transcendental subject; it produces a subject." Derrida, "*Speech and Phenomena*," 82.
54. Derrida, "Differance," 147.
55. See Derrida, *The Politics of Friendship*, 68–69, 163.
56. See Derrida, "Force of Law," 949, 961.
57. Derrida, *The Politics of Friendship*, 117.
58. Derrida, *The Politics of Friendship*, 88.
59. See Derrida, *The Politics of Friendship*, 87–89.
60. Derrida, *The Politics of Friendship*, 150–75.
61. See Derrida, *The Politics of Friendship*, 72.
62. See Derrida, *The Politics of Friendship*, 68, 88.
63. Derrida, *The Politics of Friendship*, 84.
64. Derrida, *The Politics of Friendship*, 88.
65. Schmitt's discourse "defends itself, walls itself up, reconstructs itself unendingly against what is to come; it struggles against the future with prophetic and pathetic energy. But it is also from within this threat, from within this dread that it seems to provoke in this traditionalist and Catholic thinker of European law, that he is able to see coming, better than so many others, the force of the future in this threatening figure." Derrida, *The Politics of Friendship*, 88. See Michaela and Thilo Rissing, *Politische Theologie. Schmitt-Derrida-Metz* (Munich: Wilhelm Fink, 2009), 108–11. Here a second tension or performative contradiction makes its appearance. For, as we shall see below, Schmitt considers the technological rationality in ways similar to the Derrida's interpretation of Schmitt's juridical thought, viz. as a form of determining, inquisitive, and manipulative understanding, moved by the eagerness to control and by anguish before the indeterminacy of existence.
66. Among them, these are noteworthy: "The Age of Neutralizations," in *The Concept of the Political* (80–96); *Theodor Däublers "Nordlicht." Drei Studien über die Elemente, den Geist und die Aktualität des Werkes* (Berlin: Duncker & Humblot, 1991); *Roman Catholicism and Political Form*, trans. Gary L. Ulmen (Westport, CT: Greenwood Press, 1996); *Die Tyrannei der Werte*, *Political Theology*, *Political*

Theology II, *Glossarium*, *Hamlet or Hecuba. The Intrusion of the Time into the Play*, trans. David Pan and Jennifer R. Rust (New York: Telos Press, 2009); *The Nomos of the Earth*; "The Plight," *Legality and Legitimacy*.

67. In this regard, see J. P. McCormick, *Carl Schmitt's Critique of Liberalism*, 44–45.

68. Schmitt, *The Concept of the Political*, 93; see, e.g., *Glossarium*, 238; *Political Theology*, 13–15, 35; *Theodor Däublers "Nordlicht*," 66.

69. Schmitt, *The Concept of the Political*, 93.

70. Schmitt, *The Leviathan*, 32–33.

71. Schmitt, *The Concept of the Political*, 93–94; *Roman Catholicism*, 14; see J. P. McCormick, *Carl Schmitt's Critique of Liberalism*, 41–45.

72. Schmitt, *The Concept of the Political*, 93; see Max Weber, *The Protestant Ethic and the Spirit of Capitalism*, trans. Talcott Parsons (London: Routledge, 2001), 123–24; *Economy and Society: An Outline of Interpretive Sociology*, ed. Guenther Roth and Claus Wittich (Berkeley, CA: University of California Press, 1978), 1401–1403.

73. "A life which has only death as its antithesis is no longer life but powerlessness and helplessness." Schmitt, *The Concept of the Political*, 95.

74. Schmitt's early position, as J. P. McCormick shows, resembles the one later adopted by Martin Heidegger. See *Carl Schmitt's Critique of Liberalism*, 45, 97. Heidegger writes, in similar fashion to Schmitt, that "technology is not . . . something that has to do with machines [*Maschinenartiges*]," but with "the manner in which the real reveals itself as standing-reserve [*Bestand*]." M. Heidegger, "Die Frage nach der Technik," in *Vorträge und Aufsätze* (Stuttgart: Neske, 2000), 27. Technology is above all a way in which existence can emerge and be understood. As we shall see below, for understanding to take place, there must be both a "human act" and an "unveiling [*Entbergen*]" independent of said act. "Die Frage," 27–28.

75. Schmitt, *Theodor Däublers "Nordlicht*," 60.

76. Schmitt, *Roman Catholicism*, 14–15.

77. See Schmitt, *Gesetz und Urteil*, 59; *Political Theology*, 13–15.

78. See Schmitt, *Political Theology*, 15.

79. Schmitt, *Roman Catholicism*, 16; see *Theodor Däublers "Nordlicht*," 56, 59–60, 66–67; *Political Theology*, 35.

80. Schmitt, *Roman Catholicism*, 14.

81. See Schmitt, *Roman Catholicism*, 12; *The Leviathan*, 85.

82. See Schmitt, *Ex Captivitate Salus*, 18.

83. See, e.g., Schmitt, *The Leviathan*, 32–34.

84. See Schmitt, *Glossarium*, 26, 27, 30, 70–71, 238; *Roman Catholicism*, 12–16.

85. See Schmitt, *Political Theology*, 15.

86. See Schmitt, *The Concept of the Political*, 60; *The Leviathan*, 85.

87. See Schmitt, *Political Theology*, 15.

88. See Schmitt, *Gesetz und Urteil*, 37–38, 41, 59, 68, 107.

89. Knowing the insufficiency of the norm, the law opens itself to the possibility that the judge decides in a way that differs from what would have resulted from a simple subsumption of the case under the norm—that is, by taking into account the peculiar existential meaning of the situation; see Schmitt, *Gesetz und Urteil*, 28, 32, 59–60, 112. "The judge and jury require *subtilitas*; they cannot simply, ham-fistedly, apply the law to the case. Indeed, they must treat it not as a case, as an instance of a universal, but as a unique and singular event." John D. Caputo, *Hermeneutics*, 209.

90. See Schmitt, e.g., *Political Theology*, 15; *The Concept of the Political*, 60, 85.

91. See Schmitt, *The Concept of the Political*, 28, 85; *Gesetz und Urteil*, 28, 32, 93; Schmitt, "The Plight," 427 (German ed.).

92. Schmitt, *Political Theology*, 15.

93. Schmitt, *Political Theology*, 15. He then adds a passage from Søren Kierkegaard: "The exception explains the general and itself. And if one wants to study the general correctly, one only needs to look around for a true exception. It reveals everything more clearly than the general does. Endless talk about the general becomes boring; there are exceptions. If they cannot be explained, then the general also cannot be explained. The difficulty is usually not noticed because the general is not thought about with passion but with a comfortable superficiality. The exception, on the other hand, thinks of the general with intense passion." Schmitt, *Political Theology*, 15; see S. Kierkegaard, *Repetition: A Venture in Experimenting Psychology by Constantin Constantinus*, in *Kierkegaard's Writings*, ed. Howard V. Hong and Edna H. Hong (Princeton, NJ: Princeton University Press, 1983), vol. VI, 227.

94. See Schmitt, *The Concept of the Political*, 60; *Glossarium*, 71, 160, 388.

95. See Schmitt, *Glossarium*, 136.

96. See Schmitt, *Glossarium*, 71, 160; *Political Theology*, 15.

97. Schmitt, *Political Theology*, 15.

98. See Schmitt, *Gesetz und Urteil*, 59.

99. Schmitt, *Hamlet or Hecuba*, 45.

100. A new historical era in which the world is modified; that is, the horizon within which beings emerge is altered, such that the latter acquire "a new sense." Schmitt, *Land and Sea. A World-Historical Meditation*, trans. Samuel Garret Zeitlin (New York: Telos Press, 2015), 93.

101. See Schmitt, *Political Theology*, 15; *Glossarium*, 71; *Land and Sea*, 93–94; "Drei Möglichkeiten eines christlichen Geschichtsbildes," in *Carl Schmitt and Hans Blumenberg: Briefwechsel* (Frankfurt: Suhrkamp, 2007), 165; "Die Einheit der Welt (Vortrag)," in *Frieden oder Pazifismus? Arbeiten zum Völkerrecht und zur internationalen Politik 1924–1978*, ed. Günter Maschke (Berlin: Duncker & Humblot, 2005), 851.

102. Schmitt, *Glossarium*, 64; *The Concept of the Political*, 60.
103. See Schmitt, *Ex Captivitate Salus*, 70–71.
104. Helmuth Plessner, *Macht und menschliche Natur. Ein Versuch zur Anthropologie der geschichtlichen Weltansicht*, in *Gesammelte Werke* (Frankfurt: Suhrkamp, 1981), vol. V, 231; Schmitt, *The Concept of the Political*, 60.
105. Schmitt, *Glossarium*, 64.
106. Schmitt, *Glossarium*, 64; see *Political Romanticism*, trans. Guy Oakes (London and Cambridge, MA: The MIT Press, 1986), 19.
107. Helmuth Plessner, *Die Stufen des Organischen und der Mensch* (Berlin and New York: de Gruyter, 1975), 292. Regarding this problem, Heidegger says that "Holding itself out into the nothing, Dasein is in each case already beyond beings as a whole. Such being beyond beings we call *transcendence*. If in the ground of its essence Dasein were not transcending, which now means, if it were not in advance holding itself out into the nothing, then it could never adopt a stance toward beings nor even toward itself." *What is Metaphysics?* in *Pathmarks*, translated by David Farrell Krell (Cambridge: Cambridge University Press, 1998), 91.
108. Mika Ojakangas determines the Schmittian transcendence as "transcendence *within* immanence." *A Philosophy of Concrete Life. Carl Schmitt and the Political Thought of Late Modernity* (Bern: Peter Lang, 2006), 33. That such transcendence is not conceived of as a substance in the traditional metaphysical sense, but as a necessary condition of immanence, does not amount to reducing transcendence to nothing more than what disturbs the products of modern rationalism, the "self-enclosed rationalistic systems." *A Philosophy of Concrete Life* 35. The exceptional determines human existence in its entirety.
109. Renato Cristi, *Carl Schmitt and Authoritarian Liberalism* (Cardiff: University of Wales Press, 1998), 144.
110. Carlo Galli, "Carl Schmitt's Anti-liberalism: Its Theoretical and Historical Sources and Its Philosophical and Political Meaning." *Cardozo Law Review* 21 (2000): 1607; see Michele Nicoletti, *Trascendenza e potere. La teologia politica di Carl Schmitt* (Brescia: Morcelliana, 1990), 148–49.
111. See Schmitt, *Political Theology*, 15.
112. Schmitt, *Political Theology*, 15. Panajotis Kondylis excludes the exception from juridical science. He recognizes it as a threat to juridical normality, but denies it all relevance for a specific juridical understanding. The jurist can only say "that one should consider the state of exception as possible at all times," and that an established violence is always empowered to decide on the "suppression of the law of normality." "Jurisprudence, Ausnahmezustand und Entscheidung. Grundsätzliche Bemerkungen zu Carl Schmitts 'Politische Theologie.'" *Der Staat* 34 (1995): 333. Beyond this, the jurist speaking as a jurist would have nothing to say. Certainly, a normativist conception of the law has little to add regarding the exception. However, if one notices that this situation opens the possibility for manipulative decisions, and for a juridical decision, which aims at establishing a

juridical order attending to the alterity of the other and the concrete dimension in which human beings are found, the matter emerges as juridically relevant. Furthermore, as we shall see, the juridical understanding in the normal situation is not exempt from exceptionality. Every norm, insofar as it is general, is heterogeneous with regard to concrete reality and the existential depth of the cases to be decided. Such heterogeneity implies that every norm is affected by an "indetermination," which demands a juridical decision that, if it is not to be a technical-manipulative subsumption, must take the step into the concrete dimension of the cases.

113. Schmitt, *Theodor Däublers "Nordlicht,"* 60.

114. Schmitt, *Theodor Däublers "Nordlicht,"* 15, 56.

115. See Schmitt, *Theodor Däublers "Nordlicht,"* 56–57, 60, 63; *Roman Catholicism*, 15.

116. See Schmitt, e.g., *Political Theology*, 14; *Glossarium*, 71, 121, 238, 388; *Theodor Däublers "Nordlicht,"* 56.

117. See *Glossarium*, 84; *Political Romanticism*, 19.

118. Schmitt's criticism is closely related to the observations of Martin Heidegger on this point. "Scientific existence," Heidegger writes, "possesses its simplicity and aptness in that it comports itself toward being themselves in a distinctive way, and only to them. Science would like to dismiss the nothing [i.e., 'transcendence'; *What is Metaphysics?*, 91] with a lordly wave of the hand. But in our inquiry concerning the nothing it has by now become manifest that such scientific existence is possible only if in advance it holds itself out into the nothing." *What is Metaphysics?*, 95.

119. See Schmitt, *Political Theology*, 13; "The Plight," 56; *The Nomos of the Earth*, 6 (German ed.); *Glossarium*, 136; *Roman Catholicism*, 12; *The Concept of the Political*, 26, 38; "Raum und Rom. Zur Phonetik des Wortes Raum," *Universitas* 6 (1951): 965; "Recht und Raum," in *Tymbos für Wilhelm Ahlmann* (Berlin: de Gruyter, 1951), 243.

120. See Schmitt, *On the Three Types of Juristic Thought*, 48–49, 56, 73; *Political Theology*, 13.

121. Schmitt, *The Nomos of the Earth*, 39 (translation modified); *Land and Sea*, 93; *Ex Captivitate Salus*, 72. In virtue of this meaning, human existence is in "tension [*Spannung*]" (*Ex Captivitate Salus*, 71), bestowed with "seriousness" (*Hamlet or Hecuba*, 45) and "intensity." *Political Theology*, 15.

122. See Schmitt, *Die Tyrannei der Werte*, 20, 23, 37–41; *The Nomos of the Earth*, 69; *Land and Sea*, 93; "Drei Möglichkeiten," 166; "Zu Friedrich Meineckes 'Idee der Staatsräson,'" in *Positionen und Begriffe im Kampf mit Weimar—Genf—Versailles 1923–1939*, 51–59 (Berlin: Duncker & Humblot, 2014), 58–59.

123. See Ernst-Wolfgang Böckenförde, "Konkretes Ordnungsdenken," in *Historisches Wörterbuch der Philosophie*, ed. Joachim Ritter and Karlfried Gründer (Basel: Schwabe Verlag, 1984), vol. VI, 1312–13; Bernd Rüthers, *Die unbegrenzte Auslegung* (Tübingen: Mohr Siebeck, 2012), 294.

124. See Schmitt, *Theodor Däublers "Nordlicht,"* 59–60, 66–67; *Political Theology*, 15, 35; *Glossarium*, 26 (footnote 1), 195.

125. See Schmitt, e.g., *Glossarium*, 26 (footnote 1), 27, 30, 70–71; *The Leviathan*, 85; *Theodor Däublers "Nordlicht,"* 59–60, 66–67; *Political Theology*, 15, 35; *The Nomos of the Earth*, 38–39; *Roman Catholicism*, 12–13.

126. See Schmitt, *The Concept of the Political*, 26, 38; *Der Begriff des Politischen* (Berlin: Duncker & Humblot, 1963, 120–21); *The Nomos of the Earth*, 39, 42; *Der Wert des Staates und die Bedeutung des Einzelnen* (Berlin: Duncker & Humblot, 2004), 36; *Ex Captivitate Salus*, 70–71; *Hamlet or Hecuba*, 40, 45; *Political Theology*, 35.

127. See Schmitt, *The Nomos of the Earth*, 39, 42, 67–69.

128. As in the thought of Edmund Husserl (see *The Crisis of European Sciences and Transcendental Phenomenology. An Introduction to Phenomenological Philosophy*, trans. David Carr [Evanston, IL: Northwestern University Press], 1970) or Martin Heidegger (see *Sein und Zeit* [Tübingen: Max Niemeyer 2001], 102–13), for Schmitt, space is not an empty, neutral, or objective sphere, a geometrical space, but rather a "world full of tensions between distinct elements." Carl Schmitt, "Raum und Rom," 965; see "Recht und Raum," 243. Schmitt himself, regarding his proximity with Heidegger on this point, says: "Today, a thought first becomes possible for us that would have been impossible in any other epoch and which a contemporary German philosopher has articulated: The world is not in space, rather space is in the world." *Land and Sea*, 92; see Eduardo Mendieta, "Land and Sea," in *Spatiality, Sovereignty and Carl Schmitt: Geographies of the Nomos*, edited by Stephen Legg (London: Routledge, 2011), 263.

129. The practical tension expresses itself in diverse "endeavors (*Sachgebiete*)," such as "the moral, aesthetic, and economic." In all of these, tension appears specified according to criteria of thought and action, and in different degrees of "intensity." Schmitt, *The Concept of the Political*, 26, 38 (translation modified).

130. See Schmitt, *Gesetz und Urteil*, 8, 28, 55, 59, 76; *Political Theology*, 3, 30–31; *The Concept of the Political*, 27, 85; *The Nomos of the Earth*, 39; *Land and Sea*, 93; *Die Tyrannei der Werte*, 37–41; *On the Three Types of Juristic Thought*, 54, 69.

131. See Schmitt, *Glossarium*, 27, 30, 70–71.

132. See Schmitt, *Glossarium*, 26 (footnote 1).

133. Schmitt, *Glossarium*, 26 (footnote 1).

134. See Schmitt, *Glossarium*, 27, 30, 70–71; *The Leviathan*, 85; *Theodor Däublers "Nordlicht,"* 59–60, 66–67; *Political Theology*, 15, 35; *The Nomos of the Earth*, 38–39; *Roman Catholicism*, 12–13.

135. With his allusion to the desire for power and by attempting to unveil scientific-technical rationality as an expression of human anxiety regarding the mysterious nature of existence, Schmitt is positioning himself in the tradition of Friedrich Nietzsche. "Tracing something unknown back to something known gives relief, soothes, satisfies, and furthermore gives a feeling of power. The unknown

brings with it danger, disquiet, worry—one's first instinct is to *get rid of* these awkward conditions. . . . The causal drive is therefore determined and stimulated by the feeling of fear." Nietzsche, *Twilight of the Idols*, trans. Duncan Large (Oxford: Oxford University Press, 2008), 29–30; see *Gay Science*, ed. Bernard Williams (Cambridge: Cambridge University Press, 2001), 214. In *Glossarium*, Schmitt uses words similar to Nietzsche's to raise the problem signified by the enemy: "How are we to trace back something undetermined to the determined, if we now lack common concepts?" That is why the enemy produces "angst"—because she is undeterminable. *Glossarium*, 27.

136. Schmitt, *Glossarium*, 71.
137. Schmitt, *The Crisis*, 68–69.
138. Schmitt, *Political Theology*, 15; see *Glossarium*, 71, 160, 388.
139. Schmitt, *Theodor Däublers "Nordlicht,"* 56.
140. Schmitt, *The Leviathan*, 85.
141. Schmitt, *Political Theology II*, 128.
142. Schmitt, *Political Theology*, 35 (translation modified).
143. Schmitt, *Theodor Däublers "Nordlicht,"* 61; see *Glossarium*, 40; *Political Theology*, 15.
144. "The human being, biologically and by nature an absolutely weak and needy being, endeavors to obtain, by means of technology, a new world in which he is the strongest being, or even the only being." "Die Einheit der Welt," *Merkur* 47 (1952): 9.
145. See Schmitt, *Glossarium*, 8, 40, 62–63.
146. Carl Schmitt, "Die Einheit," 9.
147. See Schmitt, *Theodor Däublers "Nordlicht,"* 59–60, 67.
148. Schmitt, *Political Theology*, 15.
149. See Schmitt, *Theodor Däublers "Nordlicht,"* 66–67.
150. Schmitt, *Theodor Däublers "Nordlicht,"* 60.
151. Ojakangas, *A Philosophy of Concrete Life*, 39.
152. See Schmitt, *The Concept of the Political*, 60.
153. See Schmitt, *Glossarium*, 64, 136.
154. See Schmitt, *Political Romanticism*, 53–54; Plessner, *Die Stufen*, 290, 292; and what is said earlier in this chapter.
155. Schmitt, "The Visibility of the Church: A Scholastic Consideration," in *Roman Catholicism and Political Form*, ed. Gary L. Ulmen (Westport, CT: Greenwood Press, 1996), 51.
156. Schmitt, "The Visibility," 51 (translation modified); see 48; *Ex Captivitate Salus*, 70–71.
157. Schmitt, "The Visibility," 48. It also speaks with itself, it "calls" itself "into question," and so can determine itself and become aware of itself and its interiority. Schmitt, *Ex Captivitate Salus*, 71.
158. Schmitt, *The Concept of the Political*, 60.

159. Schmitt, "The Visibility," 48.
160. See Plessner, *Macht*, 193; Schmitt, *Glossarium*, 277.
161. See Schmitt, *Ex Captivitate Salus*, 71; *Hamlet or Hecuba*, 45; *The Concept of the Political*, 120–21 (German ed.); *Political Theology*, 15; *The Nomos of the Earth*, 6 (German ed.); *Land and Sea*, 93; and what is said earlier in this chapter.
162. See Schmitt, *The Concept of the Political*, 26, 38, 60; *Political Theology*, 35; *Roman Catholicism*, 33; *Glossarium*, 238; "Die Einheit," 9–10.
163. Schmitt, *Glossarium*, 238; see *Ex Captivitate Salus*, 66–67.
164. Schmitt, *Roman Catholicism*, 33.
165. See Schmitt, "The Plight," 64–66; *Glossarium*, 238; *The Concept of the Political*, 36, 48–49; *Die Wendung zum diskriminierenden Kriegsbegriff* (Berlin: Duncker & Humblot, 1988), 1–8, 37–53; *Ex Captivitate Salus*, 71.
166. In juridical understanding, the principle of "legal certainty" is different from mechanical subsumption. It admits a decision *"praeter"* or even *"contra legem"* if the novelty of the case requires it. Schmitt, *Gesetz und Urteil*, 68–69, 107; see 41. In understanding in general, the ideal meaning of rules and concepts must relinquish before novelty through the "unfolding of concrete concepts" from concrete existence. "The Plight," 427 (German ed.); see *The Concept of the Political*, 85–86.
167. See Schmitt, *Der Wert des Staates*, 39–40, 80.
168. See Schmitt, *On the Three Types of Juristic Thought*, 56–57, 73; *Gesetz und Urteil*, 48–51; *Political Theology*, 13–15; *Hamlet or Hecuba*, 45; Hasso Hofmann, *Legitimität gegen Legalität. Der Weg der politischen Philosophie Carl Schmitts* (Berlin: Duncker & Humblot, 2002), 45.
169. See Schmitt, "The Plight," 427 (German ed.); *Gesetz und Urteil*, 59, 93.
170. Schmitt, *Gesetz und Urteil*, 64.
171. Schmitt, *The Concept of the Political*, 85.
172. See Schmitt, *Gesetz und Urteil*, 93; "The Plight," 427 (German ed.).
173. See Schmitt, *Gesetz und Urteil*, 28, 93. "I have a method, which is my own: let phenomena approach me, wait and think from the matter itself and not from preset categories, so to speak." Schmitt, "Gespräch über den Partisanen," in *Guerilleros, Partisanen. Theorie und Praxis*, ed. Joachim Schickel (Munich: Hanser, 1970), 11. See *On the Three Types of Juristic Thought*, 54; "The Plight," 427 (German ed.); *Political Theology*, 35.
174. See Schmitt, *The Concept of the Political*, 85.
175. Schmitt, *The Nomos of the Earth*, 16 (German ed.).
176. See Schmitt, *Gesetz und Urteil*, 28, 32, 42, 75, 93, 111–12; *Political Theology*, 30; *The Concept of the Political*, 85; Liza Mattutat, *Die vertrackte Urteilsform. Ein Argument zur Frage der Rechtsgeltung mit und gegen Hans Kelsen, Gustav Radbruch und Carl Schmitt* (Marburg: Tectum Verlag, 2016), 103.
177. Schmitt, *Gesetz und Urteil*, 28; see 35; "The Plight," 427 (German ed.). On the distinction between juridical understanding and subsumption, see

William Rasch, "Judgment: The Emergence of Legal Norms." *Cultural Critique* 57 (2004): 97–103.

178. Derrida, *The Politics of Friendship*, 88.
179. Derrida, *The Politics of Friendship*, 68.
180. Derrida, *The Politics of Friendship*, 68.
181. Schmitt, *Political Theology*, 15.
182. Regarding the juridico-political exception, J. P. McCormick notices the difference between *Dictatorship* of 1921—where Schmitt privileges the dictatorial state of exception over the exception, which, in his opinion, is negatively valued by him—and *Political Theology* of 1922—where the exception is "dangerous but good because an occasion for revivification." *Carl Schmitt's Critique of Liberalism*, 136.
183. Ojakangas, *A Philosophy of Concrete Life*, 42.
184. The broadening has been noticed by Michael Marder, who says that it places Schmitt's thought in a post-metaphysical context (see *Groundless Existence. The Political Ontology of Carl Schmitt* [New York and London: Continuum, 2010], 2–9), and by Hasso Hofmann, who even notes that by means of this broadening of the scope of the exception Schmitt works "in a way which is not different from all posterior existential philosophy." Hofmann, *Legitimität*, 59; see Ojakangas, *A Philosophy of Concrete Life*, 34 (footnote 56), 100–101, 103, 151, 203, 206.
185. Schmitt, *Political Theology*, 15.
186. Schmitt, *The Concept of the Political*, 60.
187. Schmitt, *Hamlet or Hecuba*, 45.
188. See Schmitt, e.g., *Political Theology*, 15; *The Concept of the Political*, 59–60.
189. See Schmitt, *Glossarium*, 70–71.
190. Schmitt, *Glossarium*, 71.
191. See Schmitt, *Hamlet or Hecuba*, 45; *Political Theology*, 15; *The Concept of the Political*, 60.
192. Schmitt, *Hamlet or Hecuba*, 33; see 45–49.
193. Schmitt, *Glossarium*, 64. The distance made possible by transcendence, insofar as the latter involves the subject's withdrawal from the ontic sphere, makes the subject capable of articulating an understanding of revealed existence according to rules and concepts; see Schmitt, *The Concept of the Political*, 60; Plessner, *Macht*, 231.
194. Schmitt, "The Plight," 56; see *The Nomos of the Earth*, 39; *On the Three Types of Juristic Thought*, 56–57, 73; *Political Theology*, 13; *Land and Sea*, 93.
195. Insofar as the unveiling of existence arises from a hiding, bottomless bottom of mystery, existence is always bound, also from the side of the real, to the exceptional; see Schmitt, *Political Theology*, 15; *The Concept of the Political*, 60; *Hamlet or Hecuba*, 45.
196. Schmitt, "The Visibility," 51.
197. See Schmitt, "The Visibility," 48; *Ex Captivitate Salus*, 71.

198. See Schmitt, *The Concept of the Political*, 85–87; *Gesetz und Urteil*, 28, 32, 93, 112; "The Plight," 427 (German ed.); *The Nomos of the Earth*, 67.
199. Schmitt, *Glossarium*, 136.
200. Schmitt, *Political Romanticism*, 54.
201. Schmitt, *Political Romanticism*, 53. "The self cannot be given by means of a mere concept, because concepts are only possible . . . regarding objects." Friedrich Wilhelm Joseph Schelling, *Vom Ich als Prinzip der Philosophie oder über das Unbedingte im menschlichen Wissen* (1795), in *Werke* (Historisch-kritische Ausgabe), ed. Thomas Buchheim, Jochem Hennigfeld, Wilhelm G. Jacobs, Jörg Jantzen and Siegnert Peetz (Stuttgart: Frommann-Holzboog, 1980), vol. 2, 106.
202. See Schmitt, *Political Romanticism*, 54. "The *I* is no object of thought." *Ex Captivitate Salus*, 65. Plessner indicates that consciousness involves not solely "seeing," but "seeing the act of seeing." Consciousness supposes the subject's self-knowing, not as an object, but directly in the very activity of thinking; Plessner, *Die Stufen*, 292. That is to say, the subject knows of herself not through objectifying reflection, but through direct or immediate self-access. Thinking that the subject knows of herself only when she reflectively thematizes herself implies "an absurd duplication of the subject's core" (290), which could no longer turn on herself, since otherwise we would have to ask: How does the subject know of herself, precisely insofar as she is the activity realizing the thematization of herself? A new thematization would need to be supposed, and so on ad infinitum. "[Hitherto, people reasoned as follows:] I am conscious of some object, *B*. But I cannot be conscious of this object without also being conscious of myself, for *B* is not *I* and *I* am not *B*. But I can be conscious of myself only insofar as I am conscious of consciousness. Therefore, I must be conscious of this act of consciousness; i.e., I must be conscious of this consciousness of consciousness. How do I become conscious of this? This series has no end, and therefore consciousness cannot be explained in this manner. The chief explanation for this impossibility is that consciousness has always be treated as a state of mind, i.e., as an object, for which, in turn, another subject is always required . . . The only way to avoid this objection is to discover some object of consciousness which is at the same time the subject of consciousness. One would thereby have disclosed the existence of an immediate consciousness, i.e., an object to which one would not have to oppose a new subject." Johann Gottlieb Fichte, *Wissenschaftslehre nova methodo* (1796–1798), in *Gesamtausgabe der Bayerischen Akademie der Wissenschaften*, ed. Erich Fuchs, Hans Gliwitzky, Reinhard Lauth and Peter Schneider (Stuttgart and Bad Cannstatt: Frommann-Holzboog, 1962), part 4, vol. 2, 30 (English edition, translated by Daniel Breazale [London and Ithaca, NY: Cornell University Press 1992], 112); see Frederick Neuhouser, *Fichte's Theory of Subjectivity* (Cambridge: Cambridge University Press, 1990), 84. Such direct self-knowledge explains the specific tension of the relation between the subject and the other. The other, says Plessner, is not a mere neutral other, but "the strange [*das Fremde*]," regarding

which there may be anxiety, "mistrust [*Unheimlichkeit*]." "The strange is the proper, the trusted, the secret in the other [*Das Fremde ist das Eigene, Vertraute und Heimliche im Anderen*]." *Macht*, 193; that is, an interiority, an other which also knows of herself and, therefore, knows how to discern herself from the other, of other interiorities; see Schmitt, *The Concept of the Political*, 60; *Glossarium*, 277.

203. See Schmitt, *Glossarium*, 64; *Political Romanticism*, 54–57.

204. See Schmitt, *Political Theology*, 15; *Hamlet or Hecuba*, 45; *Glossarium*, 136, 388.

205. See Peter V. Zima, *Theorie des Subjekts. Subjektivität und Identität zwischen Moderne und Postmoderne* (Tübingen: Francke Verlag, 2010), 211; Rudof Bernet, "Derrida and his Master's Voice," in *Derrida and Phenomenology*, ed. William R. Mckenna and J. Claude Evans (Dordrecht: Springer, 1995), 15, 17–20. "In Derrida *différance*, as what always already (is), renders self-presence impossible. It prevents a return to a ground because that 'ground' is always already split, and, as such, is not a ground in any meaningful sense at all." Andrew Bowie, *Schelling and Modern European Philosophy* (Oxford and New York: Routledge, 1993), 74.

206. "It is in fact true . . . that consciousness . . . presupposes, aside from its mere Being, in addition a series of opposites without which it would not be able to determine and grasp itself as that *which* it is. And what could this series of opposites be other than that which the structuralists call structure (of a language, of a discourse, of a tradition, etc.)? But this dependence on structure is not real; rather it is ideal. The dependence of any conceivable determination on a prior *Being* is real. But consciousness as the knowing subject is, in the final analysis, dependent on structure. It simply cannot concretize itself without referring to an overriding system of relations between marks; but these relations do not simply *produce* consciousness, they serve exclusively its ideal self-determination." *What Is Neostructuralism?*, trans. Sabine Wilke and Richard Gray (Minneapolis, MN: University of Minnesota Press, 1984), 283–84; see Schmitt, "The Visibility," 48, 51; *Ex Captivitate Salus*, 71.

207. Frank, *What Is Neostructuralism?* 281, 260; see Dieter Henrich, "Sebstbewusstsein. Kritische Einleitung in eine Theorie," in *Hermeneutik und Dialektik*, ed. Rüdiger Bubner, Konrad Cramer and Reiner Wiehl (Tübingen: Mohr Siebeck, 1970), vol. 1, 262–63.

208. A bare play of differences would not even allow to distinguish what is different as different. "Without remission to a moment of self-identity, differentiation (displacement of meaning, new metaphorical inscription of meanings) could not be verified; it would lack a criterion and would be indiscernible from a state of total paralysis." Manfred Frank, *Ansichten der Subjektivität* (Frankfurt: Suhrkamp, 2012), 70; see *What Is Neostructuralism?* 260. For Andrew Bowie, "if the relative differences are not transitively predicated by the Same, they cannot even *be* differences, because there would be no criterion of difference and the differences could not even be in the relative way that they are." Bowie, *Schelling*, 74.

209. A similar question was addressed by Schelling to Hegel, the question namely "of how it could be possible for the absolute spirit to recognize itself as itself . . . if it had not already had some knowledge of itself: nothing would be able to recognize itself *as* itself if it did not have a criterion for its identification in the form of a preceding (and self-familiar) knowledge." Frank, *What Is Neostructuralism?* 260. "Identification and discrimination presuppose consciousness, yet they are not able . . . to produce it." *What Is Neostructuralism?* 287.

210. Schmitt, *Political Romanticism*, 54.

211. See Fichte, *Wissenschaftslehre nova methodo*, 30.

212. Without that identity endowed with a direct self-access, it would be not even possible to understand something as significant, including the marks from which it is intended to explain the emergence of consciousness. An activity that knows itself and includes the diverse elements as parts of a relation is required beforehand. Only then can these elements reach a meaning. "Without that which is capable of interpreting them, differing marks do not *mean* anything." A. Bowie, *Schelling*, 73.

213. See Schmitt, "The Plight," 427 (German ed.).

214. See Schmitt, "The Visibility," 48, 51; *Ex Captivitate Salus*, 70–71; *Political Romanticism*, 18–19, 82–84.

215. See Schmitt, *Gesetz und Urteil*, 28, 32, 75, 93, 112; "The Plight," 427 (German ed.); *The Concept of the Political*, 85.

216. See Schmitt, *The Concept of the Political*, 85–87; *Gesetz und Urteil*, 28, 32; *The Nomos of the Earth*, 67; Ino Augsberg, *Kassiber. Die Aufgabe der juristischen Hermeneutik* (Tübingen: Mohr Siebeck, 2016), 71–73.

217. See Derrida, "Force of Law," 949; *Rogues*, 150.

218. Nick Mansfield holds that, despite the proximity of the positions of both authors (in both the point is to decide and in the decision "there will always be a sovereign dimension"), Derrida's stance is distinguished from Schmitt's because of its "openness" "to the incalculability that represents Otherness." "In its openness to incalculability, decision accepts the intrusion of that which is Other. This acceptance of intrusion means that there must be a passivity in decision, or there must be some dimension to decision beyond conscious processes of evaluation and adjudication. This 'beyond of consciousness' Derrida connects unsurprisingly with the psychoanalytic notion of the unconscious: '*In sum, a decision is unconscious*—insane as that may seem, it involves the unconscious and nevertheless remains responsible.'" "Derrida and the Culture Debate: Autoimmunity, Law and Decision." *Macquarie Law Journal* 6 (2006): 109–10. Despite there not being a detailed reflection on Schmitt's part on the reference of the decision to the psychoanalytic notion of the unconscious, in the *Glossarium*, however, there is a passage—quoted above, but to which I must return due to its importance—in which he addresses this matter. "I am not sovereign [*Herr*] of that which bursts [*dringt*] into my consciousness [*Bewußtsein*], nor of that which remains unconscious

[*unbewußt*] for me. My consciousness is not in my power . . . Every power is transcendent. Transcendence is power." *Glossarium*, 136; see *Political Theology*, 15; *Hamlet or Hecuba*, 45. Decision is, then, referred to an alterity. On the other hand, the decision is, precisely, the interruption of the logic of subsumption and of a purely active sovereignty, insofar as it opens itself to the concrete dimension of the case, to its alterity, and from the consideration of the case it returns to the rule. Such openness to the existential depth of the real implies that the decision must also be passive. As previously stated, for Schmitt, understanding, if it is not to be reductive, requires that we not only understand the case from the rule, but *the rule from the case*. See Schmitt, *Gesetz und Urteil*, 28, 32, 93, 112.

219. See Schmitt, *Gesetz und Urteil*, 7–8, 68, 107; *Political Theology*, 30–31.

220. See Schmitt, *Political Theology*, 3; *Gesetz und Urteil*, VI, 40, 75; *On the Three Types of Juristic Thought*, 73.

221. See Schmitt, *Political Romanticism*, 162; *Political Theology*, 35.

222. See Schmitt, e.g., *Gesetz und Urteil*, 1; *Political Theology*, 3, 30–31.

223. Derrida, "Force of Law," 949; see 961.

224. Derrida, "Force of Law," 961; see *Rogues*, 150.

225. Derrida, "Force of Law," 961. "The heterogeneity between justice and law does not exclude but, on the contrary, calls for their inseparability: there can be no justice without an appeal to juridical determinations and to the force of law." *Rogues*, 150. See Rupert Simon, *Die Begriffe des Politischen bei Carl Schmitt und Jacques Derrida* (Frankfurt: Peter Lang, 2006), 135–36.

226. Schmitt distinguishes, in a similar way, between a decisionism that "implements the good laws of the correctly recognized political situation" and "a degenerate decisionism, blind to the law." *Political Theology*, 3. "The legal interest in the decision . . . is derived from the necessity of judging a concrete fact concretely." *Political Theology*, 31. In *Gesetz und Urteil*, Schmitt notes that "there is no decision without justification; the justification belongs to the decision." *Gesetz und Urteil*, 66. The issue concerns the "correct decision." *Gesetz und Urteil*, 1.

227. Derrida, "Force of Law," 961.

228. See, e.g., Schmitt, *Political Romanticism*, 162.

229. Derrida, "Force of Law," 971; see John D. Caputo, *Hermeneutics*, 214–15.

230. Derrida, "Force of Law," 961.

231. Derrida, "Force of Law," 949; see 959, 961, 963, 967; Schmitt, *Gesetz und Urteil*, 48–52, 69, 71.

232. Derrida, "Force of Law," 961; *Rogues*, 150.

233. See Schmitt, *Gesetz und Urteil*, 28, 32, 46, 64, 67, 101, 103. Thorsten Hitz claims, quoting *Political Theology*, that "It is precisely the thought that the decision may be discovered to be incorrect [*falsch*] that is intolerable for Derrida. For Schmitt, on the contrary, the requirement that the decision not be incorrect is intolerable." *Jacques Derridas praktische Philosophie* (Munich: W. Fink Verlag, 2005), 143. Alexander Garcia-Düttmann states that "The 'incorrect decision' involves

a 'constitutive moment' also." In an explanation given in a footnote (no. 17), he goes on: "Schmitt makes his thought more precise by adding that the wrong decision is constitutive 'precisely because of its falseness'—every decision which is a decision in the proper sense must appear incorrect before the established norms." *Derrida und Ich. Das Problem der Dekonstruktion* (Bielefeld: Transcript Verlag, 2008), 105. It should be said, however, that if correctness and incorrectness are evaluated merely based on the norm, not only Schmitt, but also Derrida would admit that every decision must be incorrect, precisely because it should not be a mere subsumption (a product of the "calculating machine"). The recognition of the alterity of the other, of her concrete singularity and meaning, leads Derrida to claim that, in the decision, the one deciding should "conserve the law and destroy it" ("Force of Law," 961)—that it is not enough to shield oneself by means of the law, but one must take the step toward existence. See Derrida, "Force of Law," 949, 961. In the passage from *Political Theology* alluded to, the incorrectness of the decision only appears when the decision is regarded "from the perspective of the content of the underlying norm." Instead, if the situation along with the norm are taken into account, the decision may and should indeed be correct. The subject making the decision is faced with the express demand to "correctly" recognize such a situation. *Political Theology*, 3. The distancing of the decision regarding the norm and the law, beyond the limits of mere subsumption, should not, however, be complete. The "constitutive element" of the decision is only partial. If the decision is "blind to the law," the decision turns into "degenerate decisionism." *Political Theology*, 3. Schmitt here insists on what he had already said in 1912: "There is no decision without justification, the justification belongs to the decision." *Gesetz und Urteil*, 66. Moreover, Derrida and Schmitt coincide, as we have seen, on the requirement to decide—given the meaning they recognize in the other and in existence, as well as the fact that, abandoned to herself, the subject becomes prey for manipulators and calculators. That requirement implies, in turn, distancing both from the rule and calculation. See Derrida, "Force of Law," 949, 959, 961, 963, 967, 971.

234. John P. McCormick has correctly identified that the starting point for Schmitt and Derrida is the same: the "three aporias of law" put forth by Derrida in the first part of "Force of Law" "were raised by Schmitt." "Derrida on Law; Or, Poststructuralism Gets Serious." *Political Theory* 29, no. 3 (2001): 403; "Schmittian Positions on Law and Politics? CLS and Derrida." *Cardozo Law Review* 21, no. 5–6 (2000): 1710; see Derrida, "Force of Law," 949, 959. These aporias emerge from the tension between the rule and the singular, the norm and the exceptional, and leave the juridical agent before a situation of indeterminacy. For McCormick, however, Derrida distances himself from Schmitt. While Derrida "leaves open" the "aporiai," Schmitt, on the contrary, "arbitrarily resolves" the "indeterminacy of law . . . in a regressively . . . coercive manner." "Schmittian Positions," 1710; "Derrida on Law," 403. Yet if we take Schmitt's texts together into account, McCormick's claim must

be qualified. Schmitt, like Derrida, recognizes that the dilemmas faced by the juridical agent emerge from a tension that is ultimately irresolvable, for rule and situation, norm and exception, are the poles in tension between which human understanding insurmountably takes place. See *Political Theology*, 15; *Gesetz und Urteil*, 93; *Political Romanticism*, 52–54; *Glossarium*, 238. In a manner similar to Derrida, Schmitt also acknowledges that the situation must be decided upon, since detachment entails leaving justice, which is incalculable, at the mercy of the calculators. See Derrida, "Force of Law," 970; Schmitt, *Political Romanticism*, 162; McCormick, "Schmittian Positions," 1711, 1721. And, finally, Schmitt is, like Derrida, in search of a decision different from subsumption and caprice, which does justice to the situation and its singularity; see Schmitt, *Gesetz und Urteil*, 1, 7–9, 28, 32, 41, 55, 57, 59, 66, 68, 76, 82, 93, 96; *Political Theology*, 3, 30–31; *On the Three Types of Juristic Thought*, 73, and what I discuss below regarding the decision in the exceptional situation.

235. Derrida, "Force of Law," 941.

236. Derrida, "Force of Law," 945.

237. Jacques Derrida, "Before the Law," in *Acts of Literature*, ed. Derek Attridge (London: Routledge, 1992), 192, 194; see Susanne Lüdemann, *Politics of Deconstruction*, 61–62; John D. Caputo, *Hermeneutics*, 204.

238. Derrida, *Of Grammatology*, 112. Because of the "originary violence of language," there is a "loss," but "in truth the loss of what has never taken place." *Of Grammatology*, 112; see *The Beast & the Sovereign I*, 316–17, 319–20; Cristopher Johnson, *System and Writing*, 64; Hobson, *Jacques Derrida*, 30.

239. See Derrida, "Force of Law," 935; Pierre Legrand, "Derrida/Law: A Differend," in *A Companion to Derrida*, ed. Zeynep Dyrek and Leonard Lawlor (Oxford and Malden, MA: Wiley Blackwell, 2014), 592; Uwe Dreisholtkamp, *Jacques Derrida*, 141–48; Susanne Lüdemann, *Politics of Deconstruction*, 65–67. "Language [is a] human institution [which] brings up against us a whole army of *fixed ideas*. . . . Truths are men's thoughts, set down in words and therefore just as extant as other things. . . . They are human institutions." Max Stirner, *The Ego and His Own. The Case of the Individual Against Authority* (London and New York: Verso, 2015), 324–25.

240. See John Langshaw Austin, *How to do Things with Words* (Oxford: Clarendon Press, 1962).

241. Derrida, "Force of Law," 969.

242. See Derrida, "Before the Law," 199. "No law is a law unless it also applies to particular individuals. It cannot be left hanging in the air, in the abstraction of its generality. Only by thus referring it back to particular praxis can the *justice* of the law be tested, exactly as the *justesse* of any statement can only be tested by referential verifiability." Paul de Man, "Promises (Social Contract)," in *Allegories of Reading. Figural Language in Rousseau, Nietzsche, Rilke, and Proust* (London and New Haven, CT: Yale University Press, 1979), 269. "The legal or political text

makes more explicit and better reveals the very structure of the text in general. It 'defines' it better than any other text." Jacques Derrida, *Memoires. For Paul de Man*, trans. Avital Ronell and Eduardo Cadava (New York: Columbia University Press, 1989), 143.

243. Schmitt, *Glossarium*, 136.

244. See Schmitt, *On the Three Types of Juristic Thought*, 73; *Glossarium*, 64.

245. Scheuerman notices the relation between Derrida and Schmitt, with regard to the violence hiding both in the establishment of the legal order, and of the subsequent normal legal experience; see William E. Scheuerman, *Carl Schmitt: The End of Law* (Oxford: Rowman & Littlefield, 1999), 82–83.

246. Austin's relativization of the distinction between constative and performative acts makes possible to discern whether the affirmation was "*right*," not in a purely pragmatic or opportunistic sense, but in the sense of whether it was "the proper thing to say." Such discernment requires heeding what is said and the meaning of the situation and its "circumstances." J. L. Austin, *How to do Things with Words*, 144; see 145–46.

247. See Derrida, "Before the Law," 194; *Of Grammatology*, 112; *Glossarium*, 136.

248. Schmitt, *The Nomos of the Earth*, 16 (German ed.); see *The Concept of the Political*, 85. Derrida distances himself from the juridical thought of Schmitt because Derrida, although hesitantly, attributes to the notion of justice the character of a "messianic promise." Derrida, "Force of Law," 965. In the revised version of the text, he writes: "I would hesitate to assimilate too quickly this 'idea of justice' . . . to whatever content of a messianic promise (I say *content* and not form, for any messianic form, any messianicity, is never absent from a promise, whatever promise it is)." Derrida, "Force of Law," in Jacques Derrida, *Acts of Religion*, ed. Gil Anidjar (Oxford and New York: Routledge, 2002), 254. This link between the notion of justice and messianism is not, however, entirely clear. We must remember that for Derrida "justice requires us to calculate," because "it can always be reappropriated by the most perverse calculation." Moreover, for Derrida the messianic can coincide with the "worst." "Force of Law," 971. After inquiring into Walter Benjamin's efforts to distinguish two kinds of violence, one mythical or foundational, and another which is mystical or messianic, Derrida insists on the necessity of posing the question after the "possible complicity between all these [messianic] discourses and the worst." "Force of Law," 1045.

249. Despite the fact that there is no reference to Schmitt in the first part of "Force of Law," the problem addressed, its fundamental aspects, and the solution proposed are very much like those found in *Law and Judgment*. The year in which Derrida prepared that text he was already familiar with Schmitt's works, since Derrida had lectured on him. It is not implausible to suggest that his reading of Schmitt's work influenced his argument. This lack of reference produces that the similarities between both works have almost been neglected in the literature. John

P. McCormick has indicated that the "three aporias of law" put forth by Derrida in the first part of "Force of Law" "were raised by Schmitt." McCormick "Derrida on Law," 403; "Schmittian Positions," 1710. However, McCormick does not allude to *Law and Judgment*, where they are already formulated, but to later texts. Richard Wolin highlights the similarities between Schmitt's theory of law and Derrida's conception of the decision. "For Derrida Schmitt's theory of law is important insofar as Schmitt's decisionism foregrounds questions of 'undecidability'—the arbitrary bases of decision and judgment—as does deconstruction." For both, at the basis of the law there is a "groundless ground." For both, finally, "the norm fails to do justice to the specificity of the individual case in its existential immediacy." Wolin, *The Seduction of Unreason* (Oxford and Princeton, NJ: Princeton University Press, 2004), 240; see Mark Lilla, *The Reckless Mind: Intellectuals in Politics* (New York: New York Review of Books, 2001), 177, 184, 190. William W. Sokoloff notices the effort made by Derrida to understand the mediation between law and case to diminish the violence; see "Between Justice and Legality: Derrida on Decision." *Political Research Quarterly* 58, no. 2 (2005): 344. However, neither Wolin, Lilla and Sokoloff consider *Law and Judgment*, but, again, only later texts. The omission of *Law and Judgment* leaves aside Schmitt's explicit reflections on the "correction" of the judicial decision and the attention to singularity required by such correction. In *Law and Judgment*, Schmitt, like Derrida, seeks a decision that moves away from subsumption and caprice, in order to do justice to the situation. See Schmitt, *Gesetz und Urteil*, 1, 8–9, 28, 32, 41, 55, 57, 59, 76, 82, 93, 96, 111–12. Rupert Simon points out the similarity between "Force of Law" and *Law and Judgment*. He does so, however, only in passing and concentrates on the political decision, rather than on juridical understanding; see Simon, *Die Begriffe*, 6, 136 (footnote 884), 161 (footnote 1032). Desmond Manderson considers common aspects of the two works and links them to legal decisionism; Manderson, *Kangaroo Courts and the Rule of Law: The Legacy of Modernism* (Oxford and New York: Routledge, 2012), 74, 76, 77. Regarding Manderson's interpretation, see below: note 261.

250. See Schmitt, *Gesetz und Urteil*, 8, 28, 32, 40, 57–59, 75, 76, 93. In this text Schmitt distances himself from Kelsen's solution to the problem of the judicial decision. "Schmitt is not satisfied here with the facticity of an effective will." Hofmann, *Legitimität*, 32. "Schmitt's research program starts where Kelsen's theory explicitly declares its insufficiency, namely, regarding the problem of the application of the law. Thus, Schmitt, 24 years old at the time, is the one who formulates, within the context of the German Juridical Theory of the State, the first critique of Kelsen worthy of serious attention." Neumann, *Carl Schmitt als Jurist*, 21. Michael Marder considers this book by Schmitt as part of hermeneutical theory; see Marder, *Groundless Existence*, 173–75. William Rasch widely broadens the scope of this book by linking the "judgment" through which Schmitt tries to solve the problem of the tension between rule and case, with the "Kantian aesthetic judgment." Rasch, "Judgment," 100.

251. Johanna Jacques notes the connection between *Law and Judgment* and the sovereign decision. "One could argue that here [i.e., in the decision on the exception], too, the decision contains an active impulse towards correctness that can only be understood as motivated by an existing context. This context does not govern or regulate the decision's content but determines the sovereign's orientation; that is, the decision's direction towards an existing order whose meaning or 'sense' it (re-)establishes. The serious situation or *Ernstfall* arises when the contestation of meaning requires that one take a position, that one commit oneself to a 'definite' point of view. This view is never arbitrary, but is a view of the possibilities that arise as part of an existing legal order." Johanna Jacques, "Law, Decision, Necessity. Shifting the Burden of Responsibility," in *The Contemporary Relevance of Carl Schmitt. Law, Politics, Theology*, ed. Matilda Arvidsson, Leila Brännström, and Panu Minkkinen (Oxford: Routledge, 2016), 115; see 114.

252. Schmitt, *Political Theology*, 3; see *Gesetz und Urteil*, VI.

253. See earlier in this chapter, "Juridical Understanding."

254. See Schmitt, *Gesetz und Urteil*, 8, 37–38, 41.

255. Schmitt, *Gesetz und Urteil*, 64; see *Political Theology*, 30.

256. See Schmitt, *Dictatorship. From the Origin of the Modern Concept of Sovereignty to Proletarian Class Struggle*, trans. Michael Hoelzl and Graham Ward (Cambridge and Malden, MA: Polity Press, 2015, xlii–xliii, 179; McCormick, *Carl Schmitt's Critique of Liberalism*, 125–28.

257. Schmitt, *Political Theology*, 13; see Heiner Bielefeldt, *Kampf und Entscheidung. Politischer Existentialismus bei Carl Schmitt, Helmuth Plessner und Karl Jaspers* (Würzburg: Königshausen & Neumann, 1994), 27, 30.

258. Derrida, on the contrary, argues that "The sovereign does not respond. . . . He is above the law and has the right to suspend the law . . . like God, the sovereign is above the law and above humanity." *The Beast & the Sovereign I*, 57. This indication does not apply to Schmitt without major qualification. The "sovereign" he speaks of is not absolutely sovereign. In a certain sense, however, both in normality and in the exceptional situation, the one deciding is always "above the law," namely, to the extent that the law is not able to exhaust the novelty of the situation, and its correct application requires a decision.

259. Schmitt, *Political Theology*, 3. "The Sovereign . . . cannot avail himself of the burden of responsibility for its consequences [of his decision]. On the contrary, his is a responsibility for the order as a whole, and he actively assumes this burden in the struggle for a life that is more than mere existence." Johanna Jacques, "Law, Decision, Necessity," 117.

260. Schmitt, *Political Theology*, 12.

261. Desmond Manderson ignores the fact that the "insight" he attributes to David H. Lawrence is always present in Schmitt's thought, namely, "that contradiction and opposition, such as those between rules and applications, general norms and particular persons, law and justice even, should neither be separated

as the positivists would have it, nor harmonized as the romantics would have it." "Modernism, Polarity and the Rule of Law." *Yale Journal of Law and Humanities* 24, no. 2 (2012): 477. Precisely the recognition, thematization, and awareness of the basic tension between rule and case, generality and singularity, etc. is what explains Schmitt's self-understanding as a "jurist," and his rejection of the extremes of "technology," which coincides with the attitude of the "positivists," and of "theology," here related to romanticism or what Manderson also calls "transcendentalism."

262. Schmitt, *Political Theology*, 35 (translation modified); see *Glossarium*, 238.

263. The decision in the state of exception of which Schmitt speaks already supposes the constitution of existence as juridical, which Derrida considers as the establishment of the law and the language. We should, therefore, distinguish four levels: (1) the establishment of the law and language as an act of initial violence. In the context of Schmitt's thought this means: the level of the juridical unveiling of existence as tension between rule and case, on the basis of which consciousness, understanding, praxis, and decision (including the decision regarding the state of exception) are alone possible. (2) The formation of a concrete juridical (and telluric [see *The Nomos of the Earth*]) order, based on decisions made by human beings in view of the unveiled and meaningful situations they face. (3) The concrete declaration of the state of exception through a sovereign decision: sovereign insofar as it is above the juridico-positive laws that have lost their validity and efficacy because of a concrete juridico-political crisis, though not "sovereign" in the more original sense of the emergence of existence as juridical. (4) The decision within the context of valid juridico-positive norms (which are always found in a situation of relative crisis, due to the exceptionality and singularity of the individuals and situations subjected to them). In his reading, Giorgio Agamben seems to confuse the first level with the third. For him, "The sovereign *decides* . . . the *originary* inclusion of the living in the sphere of law." *Homo Sacer: Sovereign Power and Bare Life*, trans. Daniel Heller-Roazen (Stanford, CA: Stanford University Press, 1998), 26 (my emphases). The decision of the "sovereign" "produces an exception" that itself establishes the relation between "norm" and "reality." *State of Exception*, trans. Kevin Attell (Chicago: University of Chicago Press, 2005), 40, 35. This interpretation rests on a very problematic, nonthematized assumption, namely, that it would be possible to decide before understanding, i.e., previous to the emergence of existence as juridical, as tension and relation between rules of language *and of the law*, and unveiled and meaningful cases. Before existence becomes intelligible and understanding can take place, it would be possible to adopt a decision that first establishes the relation between "norm" and "reality," or that initially involves "the living in the sphere of law."

264. See Derrida, *The Politics of Friendship*, 88.

265. See Derrida, *The Politics of Friendship*, 72.

266. See Derrida, *The Politics of Friendship*, 38, 231–32, 243–44, 249.
267. Schmitt, *The Concept of the Political*, 28.
268. Schmitt, *The Concept of the Political*, 28.
269. Schmitt, *The Concept of the Political*, 27. That is why "only the actual participants can correctly recognize, understand and judge the concrete situation." *The Concept of the Political*, 27.
270. Schmitt, *Glossarium*, 277, see 238; *The Concept of the Political*, 60; *Ex Captivitate Salus*, 71.
271. See Schmitt, "The Visibility," 48, 51.
272. Jacques Derrida, *The Beast & the Sovereign II*, trans. Geoffrey Bennington (Chicago and London: University of Chicago Press, 2011), 267.
273. Derrida, *The Politics of Friendship*, 232.
274. Derrida, *The Beast & the Sovereign II*, 266–67.
275. Derrida, "Violence and Metaphysics," 153.
276. See earlier in this chapter, "The Subject" and "Closedness versus Openness to the Exceptional."
277. Plessner, *Macht*, 192–93; see Derrida, "Violence and Metaphysics," 157.
278. See Schmitt, *The Concept of the Political*, 30.
279. See Derrida, "Force of Law," 999. It must be remembered that in the second part of "Force of Law," Derrida distinguishes a mythical from a messianic violence, and demands to ask for the "possible complicity between all these [messianic] discourses and the worst." "Force of Law," 1045; see 971. The recognition of the "deconstructible" character of the "hostility" and the instability Derrida attributes to the political (Hent de Vries, *Religion and Violence: Perspectives from Kant to Derrida* [Baltimore, MD and London: Johns Hopkins University Press, 2002], 357; see "Force of Law," 971, 1045) does not preclude the admission of conflict and of the fact that, in certain cases, like those alluded to by Derrida or the ones present in Schmitt's thought, the use of force may be exigible.

Chapter 2

1. Schmitt, *Political Theology*, 36.
2. Jacob Taubes and Carl Schmitt, *Jacob Taubes—Carl Schmitt: Briefwechsel und Andere Materialien*, ed. Herbert Kopp-Oberstebrink, Thorsten Palzhoff and Martin Treml (Munich: Fink, 2011), 37.
3. Meier, *The Lesson*, xi.
4. Meier, *Leo Strauss*, 81; *Carl Schmitt and Leo Strauss*, 76. Since the publication of Meier's two main books, his interpretation has become highly influential. Hasso Hofmann recognized as early as 1994 that " 'political theology' is currently valid as a universal key" to understand Schmittian thought; Hofmann, *Legitimität*, xvii. For a similar statement, see Paul Noack, "Staatstheoretiker, Politischer

Theologe—oder was sonst? Neue Bücher von und über Carl Schmitt." *Der Staat* 43 (1996): 203; Harald Seubert, "Eigene Fragen als Gestalt: Zu neuerer Literatur über Carl Schmitt." *Der Staat* 37 (1998): 435. Among the abundant literature on the relation between Schmitt's thought and theology, see Mark Lilla, *The Reckless Mind*, 67; Ruth Groh, *Arbeit an der Heillosigkeit der Welt—Zur politisch-theologischen Mythologie und Anthropologie Carl Schmitts* (Frankfurt: Suhrkamp, 1998), 18–20, 190–91; Mathias Eichhorn, *Es wird regiert! Der Staat im Denken Karl Barths und Carl Schmitts in den Jahren 1919 bis 1938* (Berlin: Duncker & Humblot, 1994); James Wiley, *Politics and the Concept of the Political. The Political Imagination* (London and New York: Routledge, 2016), 55–56, 67–77; Marco Rampazzo Bazzan, "Die Staatslehre Fichtes unter dem Aspekt der politischen Theologie nach Carl Schmitt," in *Der Eine oder der Andere. "Gott" in der klassischen deutschen Philosophie und im Denken der Gegenwart*, ed. Christopher Asmuth (Tübingen: Mohr Siebeck, 2010), 85–95; Michaela Rissing and Thilo Rissing, *Politische Theologie*; Gerhoch Reisegger, *Wege aus dem Globalisierungs-Chaos. Grundlagen für eine neue Wirtschaftsordnung*. Tübingen: Hohenrain, 2009, 362–66; Burkhard Conrad, "Das rhetorische Moment von politischer Theologie." *Zeitschrift für Politik* 54 (2007): 408–30; François Nault, "La fraternité. En lisant Derrida, Schmitt et la Bible." *Revue d'éthique et de théologie morale* 247 (2007): 29–52; Paul W. Kahn, *Political Theology. Four New Chapters on the Concept of Sovereignity* (New York: Columbia University Press, 2011); Marc de Wilde, "Meeting Opposites: The Political Theologies of Walter Benjamin and Carl Schmitt." *Philosophy and Rhetoric* 44 (2011): 363–81; Kieran Keohane, "On the Political in the Wake: Carl Schmitt and James Joyce's Political Theologies." *Cultural Politics. An International Journal* 7, no. 2 (2011): 249–64; Bernard Bourdin, "La modernité séculière a-t-elle besoin d'une théologie politique?" *Esprit* 372 (February 2011): 125–37; Siegfried Gerlich, "Die Politische Theologie Carl Schmitts." *Sezession* (Themenheft Carl Schmitt) 42 (2011): 28–31; Helge Høibraaten, "Carl Schmitt, Henrik Ibsen und die Politische Theologie. Die Kronprätendenten, Kaiser und Galiläer und die Lehre vom Dritten Reich," in *Henrik Ibsen, Kaiser und Galiläer. Quellen—Interpretationen—Rezeptionen*, ed. Richard Faber and Helge Høibraaten (Würzburg: Königshausen & Neumann, 2011), 233–93; Christian Kierdorf, *Carl Schmitts Idee einer politischen Theologie* (Berlin: Duncker & Humblot, 2015). Bernd Wacker (ed.), *Die eigentlich katholische Verschärfung: Konfession, Theologie und Politik im Werk Carl Schmitts* (Munich: Fink, 1994); Banu Bargu, "Stasiology. Political Theology and the Figure of the Sacrificial Enemy," in *After Secular Law*, ed. Winnifried Fallers Sullivan, Robert A. Yelle, Mateo Taussig-Rubbo (Stanford, CA: Stanford University Press, 2011), 140–59.

    5. See Meier, *The Lesson*, xiv–xv.

    6. Meier, *Leo Strauss*, 84; *The Lesson*, 173.

    7. Meier, *Leo Strauss*, 84; *The Lesson*, xv; *Carl Schmitt and Leo Strauss*, 163 (German ed. Stuttgart: Metzler, 1998).

8. Meier, *Carl Schmitt and Leo Strauss*, 162 (German ed.); *The Lesson*, xiv.
9. Meier, *The Lesson*, xiii.
10. Meier, *Carl Schmitt and Leo Strauss*, 161 (German ed.); *The Lesson*, xiv; *Leo Strauss*, 84.
11. See Meier, for example, *The Lesson*, xiii–xiv, 2, 201–204; *Carl Schmitt and Leo Strauss*, 76–77; *Carl Schmitt and Leo Strauss*, 161 (German ed.).
12. Meier, *Carl Schmitt and Leo Strauss*, 80; see *The Lesson*, 19, 90–93.
13. Meier, *The Lesson*, 170.
14. See Meier, *Leo Strauss*, 84.; *The Lesson*, 19–21, 170.
15. Meier, *Carl Schmitt and Leo Strauss*, 80.
16. See Meier, *Carl Schmitt and Leo Strauss*, 80; *The Lesson* 20–21.
17. See, for example, *The Lesson*, 34–35, 71–72, 89–90; *Leo Strauss*, 82.
18. Meier, *The Lesson*, xix; *Leo Strauss*, 86; see Martin Heidegger, *Beiträge zur Philosophie (Vom Ereignis)*, in *Gesamtausgabe* 65 (Frankfurt: Klostermann, 1994).
19. Meier, *The Lesson*, xix; *Carl Schmitt and Leo Strauss*, 170, 174, 176, 177 (German ed.); *Leo Strauss*, 51, 86–87.
20. Meier, *The Lesson*, xiii; *Carl Schmitt and Leo Strauss*, 161 (German ed.).
21. Meier, *The Lesson*, xiv; *Carl Schmitt and Leo Strauss*, 161 (German ed.).
22. See Meier, *Carl Schmitt and Leo Strauss*, 161 (German ed.); *The Lesson*, xiv.
23. Meier, *The Lesson*, xviii (footnote 14); *Carl Schmitt and Leo Strauss*, 167 (footnote 16) (German ed.).
24. Meier, *The Lesson*, xviii (footnote 14); *Carl Schmitt and Leo Strauss*, 167 (footnote 16) (German ed.).
25. Meier, *The Lesson*, xviii (footnote 14); *Carl Schmitt and Leo Strauss*, 167 (footnote 16) (German ed.).
26. Meier, *The Lesson*, xviii (footnote 14); *Carl Schmitt and Leo Strauss*, 167 (footnote 16) (German ed.).
27. For the discussion about the concept and characteristics of political theology, see Michael Kodalle, *Politik als Macht und Mythos. Carl Schmitts "Politische Theologie"* (Stuttgart: Kohlhammer, 1973); Carlo Galli, *Janus Gaze. Essays on Carl Schmitt*, trans. Amanda Minervini (London and Durham, NC: Duke University Press, 2015), 33–57; the volume edited by Luigi Sartori and Michelle Nicoletti: *Teologia Politica* (Bologna: Ed. Dehonia, 1991); Ernst-Wolfgang Böckenförde, "Politische Theologie—Begriff und Bedeutung," *Neue Zürcher Zeitung*, May 30, 1981. Within the more recent context, and questioning the classical notions of theology, see Hent de Vries and Lawrence Sullivan, eds., *Political Theologies: Public Religions in a Post-Secular World* (New York: Fordham University Press, 2006); Jeffrey W. Robbins, *Radical Democracy and Political Theology* (New York: Columbia University Press, 2011); the volume ed. by Winnifried Fallers Sullivan, Robert A. Yelle and Mateo Taussig-Rubbo, *After Secular Law*.
28. See Meier, *The Lesson*, xiii–xv, 2, 173; *Leo Strauss*, 84; *Carl Schmitt and Leo Strauss*, 161–63 (German ed.) 161–63; *Carl Schmitt and Leo Strauss*, 76–77.

29. See Meier, *The Lesson*, xiii–xiv, 2; *Carl Schmitt and Leo Strauss* 161 (German ed.); *Carl Schmitt and Leo Strauss*, 76–77.

30. See Anselm of Canterbury, *The Mayor Works*, ed. Brian Davies and Gillian Evans (Oxford: Oxford University Press, 2008), chaps. 2 and 3.

31. See Thomas Aquinas, *Summa Theologica*, trans. Fathers of the English Dominican Province (New York: Benziger Brothers, 1948), I-I, q. 2 a. 3.

32. See Meister Eckhart, *Die deutschen Werke vol. III*. In *Die deutschen und lateinischen Werke*, edited by Joseph Quint (Stuttgart: Verlag W. Kohlhammer, 1976), 447–49.

33. See R. Descartes, *Meditationes de prima philosophia*, in *Œuvres complètes*, ed. Charles Adam and Paul Tannery (Paris: Vrin, 1996), vol. 8, third meditation.

34. Paul Tillich, *Theology of Culture*, ed. Robert C. Kimball (Oxford: Oxford University Press, 1959), 24–25; *Dynamics of Faith* (New York: Harper & Row, 1957), 1–2; Clayton Crockett, *Radical Political Theology. Religion and Politics after Liberalism* (New York: Columbia University Press, 2011), 16–17.

35. See, for example, Heidegger, "Die Frage," 9–40.

36. Though from a standpoint different from that of Schmitt, Clayton Crockett questions Meier's thesis and arrives at results similar to Schmitt's. He conceives a "theology" that is independent of the traditional theological thought on God. *Radical Political Theology*, 15–16. Such "theology" thus achieves the "freedom to think matters of ultimate concern—political, moral, existential, cosmological—without the constraint of tradition, authority, or the presumed certainty of dogmatic answers" (17). Before that "theology," the "clear distinction between political theology (Schmitt) and political philosophy (Strauss)," held by Meier, becomes questionable (82). The field of "immanence does not exclude the theological or settle questions of transcendence" (91), in the nondogmatic or philosophical sense indicated. Thus, as in Schmitt, the radical separation between immanence and transcendence is relativized.

37. Meier, *The Lesson*, 41.

38. Meier, *Leo Strauss*, 51.

39. Schmitt, *Glossarium*, 36, 39, 93–95.

40. Schmitt, *Theodor Däublers "Nordlicht,"* 62.

41. See Schmitt, *Glossarium*, 20, 70–72, 200.

42. Meier, *Leo Strauss*, 86.

43. See Schmitt, *Glossarium*, 238; "The Plight," 64–66; *Ex Captivitate Salus*, 58, 60, 71.

44. Schmitt, *Glossarium*, 238.

45. "The scientism . . . had an activist character in demanding a cosmos that would be dependent on the conscious work of men." Schmitt, *The Leviathan*, 85; see *Glossarium*, 238; *Theodor Däublers "Nordlicht,"* 66; *Political Theology II*, 128–30; Husserl, *The Crisis*, § 9, h), 51.

46. See Schmitt, for example, *Hamlet or Hecuba*, 45; *Political Theology*, 15; *Glossarium*, 388.

47. See Schmitt, *Glossarium*, 64; *Political Romanticism*, 19.

48. See Schmitt, *Glossarium*, 64, 136, 388; "The Visibility," 48, 51.

49. To the extent that here faith alone predominates, without there being a differentiated exercise of thought, this theology is such in an improper sense. In this case, Schmitt warns, it might even be better to restrain the use of the term "substantialism." Although there is an anti-functionalism that inclines toward the pole of the real, the absence of epistemological control may result in an attitude in which every cohesion tends to be diluted. See Schmitt, *Political Romanticism*, 19, 54–56.

50. See Schmitt, *Political Theology II*, 42, 58, 95; *Ex Captivitate Salus*, 59. Schmitt speaks, for example, of certain "metaphysicians" who make use of "God" when they cannot "master intellectually contradictory arguments or objections" (*Political Theology*, 39), or of theologians who fall into the religiously determined pretention "to always have the truth." *The Nomos of the Earth*, 141 (translation modified); see *Ex Captivitate Salus*, 15.

51. See Schmitt, *Political Theology*, 15; *Glossarium*, 238, 388; *Political Romanticism*, 51–53.

52. We have seen that for Schmitt the exceptional does not let itself be determined by the general concepts of normality with which the subject operates; see Schmitt, *Political Theology*, 15; *Hamlet or Hecuba*, 45; *Glossarium*, 237–38. Transcendence remains in the field of the "incomprehensible" (*Glossarium*, 160); of the "intangible" (*Glossarium*, 388); God in the field of the "unsayable." *Glossarium*, 133; see Meier, *The Lesson*, 89.

53. See Schmitt, *Glossarium*, 388, 64, 121, 237–38; *Political Romanticism*, 52.

54. See Schmitt, *Political Theology*, 15; *The Concept of the Political*, 60; *Hamlet or Hecuba*, 45.

55. See Schmitt, *Glossarium*, 64; *The Concept of the Political*, 60.

56. See Schmitt, *Political Theology*, 13, 15, 35; "The Plight," 56; *The Nomos of the Earth*, 39; *Roman Catholicism*, 12; *The Concept of the Political*, 26, 38; *The Concept of the Political* (German ed.) 120–21; "Raum und Rom," 965; "Recht und Raum," 243; *On the Three Types of Juristic Thought*, 56–57; *Land and Sea*, 92–93; *Die Tyrannei der Werte*, 45; *Ex Captivitate Salus*, 71, 72; *Hamlet or Hecuba*, 45. "Drei Möglichkeiten," 166; *Theodor Däublers "Nordlicht,"* 59–60, 66–67; *Glossarium*, 26 (footnote 1), 136; Böckenförde, "Konkretes Ordnungsdenken," 1312–13; Rüthers, *Die unbegrenzte Auslegung*, 294.

57. Schmitt, *Political Romanticism*, 19, 56.

58. See Schmitt, *Political Romanticism*, 55.

59. See Schmitt, *Political Theology*, 52, 65–66.

60. See Schmitt, *On the Three Types of Juristic Thought*, 73.

61. See Schmitt, *The Nomos of the Earth*, 38–39; *Land and Sea*, 92–93; *Glossarium*, 136; "Raum und Rom," 965; "Recht und Raum," 243; *On the Three Types of Juristic Thought*, 56–57; *Roman Catholicism*, 12; *The Concept of the Political*, 26, 38; *Political Theology*, 13, 15, 35; *Die Tyrannei der Werte*, 45; *Ex Captivitate Salus*, 72.

62. See Schmitt, *Glossarium*, 26 (footnote 1), 27, 30, 70–72, 147; *The Leviathan*, 85; *Theodor Däublers "Nordlicht*," 59–60, 66–67; *Political Theology*, 15, 35; *The Nomos of the Earth*, 38–39; *Roman Catholicism*, 12–13.

63. See Schmitt, *Glossarium*, 100.

64. See Schmitt, *Ex Captivitate Salus*, 72; *The Nomos of the Earth*, 39 (German ed.: 6); "The Plight," 56, 66–67.

65. Schmitt, *Glossarium*, 277.

66. See Schmitt, *Glossarium*, 238, 388; *Political Theology*, 13–15; *Political Theology II*, 117; *Constitutional Theory*, 22; *The Leviathan*, 31–37.

67. See Schmitt, *The Nomos of the Earth*, 38–39.

68. See Schmitt, *Political Romanticism*, 162; *Roman Catholicism*, 32. The institution must withdraw itself, however, from the "totalitarian" extreme of technological functionalism. The law separates itself from technical manipulation, insofar as it aims to establish an "order of meaning" in which the other is recognized. Juridical understanding is "*ad alterum*." For the technological rationality, on the contrary, insofar as it carries out an objectifying consideration of existence, the other, in the end, "does not exist." *Glossarium*, 238; see "The Plight," 64–66; *Ex Captivitate Salus*, 58–61.

69. For Schmitt, in less sophisticated versions of theology, the question of institutional normality loses its contours; see *Glossarium*, 388. He sees in Catholicism a rationality that lies, in fact and to a certain point, between theology and the law, since it does not set aside both the reference to transcendence and its meaning, and the institutional question. See *Roman Catholicism*, 8, 13, 14, 32. Despite its putting together the poles of the real and the ideal in a, so to speak, felicitous manner, Roman Catholicism, however, does not thematize the problem of the relation and tension between the poles in a sufficiently penetrating way. "Roman Catholicism"—writes Schmitt—"understands little of the dualisms" affecting modern consciousness and that are made explicit in it. *Roman Catholicism*, 11.

70. See Schmitt, *Roman Catholicism*, 3–4; *Political Romanticism*, 55.

71. See Schmitt, *Glossarium*, 238; *Dictatorship*, 127.

72. Schmitt, *The Nomos of the Earth*, 141.

73. Schmitt, *The Nomos of the Earth*, 141 (translation modified).

74. Schmitt, *The Nomos of the Earth*, 142; see *The Concept of the Political*, 36; *Ex Captivitate Salus*, 15, 59.

75. Schmitt, *Ex Captivitate Salus*, 71.

76. Schmitt, *Glossarium*, 238.

77. Schmitt, "The Plight," 66.

78. See Schmitt, "The Plight," 66–67; *On the Three Types of Juristic Thought*, 52–57; *Glossarium*, 238.
79. See Schmitt, *Constitutional Theory*, 59–60.
80. See chapter 1, the sections "Closedness versus Openness to the Exceptional" and "Understanding."
81. Schmitt, "The Plight," 66–67.
82. The interpretive decision requires balancing between the pretensions of the different others; see *Glossarium*, 238.
83. Schmitt, *Constitutional Theory*, 208. See 208–12.
84. See Schmitt, e.g., *The Nomos of the Earth*, 187, 189; *The Concept of the Political*, 36.
85. See the third section of chapter 1.
86. In *Glossarium*, Schmitt shows the relation between law and theology, in this sense of the term (T4). An "inner tension [*innere Spannung*]" is "essential [*wesentlich*]" to both, since in them the relation between conceptuality and reality, immanence and transcendence, is considered. Built on an original "'revelation' ['*Offenbarung*']," theology in this broad sense realizes a first conceptualization on which basis the law accomplishes its work of thematizing the relation between rule and case. *Glossarium*, 388–89. But we are then speaking of theology in the widest sense of the term, as a thought in which the reflection on the conditions of understanding is brought forth.
87. Schmitt, *Glossarium*, 388.
88. See Schmitt, *Glossarium*, 133, 160, 388; *Hamlet or Hecuba*, 45; *Political Theology*, 15.
89. See Schmitt, *Political Theology*, 36.
90. See Schmitt, *Political Theology*, 64–65.
91. Schmitt, *Political Theology*, 49.
92. Schmitt, *Political Theology*, 36.
93. Schmitt, *Political Theology*, 37.
94. Schmitt, *Political Theology*, 45.
95. "The starting point" of "[Schmitt's] expositions is the coincidence of the social structure of an epoch [more precisely: the juridical conceptualization brought forth in it] with the metaphysical worldview of that same epoch." Hans Maier, *Kritik der politischen Theologie* (Einsiedeln: Johannes Verlag, 1970), 14.
96. Schmitt, *Political Theology*, 46.
97. Schmitt, *Political Theology*, 46. Rae states in this regard: "Schmitt understand[s] "metaphysics" to be the branch of philosophy that deals with the nature of reality. While naturalism thinks of itself as the abandonment of metaphysical superstition or belief, Schmitt claims that naturalism is also a metaphysical theory because it proposes a theory of reality based in the claim that nature, physical appearance or that which presents itself, defines reality." Garin Rae, *The Problem*

of Political Foundations in Carl Schmitt and Emmanuel Levinas (London: Palgrave MacMillan, 2016), 35. See Catherine Coillot-Thélène, "Carl Schmitt versus Max Weber: Juridical Rationality and Economic Rationality," in *The Challenge of Carl Schmitt*, ed. Chantal Mouffe (London: Verso, 1999), 143.

98. This idea of "theology" or "metaphysics" as the most radical way of an epoch's self-understanding certainly implies an improperly and even confusing use of the terms. But to state that such an idea attests to there being dogmatic theology in Schmitt—when he in fact may be in its antipodes—is a mistake.

99. See Schmitt, *Political Theology*, 47–49.

100. Schmitt, *Political Theology*, 41.

101. Schmitt, *Political Theology*, 45–46, 49; see: *Dialogues on Power and Space*, trans. Samuel Garrett Zeitlin (Cambridge and Malden, MA: Polity Press, 2015), 43; *Political Romanticism*, 3, 17–18. Donoso Cortés presents a similar kind of sociology of concepts. He detects that the "metaphysics" of his time is what has brought monarchy to an end. This author, however, does not reach a properly philosophical level of reflection, since, in order to do that, he would have to thematize scientific-technical rationality and formulate a critique that exhibits its scope and limits based on a consideration of the conditions of human understanding. He betrays, instead, "ignorance of the mathematical natural-scientific thinking." Schmitt, *Political Theology*, 52. But he does reach the level of a jurist in the strict sense of the sociology of concepts, and he is in fact aware of the "metaphysical kernel of all politics" (PT 51; *Donoso Cortés in gesamteuropäischer Interpretation. Vier Aufsätze* [Cologne: Greven Verlag 1950], 108)—that is, of the said relation between the political order of an epoch and its metaphysical conception.

102. Kant had a similar problem in view when criticizing the skeptics: in rejecting metaphysics, the skeptics are unaware of the fact that their understanding is already being developed within a metaphysical context. The "pretended indifferentists" regarding metaphysics, "however they may try to disguise themselves by substituting a popular tone for the language of the Schools, inevitably fall back, in so far as they think at all, into the very metaphysical assertions which they profess so greatly to despise." *Critique of Pure Reason*, trans. Norman Kemp Smith (Hampshire and New York: Palgrave MacMillan, 2007), A x.

103. See Schmitt, *Glossarium*, 64; *Political Theology*, 15; *Hamlet or Hecuba*, 45; *The Concept of the Political*, 60; and what was noted earlier in chapter 1.

104. Schmitt, *Political Romanticism*, 17, 18.

105. See Schmitt, *Political Romanticism*, 17–18; *The Concept of the Political*, 95–96; *Political Theology*, 50–51, 65.

106. From the recognition of the "structural interrelationship" (*Radical Political Theology* 79) between theological and political concepts, and of the possibility of considering theology in a nondogmatic way—free "to think matters of ultimate concern" (16–17)—Clayton Crockett argues that Schmitt's sociology of concepts permits opening the path to the formulation of practical and political

orientations and critiques, also within a contemporary context. The extremes of human understanding, namely theology and technology, are the points between which, in turn, the history of modernity develops for Schmitt. See "The Age of Neutralizations and Depoliticizations," in *The Concept of the Political*, 80–96; *Political Romanticism*, 51–53; *Political Theology*, 13–15. Schmitt is critical of the loss of attention to the exceptional and the meaning of existence betrayed by the process. He may now be called a "theologian" with respect to history, but his position is that of the jurist. Schmitt values the emergence of jurisprudence as a way of understanding independent of theology, which takes place from the twelfth century onward and settles during modernity. "European jurisprudence is the first-born child of the modern European spirit; of the 'occidental rationalism' of the modern age. The modern natural sciences followed later." Schmitt, "The Plight," 65. In a theoretical and practical sense, the inclination toward the theological pole, as we have seen, is encumbered by severe difficulties. Nevertheless, the evolution cannot rightly finish with immanentism, whose insufficiencies are also pointed out by Schmitt. See "The Plight," 64–66; *Political Theology*, 15.

107. Meier, *Carl Schmitt and Leo Strauss* (German ed.), 161; *The Lesson*, xiv.

108. See Meier, *The Lesson*, 20–21, 27; *Leo Strauss*, 81–84. Ruth Groh states, in a similar vein, that Schmitt's thought is "marked by previous theological decisions and not simply motivated by them." Groh, *Arbeit*, 18.

109. "Such political theology," like the one Meier postulates regarding Carl Schmitt, "could only be elaborated based on the consideration of Schmitt's works on political theory, the theory of the state, constitutional theory, and the theory of international public law, which constitute about 90 per cent of his whole output." Günther Maschke, "Carl Schmitt in den Händen der Nicht-Juristen." *Der Staat* 34 (1995): 105; see "Vorwort" to C. Schmitt, *Staat, Großraum, Nomos. Arbeiten aus den Jahren 1916–1969* (Berlin: Duncker & Humblot, 1995), xiii. Maschke's thesis is followed by Paul Noack ("Staatstheoretiker," 198) and Harald Seubert ("Eigene Fragen als Gestalt," 441). Seubert states: "It must be acknowledged in favor of Günther Maschke . . . that Schmitt's work does not allow the dissolution of political and juridical theory into political theology." For studies in which the massive amount of theoretico-juridical doctrines in Schmitt's works is acknowledged, see Volker Neumann, *Carl Schmitt als Jurist*; Jens Meierhenrich and Oliver Simons (eds.), *The Oxford Handbook of Carl Schmitt* (New York: Oxford University Press, 2016); Michael Stolleis, *Geschichte des Öffentlichen Rechts in Deutschland*, vol. 4, 1995–1990 (Munich: Beck, 2012).

110. See (as examples), Helmuth Plessner, *Macht*, 139–234; Chantal Mouffe, *The Return of the Political* (London and New York: Verso, 1993); "Carl Schmitt and the Paradox of Liberal Democracy," in *The Challenge of Carl Schmitt*, ed. Chantal Mouffe (London and New York: Verso, 1999), 38–53; *On the Political* (London: Routledge, 2005); Ernst-Wolfgang Böckenförde, "The Concept of the Political. A Key to Understanding Carl Schmitt's Constitutional Theory," in *Law as*

Politics. Carl Schmitt's Critique of Liberalism, ed. David Dyzenhaus (London and Durham, NC: Duke University Press, 1998), 37–55; Ernst Forsthoff, *Rechtsstaat im Wandel. Verfassungsgeschichtliche Abhandlungen 1954–1973* (Munich: Beck, 1976); Leo Strauss, "Notes on Carl Schmitt, The Concept of the Political," in Heinrich Meier, *Carl Schmitt and Leo Strauss. The Hidden Dialogue* (Chicago and London: University of Chicago Press, 1995), 91–119; Helmuth Kuhn, *Der Staat. Eine philosophische Darstellung* (Munich: Kösel, 1967); Michael Marder, *Groundless Existence*; Ojakangas, *A Philosophy of Concrete Life*; Werner Weber, *Spannungen und Kräfte im westdeutschen Verfassungssystem* (Berlin: Duncker & Humblot, 1970); Roman Schnur, *Revolution und Weltbürgerkrieg. Studien zur Ouvertüre nach 1789* (Berlin: Duncker & Humblot, 1983); Joseph H. Kaiser, *Die Repräsentation organisierter Interessen* (Berlin: Duncker & Humblot, 1956); Reinhart Koselleck, *Kritik und Krise. Eine Studie zur Pathogenese der bürgerlichen Welt* (Frankfurt: Suhrkamp, 1973); Otto Kirchheimer, *Von der Weimarer Republik zum Faschismus. Die Auflösung der demokratischen Rechtsordnung* (Frankfurt: Suhrkamp, 1976); Franz Neumann, *Witschaft, Staat, Demokratie. Aufsätze 1930–1954*, ed. Alfons Söllner (Frankfurt: Suhrkamp, 1978); David Dyzenhaus, "Why Carl Schmitt?" in *Law as Politics. Carl Schmitt's Critique of Liberalism*, ed. David Dyzenhaus (London and Durham, NC: Duke University Press, 1998), 1–20; *Legality and Legitimacy. Carl Schmitt, Hans Kelsen and Hermann Heller in Weimar* (Oxford: Oxford University Press, 1997); Bernard Willms, "Carl Schmitt—Jüngster Klassiker des politischen Denkens?" in *Complexio Oppositorum. Über Carl Schmitt*, ed. Helmut Quaritsch (Berlin: Duncker & Humblot, 1988), 577–97; Jorge E. Dotti, "*Filioque*. Una tenaz apología de la mediación teológico-política," in Carl Schmitt, *La tiranía de los valores* (Buenos Aires: Hydra, 2009), 9–86; Miguel Vatter, "The Idea of Public Reason and the Reason of State: Schmitt and Rawls on the Political." *Political Theory* 36 (2008): 239–71; Neumann, *Carl Schmitt als Jurist*; Rüthers, *Die unbegrezte Auslegung*, 293–302; Andreas Kalyvas, *Democracy and the Politics of the Extraordinary. Max Weber, Carl Schmitt, and Hannah Arendt* (Cambridge: Cambridge University Press, 2008), 79–253, 292–300. On the reception of the thought of Schmitt, see Reinhard Mehring, *Carl Schmitt* (Hamburg: Junius, 2001), 117–25; *Carl Schmitt: Denker im Widerstreit. Werk—Wirkung—Aktualität* (Freiburg: Verlag Karl Alber, 2017), 353–72; Daniel Hitschler, *Zwischen Liberalismus und Existentialismus. Carl Schmitt im englischsprachigen Schrifttum* (Baden-Baden: Nomos, 2011).

    111. Meier, *The Lesson*, 22.

    112. See Schmitt, *On the Three Types of Juristic Thought*, 56–57; *Political Theology*, 13; *Constitutional Theory*, 65, 76. Moreover, normativism ignores the problem of correction or justice criterion of the juridical decision. The norm as operative representation is not self-sufficient, but is referred to a concrete instance—the judge. See *On the Three Types of Juristic Thought*, 51. Insofar as the generality of the rule differs from the concrete situation in a way that no norm is able to annul, the margin for the judge to act comprises not only a mechanical

subsumption of the case under the rule, but also the interpretation of the norm. Thus arises the problem of the criterion for the right decision. This problem cannot be solved within the confines of normativism, which pays no heed to the practical and concrete character of the situation. See Schmitt, *Gesetz und Urteil*, 8, 9, 28, 32, 41, 57, 59, 66, 76, 82, 93-94, 111-12; Neumann, *Carl Schmitt als Jurist*, 21.

113. See Meier, *The Lesson*, 80.

114. Meier, *The Lesson*, 81. These examples evince that Meier's reading impedes or hinders a grasp of Schmitt's thought that approaches it in its specific theoretical complexity. Harald Seubert says about *The Lesson*: "In his 'The Lesson of Carl Schmitt' political philosophy is reduced to political theology." "Eigene Fragen als Gestalt," 447. To affirm that Schmitt's theoretical attitude is conditioned by his faith restricts its systematic validity and scope, to the point that, regarding this reading, one is justified in asking, as Hasso Hofmann does: "What is, however, the objective contribution of this political theology, beyond that of an enormous increase in *pathos*?" Hofmann, *Legitimiät*, xxxix; see Werner von Simson, "Carl Schmitt und der Staat unserer Tage." *Archiv des öffentlichen Rechts* 114 (1990): 213-14. Bernhard Schlink, "Why Carl Schmitt?" *Rechtshistorisches Journal* 10 (1991): 167. To say that the basis of Schmitt's theories is conditioned by faith in revelation, can in itself be a contribution toward the effort to inquire into Schmitt's motivations. Elucidating the intrinsic theoretical validity of his arguments is made more difficult under such an assumption because from a strictly philosophical perspective, they become as theoretically questionable as mere faith itself. That in Meier's interpretation the systematic relevance of Schmitt's thought is ultimately not recognized is attested in a final passage in *The Lesson*, where he states that Schmitt's "greatest lesson" is the "contribution" that his "political theology makes to" the "clarification" of the "own cause" of "political philosophy." Meier, *The Lesson*, 173. The contribution of Schmitt's political theology ends up being a residual one. It serves as a means of contrasting theology with philosophy in such a way that by so doing we become aware of what philosophy isn't. Nevertheless, this contribution requires a positive knowledge of what political philosophy is, without which we stand little chance of determining what it isn't. In fact, Meier seems to already have acquired that knowledge; see *Leo Strauss, Carl Schmitt and Leo Strauss*, *The Lesson*. Only then and in particular when dealing with doubtful topics, it might be necessary to define what philosophy isn't.

115. Schmitt, *Glossarium*, 99. In that same passage, however, Schmitt is concerned with distinguishing his religious Catholicism, or faith, both from "theology" and from the law. Faith operates in the field of the "unfathomableness" of "enigmatically individual events." The law as a discipline is placed "between theology and technology." Theology is, like the law and technology, understood as a hermeneutical discipline. Within this context, it is possible for Schmitt to have faith and not become a "theologian," but to remain a "jurist." That is to say, faith should have a motivating, not a conditioning, role. Remaining a jurist,

"conscious of one's own specific task [*Aufgabe*]" requires—says Schmitt—holding the distance from both the substantialist extreme of theology and the functionalist extreme of technology. Put in positive terms: it requires keeping the awareness of the presuppositions and limits of understanding and of the tension and relation between the conceptual and the real. *Glossarium*, 100; see 237–38.

116. Catholicism influences Schmitt's conception of the incarnation, which in turn influences his grasp of what he sees as a Christian view of history. In the texts where he refers to these ideas, also when he speaks of the Katechon (e.g., *Glossarium*, 215), Schmitt usually makes it explicit that such texts contain approaches which are valid within the context of Christianity, that is, under the presupposition of Christian faith. In *Glossarium* he writes: "I *believe* in the Katechon; it is, for me, the only possibility, *as a Christian*, to understand history and find meaning in it." *Glossarium*, 47 (my emphases). In "The Visibility of the Church," where he speaks of the incarnation, the institutionality of the Church, and the Christian God, he indicates that he shall proceed "as if conversing with a Christian." "The Visibility," 47. Already the title of "Drei Möglichkeiten eines christlichen Geschichtsbildes" (correspondence with Blumenberg, 161) explicitly hints at the fact that it is concerned, if not exclusively, with a matter of faith. In this text, Schmitt restricts the scope of the doctrine of "incarnation" to "Christianity," to "Christian belief," and "the Christian." "Drei Möglichkeiten," 163–65; see *Glossarium*, 215; "The Visibility," 52.

The notion of incarnation as a historical event, and of the Katechon as irruption of the divinity in the midst of times, although in principle matters of faith, may nonetheless reach beyond it, insofar as they enable one to gain a perspective regarding the exceptional character of existence, of the unforeseeability of historical events, and of history as operating in the tension between conforming forces and the tendencies resisting conformation. The Katechon is considered as a "sustaining force" operating in history, able to overcome chaos, though in a form different from that of a technological control of the world; "Drei Möglichkeiten," 162, 164. Katechon is a notion that makes possible to think of a power that operates in history in a creative but nonprogressive way, a power able to institute order, an order that is, however, vulnerable. One need not be a dogmatic theologian to understand history based on concepts such as "sustaining forces and powers" and chaos, instability and manipulation, or on those of conformation, subsumption and anomie, but rather, they seem in fact to be the usual way in which historical thought is articulated and can be articulated; an historical thought namely that is aware of the eventual character of history, of the contingency of historical situations. Schmitt understands this doctrine in this broader sense when he states in this very text that this "idea of sustaining forces and powers can be confirmed in some form in every great historian" ("Drei Möglichkeiten," 164), not only in those who are believers. "Drei Möglichkeiten" is a commentary on a book by Karl Löwith on various possible conceptions of history, and it is within this context that Schmitt makes a characterization of the Christian conception of history and considers what he calls a historical-philosophical view. Regarding the Christian conception of history, he distinguishes a dogmatical appearance—which could be dismissed as "mere historical mysticism"—and what he calls the "dark truth" hidden in the Christian dogma. "Drei Möglichkeiten," 165. The dogma of the incarnation allows one to open an understanding of history that is distinct from a strictly immanent—historical-philosophical—vision. See "Drei Möglichkeiten," 165–66. Here Schmitt seems to stress the existential exception, the "infinite uniqueness of the historical real [*unendliche Einmaligkeit des geschichtlich Wirklichen*]" ("Drei Möglichkeiten," 165), and the relativity of all efforts toward rationalization. The historical-philosophical view, instead, tries to avoid this exceptionality by means of calculation and "planning." "Drei Möglichkeiten," 162. The dogma here arises illustrating a "dark truth," but the meaning of this truth is not necessarily bound to dogma, insofar as it rests on a reflection on the exceptional character of existence.

117. Meier cites a text in which Schmitt affirms: "This is the secret keyword of my entire spiritual and public existence: revolving around the authentic Catholic intensification." Schmitt, *Glossarium*, 165. In the quoted passage, Schmitt opposes "Catholic intensification" to the position of "neutralizers." This position ultimately seeks to ignore the tension between an existence emerging in a plethoric way, on one hand, and rules and concepts, on the other, in order to make the latter pole (that of rules and concepts) prevail. That is, the expression refers to technological understanding. See *The Concept of the Political*, 78–96; *Political Theology II*, 129. Schmitt, as "jurist," distances himself from that form of rationality because of his reflection on the conditions of understanding. Within this context, the allusion of Schmitt to Catholicism cannot mean a religious conditioning of his thought. His criticism of technological rationality is a philosophical one. Schmitt values Catholicism, because he sees in it a form of rationality that recognizes the significance of the poles of the ideal and the real, understands existence as a unity of opposites ("*complexio oppositorum*"), and distances itself from gnostic and modern dualism. See Schmitt, *Roman Catholicism*, 9–11; *Political Theology II*, 122–26; *Political Romanticism*, 52–54 (in this sense, Groh's interpretation should be criticized, which binds Schmitt to Gnostic dualism; see *Carl Schmitt gnostischer Dualismus* [Berlin: Lit, 2014], 16, 30). The form of Catholic rationality is expressed in the Catholic institution. The Church emerges as an attempt at meditation between the idea and the real. Its "formal character" is to be a "sustaining configuration of historical and social reality," which takes "concrete existence" into account, and which remains itself both "vital and yet rational." *Roman Catholicism*, 8. Its articulation rests on the notion of "representation," which is sharply distinguished from subsumption or the subjection of vital and concrete reality carried out by the functionalism of "technology" (*Roman Catholicism*, 8, 13); from detachment (see *Roman Catholicism*, 32); and from the "fanatical excesses." *Roman Catholicism*, 14. The representation achieved by the Catholic Church is due to its

institutional character; to an articulation of the vital according to some form. In the case of the Church, that representation rests on faith in revelation, shared by its members and authorities. If that faith in revelation can "still [be] a living idea," is for Schmitt an open question; *Roman Catholicism*, 17. Schmitt values the Catholic rationality and the Church, because of its institutional capacity, the capacity namely to give expression to the real in a stable manner and according to an "idea." *Roman Catholicism*, 17, 21, 8. Despite his assessments regarding Catholicism, the "Catholic intensification" and the Church, Schmitt is, however, also fully aware of the limits of Catholic thought. As we have seen, he considers that Catholicism does not sufficiently thematize the problem of the relation and tension of the opposites: "Roman Catholicism understands little of the dualisms" affecting modern consciousness. *Roman Catholicism*, 11. It does not reach the level of radicalness with which the problem of the tension and relation between the poles of the ideal and the real is posed by modern thought, which is the starting-point of Schmitt's reflection on understanding.

118. Meier also cites a letter from Schmitt to Jacob Taubes, where he writes: "All that still concerns me today, is for me a question of political theology." *Jacob Taubes—Carl Schmitt: Briefwechsel*, 37. In the same letter to Taubes, Schmitt makes it clear, nonetheless, that he is using the term improperly, in a sense different from the usual one—in any case distinct from a thought determined by faith. He remarks that his position is similar, in his opinion, to the one Max Weber held at the end of his life. Weber, in so doing, in no way became a dogmatic theologian. The point is a recognition of the limits of technological rationality in government and the importance a specifically political leadership acquires in counterweighing it, a leadership capable of effectively guiding large human groups; that is, Weber distances himself from technology. See the note of the editors of the Schmitt-Taubes correspondence (*Briefwechsel*, 39), and the text to which they allude: "Parlament und Regierung im neugeordneten Deutschland," in Max Weber, *Gesammelte politische Schriften*, ed. Johannes Winckelmann (Tübingen: Mohr Siebeck, 1988), 348; see also McCormick, *Carl Schmitt's Critique of Liberalism*, 176–77. In the same letter, Schmitt expressly determines what being a political theologian consists of. His assessment is consistent with his reference to Weber as a theologian. "For me this means something like what Hugo Ball said in 1924. 'He (C[arl] S[chmitt]) experiences his time in the form of consciousness of his capability.'" Schmitt explains: "For me this is a specifically *juridical* capability." *Briefwechsel*, 37 (my emphasis). For Schmitt, being a political theologian means, in this context, taking on a juristic way of understanding: to be a "jurist" and all that that implies, including the distinction he repeatedly makes between the position of the "jurist" and that of the theologian in the more usual senses of a dogmatic stance or of rational theology. Finally, in the text to which I refer, Schmitt also explains what the "specifically juridical capability" to which he alludes consists of: "In other words, I am able to distinguish between *nomos* and

norm, a fundamental, constituent distinction, which contemporary positivism has deprived itself of by self-mutilation." *Briefwechsel*, 37. This being the case, in this context the "theological" nature of his thought refers to—rather than a worldview conditioned by faith—the recognition that law is not simply a technical device of positive norms, but also a concrete order of meaning; see *The Nomos of the Earth*, 42, 67-79; *Glossarium*, 18. Against the attempt to bring law down to a mere technology, to reduce it to its functional aspect, Schmitt restores its implications of meaning by calling himself a theologian. But ultimately, and beyond the unusual language employed by Schmitt, this is more to safeguard the place that law still occupies *between* theology and technology than to assert a dogmatic theology.

119. I have already referred to Schmitt's assertion, in the context of the "sociology of juridical concepts," that "All significant concepts of the modern theory of the state are secularized theological concepts." In *Political Romanticism*, he writes: "Every expression in the intellectual sphere has, consciously or unconsciously, a dogma—orthodox or heretical—as its premise." Schmitt, *Political Romanticism*, 3. Meier interprets this passage as a manifestation of Schmitt's theology. See *Carl Schmitt and Leo Strauss*, 77-78. Religious dogmatism is, however, incompatible with this statement, because the action of revealing the dogmatic nature of dogma, that is, showing that it has to do with an assertion that is simply believed but not justified, prevents dogma to function thereafter as a basis for justification. If Schmitt were actually trying to turn "faith against faith," in the context of a public discussion, that would immediately require showing which faith is better justified. Schmitt would thereby depart from the dimension of mere faith. And that is precisely what he does when, for example, he shows, in that same book, the insufficiencies of romanticism.

120. Along with the justifications and arguments to which I have alluded, it must be remembered that Schmitt explicitly distinguishes faith as an "enigmatically individual" matter—which takes place in a sphere of "unfathomableness"—from the "proper and specific task" of the "jurist." *Glossarium*, 100.

121. See Marder, *Groundless Existence*, 2-9.

122. See Hofmann, *Legitimität*, 59.

123. See Ojakangas, *A Philosophy of Concrete Life*, 18, 30-34, and *passim*.

124. Schmitt, "The Plight," 66-67.

125. Meier, *Carl Schmitt and Leo Strauss*, 167; see 159 (German ed.); *The Lesson*, xviii.

126. See Meier, *Carl Schmitt and Leo Strauss*, 167 (footnote 16) (German ed.); *The Lesson*, xviii (footnote 14).

127. See Schmitt, *Political Theology*, 15; *The Concept of the Political*, 60, *Hamlet or Hecuba*, 45, etc.

128. Meier, *The Lesson*, 89; see Schmitt, *Glossarium*, 133, 160, 388.

129. Meier, *The Lesson*, 19.

130. See, for instance, Meier, *The Lesson*, 30.

131. Schmitt, *Glossarium*, 388.
132. See Meier, *The Lesson*, 20–21, 90–93.
133. Meier, *The Lesson*, 93.
134. Meier, *The Lesson*, 20.
135. Meier, *The Lesson*, 19. On Schmitt's historicism, see Kuhn, *Der Staat*, 42–43, 447; Hofmann, *Legitimität*, 224, 230, 238–44.
136. Schmitt, "Die Einheit," 851.
137. See Schmitt, *Political Theology*, 15; *Hamlet or Hecuba*, 45.
138. See Schmitt, *Political Theology*, 3; *Gesetz und Urteil*, vi, 40, 75; *On the Three Types of Juristic Thought*, 73.
139. See Schmitt, *Political Romanticism*, 162. Schmitt criticizes Hegel because his system doesn't allow a radical exception (*Ausnahme*) that "comes from outside" into existence. He criticizes Hegel further because in his dialectic all opposites are synthesized in such a way that the "either/or of moral decision . . . has no place in this system." Hegelian philosophy would remain, therefore, "in the contemplative." Schmitt, *The Crisis*, 56–57. For Meier, Schmitt criticizes Hegel's rejection of an exception that penetrates into existence from the outside because it implies the rejection of the irruption of the divine mandate into human life. And the critique of Hegel's tendency to the contemplative—which for Meier coincides with Schmitt's critique of philosophers in general—is made because it is incompatible with the mandate of "obedience" to which the political theologian is subject; Meier, *The Lesson*, 15–16. Schmitt's objections to Hegel have, nonetheless, justifications that are autonomous from faith. The first is directed at noting the inevitability of the exception. In Schmitt's view, in Hegel's system the exception results repressed. On this point, Mika Ojakangas states: "According to Meier, Schmitt rejects Hegel because Hegel's denial of the other entering from the outside entails the denial of God's sovereignty. . . . To my mind, however, Schmitt . . . abandons Hegel . . . because the Hegelian absorption makes all interruption counterfeit. In Hegel's philosophy, there is no genuine interruption and thereby, no space for an event of the concrete. . . . On the other hand, Schmitt rejects Hegel's philosophy because for the latter that which remains outside the concept—outside objective knowledge—is identical to nothing." Ojakangas, *A Philosophy of Concrete Life*, 205. While the exception is resistant to any adequate conceptualization, and, seen from this perspective, it is to a certain extent a "nothing," this does not mean that one can close herself off to the exception as if it were a pure and simple nothing, given that it is a condition of human existence. In said existence normality emerges from, and is always affected by, the exception. Additionally, the recognition of the exception is a requirement of an authentic life; namely, of a life that is aware of its existential situation. Further, for Schmitt, the recognition of the exception is a condition of practical decision, as he points out in his second critique of Hegel. Moral decision, understood as a decision regarding the way of living human life and open to the radically indeterminate, has no place in a world where the exceptional is

marginalized. In such a world, a proper decision ceases to exist and what remains are options amongst predetermined possibilities. See Schmitt, *The Crisis*, 56–57.

140. See Schmitt, *Gesetz und Urteil*, 28, 32, 93, 111–12; *On the Three Types of Juristic Thought*, 56–57.

141. See the above section "Omissions."

142. See Schmitt, *Gesetz und Urteil*, 40, 75.

143. See Schmitt, *On the Three Types of Juristic Thought*, 52–57, 73.

144. See Schmitt, *Roman Catholicism*, 32; *Political Romanticism*, 162.

145. Meier, *The Lesson*, 82.

146. Meier, *The Lesson*, 84–85.

147. "To anyone who wishes to 'disregard' the sovereignty of God, the meaning of the doctrine of original sin and of grace has to remain closed." Meier, *The Lesson*, 82; see 84–88. Schmitt's political theology is also evident for Meier in Schmitt's understanding of the evil of the human being as one that, unlike that of animals, involves a religiously grounded guilt. "Original sin is the central point around which everything turns in [Schmitt's] anthropological *confession* of faith." Meier, *Carl Schmitt and Leo Strauss*, 57. Meier, however, does not support his claim with direct textual evidence. See *Carl Schmitt and Leo Strauss*, 56–59. He refers to two passages: in one of them, Schmitt states that humans are capable of the friend-enemy distinction, that does not exist in animals, because humans are "spiritual" and animals not; *The Concept of the Political*, 9, 41–42 (German ed. of 1933, Hamburg: Hanseatische Verlaganstalt). In the other text, Schmitt states that the tension between human beings "far transcends the natural." "Die geschichtliche Struktur des heutigen Welt-Gegensatzes von Ost und West," in *Freundschaftliche Begegnungen. Festschrift für Ernst Jünger zum 60. Geburstag*, ed. Armin Mohler (Frankfurt: Klostermann, 1955), 149. But in neither of these texts does Schmitt speak of a—religiously understood—guilt of humans.

148. Plessner, *Macht*, 231; Schmitt, *The Concept of the Political*, 60–61.

149. See Schmitt, *Ex Captivitate Salus*, 70–71.

150. Schmitt, *Glossarium*, 277; see *The Concept of the Political*, 60.

151. See Schmitt, *Glossarium*, 26 (footnote 1), 27, 30, 70–72; "The Plight," 56; *The Leviathan*, 85; *Political Theology*, 13–15, 35; *The Nomos of the Earth*, 38–39.

152. Schmitt, *The Concept of the Political*, 58–61.

153. Schmitt, *The Concept of the Political*, 59. On the relation between Schmitt's and Machiavelli's thought, see Galli, *Janus Gaze*, 58–77.

154. Schmitt, *The Concept of the Political*, 65.

155. Hobbes, *Leviathan* (Cambridge: Cambridge University Press, 1996), chaps. 6 and 11; see Schmitt, *Glossarium*, 30.

156. Schmitt, *The Concept of the Political*, 59; *The Leviathan*, 31. See Mouffe, *The Return of the Political*, 6; McCormick, *Carl Schmitt's Critique of Liberalism*, 250–53; Helmut Rumpf, *Carl Schmitt und Thomas Hobbes: Ideelle Beziehungen und aktuelle Bedeutung* (Berlin: Duncker & Humblot, 1972).

157. Conflict and distance do not take place with respect only to the other "outside." Like Hobbes, Schmitt understands that the roots of conflict lie already within the human being. But the inner tension, in Schmitt, acquires a discursive character. The human being can enter into a relation with itself and question itself. The relation may be conflictual. "Whom in the world can I acknowledge as my enemy? Clearly only him who can call me into question. By recognizing him as enemy I acknowledge that he can call me into question. And who can really call me into question? Only I myself. Or my brother." Schmitt, *Ex Captivitate Salus*, 71.

158. Plessner, *Macht*, 192–93.

159. On the relation between Schmitt and Plessner regarding the justification of the political, see Rüdiger Kramme, *Helmuth Plessner und Carl Schmitt: eine historische Fallstudie zum Verhältnis von Anthropologie und Politik in der deutschen Philosophie der zwanziger Jahre* (Berlin: Duncker & Humblot, 1989).

160. See Schmitt, *The Concept of the Political*, 30.

161. See section "Friend and Enemy" in chapter 1.

162. Meier, *The Lesson*, 57 (footnote 88).

163. Meier, *The Lesson*, 80.

164. Meier, *The Lesson*, 81. See Danijel Paric, *Anti-römischer Affekt. Carl Schmitts Interpretation der Erbsündenlehre und ihre wissenschaftliche Funktion* (Berlin: Lit, 2012), 90.

165. There are *four* other ways in which Meier tries to prove that Schmitt's argumentation is theologically determined: (1) He notices that for Schmitt the political is not simply one more human sphere, but ends up becoming "the total." *The Lesson*, 71; see 31. It becomes the total because in this sphere the individual is placed before a radical either/or, in which "everything is at stake." *The Lesson*, 35, see 32. Such radical either/or can make sense only when the mandatory command of a revealed God is posited; see *The Lesson*, 74, 76. (2) The political is theologically determined also because, for Schmitt, the enemy is the condition for the authenticity of human existence. By means of her presence, she "preserves" individuals "from self-deception [*Selbstbetrug*]" that comes about in a mere individualistic world. *The Lesson*, 45–46. The enemy is "the tool the supreme authority uses in order to place us in an objective event, . . . one in which we are confronted with 'our own question' and must 'answer in doing.'" *The Lesson*, 45–46; see 47, 49; Schmitt, *Ex Captivitate Salus*, 71. (3) Theological determination is evinced, for Meier, also in the importance Schmitt attributes to the existential participation in the political community. Schmitt states: "For political decisions even the mere possibility of correctly knowing and understanding, and therewith the entitlement to participate in discussion and to make judgments, is based only on existential sharing and participating, only on the genuine *participatio*." *The Concept of the Political* (1933), 8. This requirement, according to Meier, "If it holds anywhere, then nowhere more than in the case of the community of faith." *The Lesson*, 61; *Carl Schmitt and Leo Strauss*, 56.

(4) The theological status of the political would be expressed, finally, in Schmitt's conception of war and conflict. The decision to go to war has to do with taking a position "based on the question of what is right." *The Lesson*, 40. The "right," however, is not a philosophical-political problem; see *The Lesson*, 40–43. The issue, instead, concerns the right thing to do in action in the extreme case where the human is placed before a theological "commandment" that demands "obedience." *The Lesson*, 43–44. In the 1933 version of *The Concept of the Political*, Schmitt states that wars "can rest on a decision of enmity that is especially authentic and profound" (30), which is a statement that implies, for Meier, an approval "of the holy wars and crusades of the Church." *Carl Schmitt and Leo Strauss*, 66. In *The Lesson*, 58–59, Meier mentions, in support of his thesis, a quotation of Cromwell cited by Schmitt, where Cromwell identifies the Spaniard as "providential enemy." Meier's four arguments are disputable: (1) Faith is not required to understand that the political is the total. It is sufficient to attend to the intensity that any practical tension may reach, and to the fact that the superior intensity having place in political conflict and war completely implicates those involved in it (and, by extension, all those who are affected by its eventuality). (2) Nor is faith required for understanding that the lucid consideration of the tension of human relations is a condition for an authentic existence. (3) Regarding the Schmittian demand of participation, Meier does not ask himself whether it has to do with the hermeneutical principle, valid for any human sphere and also for the political, and according to which understanding requires a certain proximity between the one making the decision and the concrete context within which a decision has to be made. (4) Concerning war, it needs to be said that, in Schmitt's thought, there is a permanent effort to limit the scope and influence of theology on such event. Schmitt thinks the "*Silete Theologi*" of Albericus is a valuable advance, just as he values the process by means of which jurisprudence was made independent of theology; "The Plight," 64–66; *The Nomos of the Earth*, passim; *Political Theology II*, 117–18; *Ex Captivitate Salus*, 56. He persistently condemns the moralization and theologization of war and their pernicious effects; see *The Concept of the Political*, 36; *Theory of the Partisan. Intermediate Commentary on the Concept of the Political*, trans. Gary L. Ulmen (New York: Telos Press, 2007), 94; *The Nomos of the Earth*, 141–42, 169; *The Leviathan*, 48; *Ex Captivitate Salus*, 55, 59. Ojakangas, *A Philosophy of Concrete Life*, 111–12, 201; William Hooker, *Carl Schmitt's International Thought. Order and Orientation* (Cambridge: Cambridge University Press, 2009), 21–22, 79–80. Regarding the reference to Cromwell, I concur with Maschke: Schmitt is alluding to the fact that "in the great moments in politics, 'in which the enemy is viewed with particular clarity as an enemy,' leaders of States, parties or warring factions gladly declare that God speaks through them. . . . Meier argues that Schmitt is convinced that at the climax of monumental politics, faith battles heresy, but what Schmitt really thinks is that therein each party disqualifies the other as a criminal that must be exterminated, as an unjust enemy. Meier,

however, identifies the logic that results from a particular political theology, laid bare by Schmitt, with Schmitt's own program." Günter Maschke, "Carl Schmitt," 108. See Schmitt, *The Concept of the Political*, 67.

166. See Meier, *Carl Schmitt and Leo Strauss*, 161 (German ed.); *The Lesson*, xiv.

167. Meier, *The Lesson*, xiv; *Carl Schmitt and Leo Strauss*, 161 (German ed.).

168. See Meier, *The Lesson*, 19–20.

169. Meier, *Carl Schmitt and Leo Strauss*, 167; see 159 (German ed.); *The Lesson*, xviii.

170. Meier, *Carl Schmitt and Leo Strauss*, 167 (footnote 16) (German ed.); *The Lesson*, xviii (footnote 14).

171. See Meier, *The Lesson*, xiv; *Carl Schmitt and Leo Strauss*, 161 (German ed.).

172. Meier, *The Lesson*, xviii (footnote 14); *Carl Schmitt and Leo Strauss*, 167 (footnote 16) (German ed.).

173. See Meier, *The Lesson*, 57 (footnote 88), 81.

174. See Meier, *The Lesson*, 22, 30 (footnote 12), 57 (footnote 88), 80–81, 201–203.

175. Meier, *The Lesson*, 2. Meier ignores the eventual contradiction implied in affirming that Schmitt seeks both to hide his theological center (see *The Lesson*, 2) and to exhibit dogmas; see *The Lesson*, 81.

Schmitt's ability concerning the endeavor of cover-up would be quite notable. For Meier, Leo Strauss errs pursuing "his confrontation with Schmitt on the plane of political philosophy." Meier believes that Strauss does not realize that in *The Concept of the Political*, Schmitt writes as a political theologian; see Meier, *Carl Schmitt and Leo Strauss*, 50. Leo Strauss, in a thorough and detailed comment on the brief text of Schmitt, in which Strauss makes use of sophisticated arguments supported by a rich and complex philosophical-political background, precisely in order to reveal the connections of the Schmittian arguments and to analyze them meticulously, in such a text—by Meier's account—Strauss does not realize that in Schmitt's book there are really no arguments and justifications at the basis, but rather something akin to sleights of hand that at the end are grounded in no more than mere faith in revelation.

Chapter 3

1. Hans-Georg Gadamer, *Truth and Method*, trans. revised by Joel Weinsheimer and Donald G. Marshall (London: Bloomsbury, 2013), 334.

2. Gadamer, *Truth and Method*, 338.

3. Gadamer, *Truth and Method*, 322, 323, 324, 328.

4. See Gadamer, *Truth and Method*, 323, 331.

5. Gadamer, *Truth and Method*, 318–19, 328, 333, 339; see 334–50.
6. Schmitt, *Gesetz und Urteil*, 93; see 58–59.
7. See Schmitt, *On the Three Types of Juristic Thought*, 56–57; *Political Theology*, 13; "The Plight," 427 (German ed.); *Gesetz und Urteil*, 93.
8. See Schmitt, *Gesetz und Urteil*, 64; *Political Theology*, 30.
9. Schmitt, *Gesetz und Urteil*, 93; see *The Concept of the Political*, 85, 87, 95.
10. Schmitt, *Gesetz und Urteil*, 93; see 28, 32, 59, 112; Rasch, "Judgment," 100.
11. Gadamer, *Truth and Method*, 350, 339; see 333.
12. Gadamer, *Truth and Method*, 318–19.
13. See Gadamer, *Truth and Method*, 323, 331.
14. Gadamer, *Truth and Method*, 337; see 319, 349.
15. See Gadamer, *Truth and Method*, 318–19, 339.
16. Gadamer, *Truth and Method*, 341.
17. Gadamer, *Truth and Method*, 333; see Jean Grondin, *The Philosophy of Gadamer*, trans. Kathryn Plant (Montreal and Kingston: McGill-Queen's University Press, 2003), 107–108.
18. Karl Larenz, *Methodenlehre der Rechtswissenschaft* (Berlin and New York: Springer, 1991), 404 (footnote 91).
19. Larenz, *Methodenlehre*, 404.
20. Larenz, *Methodenlehre*, 403–404.
21. See third section of chapter 1; Derrida, "Force of Law," 935, 941, 945, 969. *Of Grammatology*, 112; "Before the Law," 199.
22. See Schmitt, *Gesetz und Urteil*, 5, 8, 37, 76.
23. See Schmitt, *Gesetz und Urteil*, 8, 76.
24. In virtue of this meaning, which bestows the "concrete" case with a fundamentally distinct intensity from that of the case merely thought of "as possible," judicial understanding acquires a practical character. Schmitt, *Gesetz und Urteil*, 58–59; see 8, 28, 32, 41, 55, 76, 82, 96, 111–12; *Political Theology*, 13, 15; *On the Three Types of Juristic Thought*, 56.
25. See Schmitt, *Gesetz und Urteil*, 28, 32, 41, 59, 76, 93, 111–12.
26. See Schmitt, *Gesetz und Urteil*, 37–38, 41, 68, 107.
27. Schmitt, *Gesetz und Urteil*, 66; *Political Theology*, 3.
28. Schmitt, *Gesetz und Urteil*, 1.
29. See Schmitt, *Gesetz und Urteil*, 93.
30. Schmitt, *Gesetz und Urteil*, 28.
31. Schmitt, *Gesetz und Urteil*, 8.
32. Schmitt, *Gesetz und Urteil*, 76 (footnote 1); see 68, 107.
33. See Schmitt, *Gesetz und Urteil*, 28, 32, 93 94, 111–12.
34. See Schmitt, *Gesetz und Urteil*, 5–9.
35. On Schmitt's understanding of law and decision in his early writings, see, e.g., Paul Oertmann, "Besprechung der Schrift 'Gesetz und Urteil' von Carl Schmitt." *Literatursbeilage zur Deutschen Juristenzeitung* XVIII, no. 12 (1913):

817–18; Felix Halldack, "Beschprechung der Schrift 'Gesetz und Urteil' von Carl Schmitt." *Kant-Studien* 17 (1912): 464–67; Walsmann, "Besprechung des Buches 'Gesetz und Urteil' von Carl Schmitt." *Rheinische Zeitschrift für Zivil- und Prozessrecht* 5 (1913): 431–32; Walter Jellinek, "Besprechung der Schrift 'Gesetz und Urteil' von Carl Schmitt." *Archiv für öffentliches Recht* 23 (1914): 296–99; "W.I.," "Besprechung der Schrift *Gesetz und Urteil* von Carl Schmitt." *Fischers Zeitschrift für Praxis und Gesetzgebung der Verwaltung* 42 (1913): 148–49; F. Doerr, "Besprechung des Buches *Gesetz und Urteil* von Carl Schmitt." *Zeitschrift für das Gesamte Handelsrecht und Konkursrecht* 73 (1913): 537–39; Hofmann, *Legitimität*, 25–37; L. Kiefer, "Begründung, Dezision und Politische Theologie." *Archiv für Rechts—und Sozialphilosophie* LXXVI, no. 4 (1990): 480–82; Ulrich Habfast, "*Das normative Nichts. Eine Studie zum Dezisionismus in den frühen Schriften Carl Schmitts*" (PhD diss., University of Frankfurt, 2010), 8–36; Gary Ulmen, *Politischer Mehrwert. Eine Studie über Max Weber und Carl Schmitt* (Weinheim: Wiley-VCH, 1991), 102–103; Neumann, *Carl Schmitt als Jurist*, 20–21; William E. Scheuerman *Carl Schmitt*, 4, 19–20; Armin Adam, *Rekonstruktion des Politischen. Carl Schmitt und die Krise der Staatlichkeit 1912-1933* (Weinheim: Wiley-VCH, 1992), 56; Ingeborg Maus, *Bürgerliche Rechtstheorie und Faschismus. Zur sozialen Funktion und aktuellen Wirkung der Theorie Carl Schmitts* (Munich: Wilhelm Fink, 1980), 86–88; Marder, *Groundless Existence*, 173–74; McCormick, *Carl Schmitt's Critique of Liberalism*, 211–12; "Three Ways of Thinking 'Critically' about the Law." *The American Political Science Review* 93, no. 2 (1999): 413–28; Carlo Galli, *Genealogia della politica. Carl Schmitt e la crisi del pensiero politico moderno* (Bologna: Il Mulino, 1996), 313–31; Heiner Bielefeldt, *Kampf und Entscheidung*, 20–23.

36. Rasch, "Judgment," 100.
37. Schmitt, *Gesetz und Urteil*, 93; see 58–59.
38. See Rasch, "Judgment," 100; Schmitt, *Gesetz und Urteil*, 28, 32, 59, 112.
39. Schmitt, *Gesetz und Urteil*, 93.
40. Schmitt, *Gesetz und Urteil*, 93.
41. Schmitt, *Gesetz und Urteil*, 93. See I. Kant, *Critique of the Power of Judgment*, trans. Paul Guyer and Eric Matthews (Cambridge and New York: Cambridge University Press, 2000), §§ 39–41 (171–78). On the importance of aesthetic judgment for political understanding, see Hannah Arendt, *Lectures on Kant's Political Philosophy*, ed. Ronald Beiner (Chicago: University of Chicago Press, 1992), 65–77.
42. Schmitt, *Gesetz und Urteil*, 68.
43. This idea shall persist in Schmitt's thought; see *Political Theology*, 15; *Glossarium*, 64, 388.
44. Schmitt, *Theodor Däublers "Nordlicht,"* 51.
45. Schmitt, *Theodor Däublers "Nordlicht,"* 51.
46. See Schmitt, *Theodor Däublers "Nordlicht,"* 51, 66.

47. Schmitt, *Theodor Däublers "Nordlicht,"* 31, 63, 70.
48. See Schmitt, *Theodor Däublers "Nordlicht,"* 52, 55.
49. Schmitt, *Theodor Däublers "Nordlicht,"* 57.
50. Schmitt, *Theodor Däublers "Nordlicht,"* 56.
51. See Schmitt, *Theodor Däublers "Nordlicht,"* 47, 51.
52. Schmitt, *Theodor Däublers "Nordlicht,"* 51.
53. Schmitt, *Theodor Däublers "Nordlicht,"* 63.
54. Schmitt, *Theodor Däublers "Nordlicht,"* 66.
55. Schmitt, *Theodor Däublers "Nordlicht,"* 66.
56. Schmitt, *Political Romanticism*, 52.
57. Schmitt, *Political Romanticism*, 52.
58. See Schmitt, *Political Romanticism*, 16–17, 124, 161.
59. Schmitt, *Political Romanticism*, 19.
60. Schmitt, *Political Romanticism*, 77; see 19, 162.
61. Schmitt, *Political Romanticism*, 77.
62. Schmitt, *Political Romanticism*, 19; see 16–17, 124, 161.
63. Schmitt, *Political Romanticism*, 19, see 74–75.
64. Schmitt, *Political Romanticism*, 96.
65. Schmitt, *Political Romanticism*, 76.
66. See Schmitt, *Political Romanticism*, 96. Romanticism must be distinguished from a mystical or religious devotion directed toward the pole of the real. See Schmitt, *Political Romanticism*, 56. "The romantic," writes Schmitt, "is always in flight," withdrawing "from reality." *Political Romanticism*, 71. With its uprooted elaborations, and despite its initial surrendering to the real, it is the opposite of a devotion: a "negation of the here and now." *Political Romanticism*, 70.
67. Schmitt, *Political Romanticism*, 84.
68. Schmitt, *Political Romanticism*, 19.
69. See Schmitt, *Political Romanticism*, 18–19, 82–84.
70. Schmitt, *Political Romanticism*, 52.
71. See, for example, Salomon Maimon, *Essay on Transcendental Philosophy*, trans. Nick Midgley, Henry Somers-Hall, Alistair Welchman, and Merten Reglitz (London and New York: Continuum, 2010), 37–38; Schmitt, *Political Romanticism*, 52; *Political Theology*, 13; *On the Three Types of Juristic Thought*, 56–57.
72. Schmitt, *Political Theology*, 15.
73. See Schmitt, *Political Theology*, 13–14.
74. See Schmitt, *Political Theology*, 12.
75. Schmitt, *Political Theology*, 15.
76. See Schmitt, *Hamlet or Hecuba*, 45; *Political Theology*, 13–15; *The Concept of the Political*, 60; *Glossarium*, 277.
77. See Schmitt, *Political Theology*, 13–15.
78. See Schmitt, *Political Theology*, 15.

79. See Schmitt, *Political Theology*, 13–15; *Gesetz und Urteil*, 8, 28, 68, 76, 107; *Theodor Däublers "Nordlicht,"* 47, 51; *Political Romanticism*, 52–53; *On the Three Types of Juristic Thought*, 54–57, 73.

80. Schmitt, *The Concept of the Political*, 27.

81. Schmitt, *The Concept of the Political*, 28 (translation modified).

82. Schmitt, *The Concept of the Political*, 28.

83. Schmitt, *The Concept of the Political*, 85; see "Staatsethik und pluralistischer Staat," in *Positionen und Begriffe im Kampf mit Weimar—Genf—Versailles 1923–1939* (Berlin: Duncker & Humblot, 2014), 162.

84. Schmitt, *The Concept of the Political*, 95.

85. Schmitt, *The Concept of the Political*, 85.

86. Schmitt, *The Concept of the Political*, 85.

87. Schmitt, *The Concept of the Political*, 96.

88. Schmitt, *On the Three Types of Juristic Thought*, 73.

89. See Schmitt, *On the Three Types of Juristic Thought*, 54–56.

90. See Schmitt, *On the Three Types of Juristic Thought*, 49–57, 73.

91. Schmitt, *On the Three Types of Juristic Thought*, 54, 74.

92. Schmitt, *On the Three Types of Juristic Thought*, 52–55, 74.

93. Schmitt, *On the Three Types of Juristic Thought*, 73; see 56–57.

94. Schmitt, "The Plight," 427 (German ed.).

95. See Schmitt, "The Plight," 427 (German ed.).

96. See Schmitt, "The Plight," 56; *Political Theology*, 13; *On the Three Types of Juristic Thought*, 56–57; *The Nomos of the Earth*, 38–39; *Land and Sea*, 93.

97. Schmitt, *Die Tyrannei der Werte*, 32, 35.

98. Schmitt, *Die Tyrannei der Werte*, 31, 38. In his commentary to the new German ed. of the text, Christoph Schönberger notes Schmitt's self-understanding as a jurist as placed between theology and technology. He limits, however, the scope of Schmitt's juridical consideration to the contours of the law as it is usually construed. Hence, Schönberger is perplexed and asks himself: "At which level does Schmitt's argument really operate? . . . His text chooses from the beginning a difficult intermediate position between philosophy and jurisprudence." Schönberger, "Werte als Gefahr für das Recht? Carl Schmitt und die Karlsruher Republik." In Carl Schmitt, *Die Tyrannei der Werte* (Berlin: Duncker & Humblot, 2011), 58. On the contrary, once one has noted Schmitt's reflections on the poles of understanding and the admissible hermeneutical positions, the law acquires a broader scope than that which it is usually considered to possess, so that a *juridical* critique of the rationalizing and aestheticizing manners of understanding makes sense.

99. See Schmitt, "The Plight" (German ed.), 427.

100. Schmitt, *Die Tyrannei der Werte*, 30, 35.

101. Schmitt, *Die Tyrannei der Werte*, 24, 29–30, 38.

102. See Schmitt, *Die Tyrannei der Werte*, 23, 29–30, 34, 52.

103. Schmitt, *Die Tyrannei der Werte*, 48–51.

104. Schmitt, *Die Tyrannei der Werte*, 52, 54.

105. The "world" and the subject emanate from the "depths" of the exceptional. Schmitt, *Theodor Däublers "Nordlicht,"* 51; see *Political Theology*, 15; *Hamlet or Hecuba*, 45; *The Concept of the Political*, 60; *Glossarium*, 64, 71, 160, 388.

106. See Schmitt, *Gesetz und Urteil*, 59, 93; *The Crisis*, 44.

107. Schmitt, *Hamlet or Hecuba*, 45.

108. Schmitt, *Political Theology*, 15; see *Glossarium*, 94; *Land and Sea*, 93–94; "Drei Möglichkeiten," 165.

109. See Schmitt, *Political Theology*, 13; "The Plight," 56; *On the Three Types of Juristic Thought*, 56–57, 74; *The Nomos of the Earth*, 39.

110. Richard E. Palmer, *Hermeneutics: Interpretation Theory in Schleiermacher, Dilthey, Heidegger, and Gadamer* (Evanston, IL: Northwestern University Press, 1969), 128.

111. Schmitt, *On the Three Types of Juristic Thought*, 48.

112. Schmitt, *On the Three Types of Juristic Thought*, 56.

113. Schmitt, *On the Three Types of Juristic Thought*, 48–49.

114. Schmitt, *On the Three Types of Juristic Thought*, 73. I partially follow the original German text, and render "*Intelligenz*" as "intelligence," instead of Bendersky's more limited term, "intelligentsia." See *Über die drei Arten des rechtswissenschaftlichen Denkens* (Berlin: Duncker & Humblot, 1993), 34; *On the Three Types of Juristic Thought*, 56–57; *Political Theology*, 13. The above mentioned is a problem generally recognized in the history of philosophy. Kant puts it thus: "If among the appearances which present themselves to us, there were so great a variety—I do not say in form, for in that respect the appearances might resemble one another; but in content, that is, in the manifoldness of the existing entities—that even the acutest human understanding could never by comparison of them detect the slightest similarity (a possibility which is quite conceivable), the logical law of genera would have no sort of standing; we should not even have the concept of a genus, or indeed any other universal concept; and the understanding itself, which has to do solely with such concepts, would be non-existent." *Critique of Pure Reason*, A 653/B 681–A 654/B 682 (539). Lacking homogeneity with phenomena, "no empirical concepts, and, therefore, no experience, would be possible." *Critique of Pure Reason*, A 654/B 682 (539–40).

115. Schmitt, *Political Theology*, 13; see *On the Three Types of Juristic Thought*, 56.

116. See Schmitt, "The Plight," 56; *Theodor Däublers "Nordlicht,"* 51; *The Nomos of the Earth*, 38–39, 42, 67–69; *Land and Sea*, 93; *On the Three Types of Juristic Thought*, 73; *The Concept of the Political*, 26, 38, 60, and 120–21 (German ed.); *Die Tyrannei der Werte*, 35–41, 45; "Raum und Rom," 965; "Recht und Raum," 243; *Political Theology*, 15; *Glossarium*, 388; *Hamlet or Hecuba*, 45; Böckenförde, "Konkretes Ordnungsdenken," 1312–13; Rüthers, *Die unbegrenzte Auslegung*, 294.

117. See Schmitt, e.g., *Glossarium*, 26 (footnote 1), 27, 30, 70–71; *The Leviathan*, 85; *Theodor Däublers "Nordlicht,"* 59–60, 66–67; *Political Theology*, 15, 35; *The Nomos of the Earth*, 38–39; *Roman Catholicism*, 12–13.

118. Schmitt, *On the Three Types of Juristic Thought*, 73; see 56–57; *Die Tyrannei der Werte*, 20, 23, 37–41; *The Nomos of the Earth*, 69; *Land and Sea*, 93; "Drei Möglichkeiten," 166; "Zu Friedrich Meineckes 'Idee der Staatsräson,' " 58–59.

119. See Schmitt, *On the Three Types of Juristic Thought*, 54, 56, 69.

120. Schmitt, *The Nomos of the Earth*, 6 (German ed.); *Land and Sea*, 93; *Die Tyrannei der Werte*, 45.

121. Rüthers, *Die unbegrenzte Auslegung*, 294.

122. Schmitt, "The Plight," 56. See Böckenförde, "Konkretes Ordnungsdenken," 1312–13.

123. See Schmitt, *Glossarium*, 27, 30, 70–71.

124. See Schmitt, *Glossarium*, 26 (footnote 1).

125. Without a "given" "meaning," without a "world that presents us with a meaning to be interpreted," "language would remain empty of significance." Even a "hermeneutic of suspicion," "that reduces claims to meaning to the economy of energies that function behind them (impulses, class interest, will to power)," can only perform "its destructions by appeal to a 'true' consciousness," which implies a true meaning. Jean Grondin. *Introduction to Philosophical Hermeneutics*, trans. Joel Weinsheimer (London and New Haven, CT: Yale University Press, 1994), 15.

126. Meaning is also not to be understood as a reified whole. Due to the indeterminability of the pole of the real, there is an insurmountable difference between word and meaning. Understanding is an activity that occurs precisely in that difference. See Hans-Georg Gadamer, "Grenzen der Sprache," in *Gesammelte Werke* (Tübingen: Mohr Siebeck, 1993), vol. 8, 361.

127. The awareness of this limit of knowledge, and of the exceptional as background from which existence emerges, also involves, according to Schmitt, a certain kind of knowing. It is, however, a knowledge that escapes the ontic sphere; see *Political Theology*, 15.

128. Schmitt, *Glossarium*, 64; *The Concept of the Political*, 60 (German ed.); Plessner, *Macht*, 231; *Stufen* 292.

129. Schmitt, *Glossarium*, 64.

130. See Schmitt, *Glossarium*, 388.

131. That transcendence is the source of both the mental activity and the real. See Schmitt, *Theodor Däublers "Nordlicht,"* 51; *Glossarium*, 388.

132. See Schmitt, *Political Theology*, 15; *Hamlet or Hecuba*, 45; *Glossarium*, 388.

133. Schmitt, *Political Romanticism*, 54.

134. See Schmitt, *Political Romanticism*, 53.

135. See Schmitt, *Political Romanticism*, 54; *Ex Captivitate Salus*, 65.

136. See Schmitt, e.g., *Political Theology*, 6, 13, 15; *The Concept of the Political*, 27–28; *Political Romanticism*, 52; *Theodor Däublers "Nordlicht,"* 51; *Glossarium*, 121, 388.

137. See Schmitt, *Glossarium*, 64.

138. See Schmitt, *Der Wert des Staates*, 39; *Glossarium*, 388.

139. Schmitt, *Political Theology*, 15.

140. The consciousness of the concrete can be lost in a generalizing thought. The recovery of consciousness requires to notice that initial access to the concrete; see Stirner, *The Ego and His Own*, 324.

141. Schmitt, *Gesetz und Urteil*, 64.

142. Schmitt, *The Concept of the Political*, 85.

143. See Schmitt, *Gesetz und Urteil*, 28, 68, 76, 93, 107; "The Plight," 427 (German ed.); *The Concept of the Political*, 27; *The Crisis*, 44.

144. See Schmitt, *Gesetz und Urteil*, 8, 28, 32, 41, 59, 96, 111–12; *Political Theology*, 3, 30; *The Concept of the Political*, 85, 96.

145. See Schmitt, *Glossarium*, 84; Schmitt, *The Concept of the Political*, 60 (translation modified).

146. See Schmitt, *Political Romanticism*, 18–19, 84.

147. Schmitt, *Political Romanticism*, 18–19; see *On the Three Types of Juristic Thought*, 56–57; *The Nomos of the Earth*, 39.

148. See Schmitt, *Ex Captivitate Salus*, 70–71; "The Visibility," 48, 51.

149. See Schmitt, *On the Three Types of Juristic Thought*, 56–57; *The Nomos of the Earth*, 39.

150. Schmitt, *Political Romanticism*, 84.

151. See Schmitt, *Political Romanticism*, 18–19, 82–84.

152. Schmitt, *Gesetz und Urteil*, 68; see 69, 86, 106; *Political Romanticism*, 161–62; *Theodor Däublers "Nordlicht,"* 57.

153. As it happens, for example, in the case of a theology that determines transcendence using the properties of a being; see Schmitt, *Glossarium*, 238, 388.

154. "There is no rule for the application of rules." Friedrich Schleiermacher, *Hermeneutik und Kritik*, ed. Manfred Frank (Frankfurt: Suhrkamp, 1977), 81, 360.

155. See Schmitt, *Gesetz und Urteil*, 59.

156. See Schmitt, *The Concept of the Political*, 85; *Gesetz und Urteil*, 28, 32, 59, 69, 93.

157. See Schmitt, *The Concept of the Political*, 28, 30; *On the Three Types of Juristic Thought*, 57; *Political Romanticism*, 54; *Political Theology*, 14; *The Nomos of the Earth*, 72.

158. Schmitt, *The Concept of the Political*, 28, 85; "The Plight," 427 (German ed.).

159. See Schmitt, *Gesetz und Urteil*, 28, 32, 93; *The Concept of the Political*, 85; *Legality and Legitimacy*, 32; *Political Theology*, 3; "The Plight," 427 (German ed.).

160. Schmitt calls them "rationalist scheme[s]," "abstractions," "normative ideals" (*The Concept of the Political*, 28, 30), "empty generalities," "constructed abstraction[s]" ("Staatsethik," 162), "mechanistic scheme[s]" (*The Crisis*, 69), "calculable function[s] without substance" (*The Nomos of the Earth*, 72; see *Hamlet or Hecuba*, 37; *The Crisis*, 44; *On the Three Types of Juristic Thought*, 73), "abstract concepts" (*Political Romanticism*, 54), "predetermined rules" (*On the Three Types of Juristic Thought*, 57).

161. See Schmitt, *Gesetz und Urteil*, 8, 41, 68, 93, 107.

162. See Schmitt, *Gesetz und Urteil*, 59; *Political Theology*, 15.

163. See Schmitt, e.g., "Staatsethik," 162; *Die Tyrannei der Werte*, 53–54. In the juridical case in the strict sense, the reduction is expressed as a decision "conforming to the law [*gesetzmäßig*]," and yet incorrect. Further, such reduction also expresses itself as indecision, due to the generality of the rule, regarding a matter that does indeed require a concrete decision; see Schmitt, *Gesetz und Urteil*, 7–9, 93. Insofar as practical situations that demand a decision are an insurmountable fact of juridical life, Schmitt proposes abandoning the principle of "conformity to the law." He also recognizes that "to a certain extent" (*Gesetz und Urteil*, 46) or "under certain circumstances" (*Der Wert des Staates*, 80), "it is more important *that*" a decision be adopted than its "content." From these reflections, he proposes, as I have indicated, a criterion for the correctness of judicial decisions. This, while taking into account the requirement of making a decision, is also far apart from subsumption. That criterion is provided by a reflective judgment: "a judicial decision" is "correct, when one can assume that another judge would have decided in the same way [*ebenso entschieden hätte*]." Schmitt, *Gesetz und Urteil*, 68.

164. See Schmitt, *On the Three Types of Juristic Thought*, 54; "The Plight," 427 (German ed.); *Political Theology*, 35; *Theodor Däublers "Nordlicht,"* 51; *The Concept of the Political*, 85–86; *The Nomos of the Earth*, 45.

165. Schmitt, *The Concept of the Political*, 27. The recognition of the situation and its meaning can lead the judge or politician to deem that what is most correct is to keep the "original" meaning of the rule without modifying it. This indication especially operates regarding the rules which are meant to protect fundamental aspects of human existence, whether individual or collective. What is relevant, however, is that only she who finds herself in the situation is in position to know the correctness of that decision; see Schmitt, *Gesetz und Urteil*, 82–83.

166. See Schmitt, *Gesetz und Urteil*, 93. For the problem of application in Schmitt's thought, see Miguel Vatter, "The Idea of Public Reason," 248; Carlo Galli, *Genealogia*, 313–31.

167. See Schmitt, *Land and Sea*, 93; *Hamlet or Hecuba*, 45; *The Concept of the Political*, 85–86; *Political Theology*, 15. With regard to judicial understanding, for example, Schmitt states that the principle of "legal certainty," insofar as it is different from mechanical subsumption, admits a decision "*praeter*" or even

"*contra legem*," if the novelty of the case requires it. Schmitt, *Gesetz und Urteil*, 68, 107; see 8, 93, 111–12.

168. See Schmitt, "The Plight," 427 (German ed.); *The Concept of the Political*, 28, 85–86.

169. Schmitt, *The Nomos of the Earth*, 45 (translation modified).

170. Schmitt, *The Concept of the Political*, 28.

171. Schmitt, *Gesetz und Urteil*, 32; see 28, 35; Rasch, "Judgment," 97–103.

172. See Schmitt, *Gesetz und Urteil*, 28, 32, 75, 93. "The choice that is right cannot be determined in advance or apart from the particular situation, for the situation itself partly determines what is right." Joel C. Weinsheimer, *Gadamer's Hermeneutics: A Reading of "Truth and Method"* (New Haven, CT: Yale University Press, 1985), 190.

173. Henri Bortoft, *Taking Appearance Seriously. The Dynamic Way of Seeing in Goethe and European Thought* (Croydon: Floris Books, 2012), 100; see 107; "The Plight," 427 (German ed.); *Political Theology*, 15.

174. Schmitt, *The Concept of the Political*, 85. "The relationship between the universal and the particular . . . is not unilateral, because . . . the universal itself is reciprocally determined by the individual case to which it is applied. So . . . the particular contributes to the universal, which therefore cannot be understood in advance of its application to individual cases." H. Bortoft, *Taking Appearance Seriously*, 125.

175. Gadamer, *Truth and Method*, 446 (translation modified).

176. Schmitt, *Gesetz und Urteil*, 93; see *The Concept of the Political*, 85, 87, 95.

177. See Schmitt, *Gesetz und Urteil*, 59, 93.

178. The recognition of this implication for understanding explains that Schmitt resolves the tension between a markedly functionalist conception in *The Value of the State and the Importance of the Individual*, in favor of a juridical understanding, open to the consideration of the tension and relation of the hermeneutical poles, and to the meaning that emerges with existence. This resolution implies, already in this work, a recognition of the perspective of the "praxis." Schmitt, *Der Wert des Staates*, 74–75; see *Gesetz und Urteil*, 58–59.

179. See Schmitt, *Gesetz und Urteil*, 28, 32, 75, 93, 111–12; *The Concept of the Political*, 85; "The Plight," 427 (German ed.); *Political Theology*, 14–15, 35; *On the Three Types of Juristic Thought*, 54–55.

180. See Schmitt, *Gesetz und Urteil*, 111–12; "The Plight," 427 (German ed.); *The Concept of the Political*, 85–87.

181. Schmitt, *Theodor Däublers "Nordlicht*," 51. Johannes Türk argues that, from these considerations on the scope of language, Schmitt develops an "investigation of myth as a political force." Türk, "At the Limits of Rethoric. Authority, Commonplace, and the Role of Literature in Carl Schmitt," in *The Oxford Handbook of Carl Schmitt*, ed. Jens Meierhenrich and Oliver Simons (New York: Oxford University Press, 2016), 768; see 766–68, 772. The reflection on myth takes

various forms throughout Schmitt's works. In his book on Hobbes's *Leviathan*, to which Türk alludes, Schmitt speaks of the "mythical power" of this image; Schmitt, *The Leviathan*, 5. "In his mixture of huge animal and huge machine, the image of the leviathan attains the highest level of mythical force." *The Leviathan*, 49. In *The Crisis of Parliamentary Democracy*, Schmitt refers to Sorel's "theory of myths," "that possess the starkest contradiction of absolute rationalism." Sorel sees that "the socialist masses of the industrial proletariat had a myth in which they believe, and this was the general strike," namely, a movement that "would provoke" a "monstrous catastrophe" and "would subvert the whole of social and economic life." Here we are not in front of a "construction of intellectuals," nor before a "utopia." Utopia is distinguished from myth because the former is "the product of a rationalist intellect that attempts to conquer life from the outside, with a mechanistic scheme." Schmitt, *The Crisis*, 68–69. Schmitt then notes that "the strongest myth is national." This claim is based on the quantity of meaningful factors that the myth may welcome; *The Crisis*, 75. In a 1922 speech, Mussolini turns this idea into a conscious exposition; see *The Crisis*, 76. Ojakangas indicates: "Myth does not attempt to rationalize the non-rational, but merely to foster its ghost and to expose this ghost in a meaningful form." Ojakangas, *A Philosophy of Concrete Life*, 213. Schmitt also approaches the subject in *Hamlet or Hecuba*, where he distinguishes between an ancient and a modern myth, such as that which emerges from Shakespeare's tragedy. What is characteristic of Shakespeare's tragedy is that unlike "ancient tragedy," it is not "simply faced with myth," but "creates" a myth. "In the case of *Hamlet* we encounter the rare (but typically modern) case of a playwright who establishes a myth from the reality that he immediately faces." Shakespeare "was capable of extracting from the confusing richness of his contemporary political situation the form that could be intensified to the level of myth." *Hamlet or Hecuba*, 49. In these passages, myth appears as an articulation of reality by means of images and words characterized by the efficacy with which it affects the understanding of a human group. Without efficacy, there is no myth; see *Hamlet or Hecuba*, 46–47; Türk, "At the Limits of Rhetoric," 765. Schmitt conducts an "investigation" of myth, through a "systematic reflection." Türk, "At the Limits of Rhetoric," 768, 772. Schmitt's is thus not a directly mythologizing thought, despite noting the articulating capacity exhibited by myth in the political sphere, and the eventual advantage that may be gained by it in order to give form to concrete political existence. If myth successfully articulates the existential, what characterizes Schmitt's juridical thought and distinguishes it from a directly mythologizing articulation is the disposition to explicitly thematize the conditions, poles, and limits of understanding, and the diverse ways in which the conceptual articulation of experience can be realized.

182. Schmitt, *Hamlet or Hecuba*, 37.
183. Schmitt, *Hamlet or Hecuba*, 37.
184. Schmitt, *Hamlet or Hecuba*, 33; see 33–37.

185. Schmitt, *Hamlet or Hecuba*, 40.

186. Schmitt, *Hamlet or Hecuba*, 45; see 49.

187. Schmitt, *Hamlet or Hecuba*, 45. In *Hamlet*'s case, Schmitt attempts to show how the "taboo surrounding the guilt of the queen and the distortion of the avenger that leads to the Hamletization of the hero" refer to historical circumstances; Schmitt, *Hamlet or Hecuba*, 44: on one hand, to the eventual instigation of Mary, Queen of Scots, to kill her husband and father of her son, the future King James; on the other, to the attitude of King James, prudent regarding Queen Elizabeth, though heedful of his mother's honor; see *Hamlet or Hecuba*, 16, 18. James, a "philosophizing and theologizing King," is a significant figure. He "embodied . . . the entire conflict of his age, a century of divided belief and religious civil war." *Hamlet or Hecuba*, 18. These "intrusions" of reality into the play are handled with subtlety, "received and respected by the play," and the play "timidly maneuvers" around them; *Hamlet or Hecuba*, 25, 44. Yet such timid delicacy suffices for the force of the real to break through in the play, and for the play to acquire its tragic quality.

188. Schmitt, *Hamlet or Hecuba*, 45; see 40, 46.

189. See Schmitt, *Hamlet or Hecuba*, 44–46. "Here, what we find in Schmitt's account is that his opposition between play and tragedy seems to recapitulate the primary opposition in politics that he identifies between the norm and the exception. Like the norm, the play functions as a self-enclosed game, with an internally coherent set of rules that allows for the uncomplicated functioning of its mechanisms. Just as the exception results from an external threat to a self-sufficient system of norms, the tragedy upsets the self-enclosed nature of the play through the intrusion of an external force." David Pan, "Tragedy as Exception in Carl Schmitt's *Hamlet or Hecuba*," in *The Oxford Handbook of Carl Schmitt*, ed. Jens Meierhenrich and Oliver Simons (New York: Oxford University Press, 2016), 732.

190. Schmitt, *Hamlet or Hecuba*, 45 (translation modified).

191. Schmitt, *Hamlet or Hecuba*, 45, 46. Gadamer puts forth a critical interpretation of Schmitt's commentary. He understands the Schmitt's reference to the "eruption of time into the play," as a placement of the "play of art within its historical and political context." This placement, in turn, is taken as a sort of redirecting of the eventual indeterminations of the play to historical and political determinations and positions. This ultimately destroys the work: "A play in which everything is completely motivated creaks like a machine. It would be a false reality if the action could all be calculated out like an equation." Gadamer, *Truth and Method*, 519–20. Schmitt's notion of reality and the kind of redirecting of the theatrical to the real, however, are not exactly those which Gadamer has in mind. The redirecting of the theatrical to the real does not aim at an erudite consideration of the specific historical background of what happens in the play. It is not about taking historical circumstances into account to compose a picture fully or mostly determined by the age. *Hamlet* opens itself to the history of its

time and refers to historical figures that emerge in the play and to the tensions affecting them at the time, but as incarnations of tensions which impact an entire historical era. Shakespeare's consideration of certain situations and circumstances of his time—James's doubts about religious conflicts, about his mother and about his position—refer the participants not simply to those situations and circumstances. That consideration has a tragic character precisely because it effectively refers the participants (actors and audience) beyond those situations and circumstances, to the "entire conflict" of an "age," as to the mystery of existence, to the "ineluctable reality that no human mind has conceived"—namely, to the tensions and the unfathomableness that impact on the whole of human existence. The tragic work is constituted and acquires its seriousness insofar as it becomes an opening toward the meaning, tension, and fate affecting historical existence. See Schmitt, *Hamlet or Hecuba*, 40, 44, 45. On Gadamer's commentary, see Jens Meierhenrich and Oliver Simons, "'A Fanatic of Order in an Epoch of Confusing Turmoil:' The Political, Legal, and Cultural Thought of Carl Schmitt," in *The Oxford Handbook of Carl Schmitt*, ed. Jens Meierhenrich and Oliver Simons (New York: Oxford University Press, 2016), 45; Marder, *Groundless Existence*, 170–73, 186–87; Michael G. Salter, *Carl Schmitt: Law as Politics, Ideology and Strategic Myth* (Oxford: Routledge, 2012), 198–99.

192. Bowie, *Schelling*, 53.

193. See Schmitt, *Gesetz und Urteil*, 68; *Hamlet or Hecuba*, 44–49; *Theodor Däublers "Nordlicht,"* 51; Rasch, "Judgment," 100–103.

194. Schmitt, *Glossarium*, 388.

195. See Schmitt, *Glossarium*, 64; *Political Romanticism*, 19.

196. Schmitt, *Glossarium*, 71; see *The Concept of the Political*, 60; *Hamlet or Hecuba*, 45; *Theodor Däublers "Nordlicht,"* 51.

197. Meierhenrich and Simons, "A Fanatic of Order," 18; see 20; Wolfram Hogrebe, *Duplex. Strukturen der Intelligibilität* (Frankfurt: Klostermann, 2018), 34.

198. McCormick, *Carl Schmitt's Critique of Liberalism*, 16–17.

199. See Schmitt, *Political Theology*, 15; *Hamlet or Hecuba*, 45; *Glossarium*, 133, 160, 238, 388; *Political Romanticism*, 51–53; *The Concept of the Political*, 60. I have also shown that, in Schmitt's thought, there is a critique of that scope, from which he sees a non-reductionist way of considering the exceptional, in which the law as a fundamental manner of understanding can coincide with a critical or nondogmatic theology. See chapter 2.

200. See Schmitt, *Glossarium*, 27, 30, 71–73; Rudolf Otto, *The Idea of the Holy* (London, Oxford, and New York: Oxford University Press, 1958), 13.

201. See Otto, *The Idea of the Holy* 12–13; *Political Theology*, 15; *Hamlet or Hecuba*, 45.

202. See Otto, *The Idea of the Holy* 31–39.

203. In this sense, Schmitt criticizes Erik Peterson in *Political Theology II* for trying to defend a purely theological conception of theology. Only a consideration

of existence that leaves the dogmatic implications of theology behind is in a position not only to elucidate existence in a pertinent way, but also to make manifest the insufficiencies of technological rationality; see *Political Theology II*, 42, 58, 95.

204. See Schmitt, e.g., *Political Theology*, 13–15; "The Plight," 56; *The Nomos of the Earth*, 39; *Roman Catholicism*, 12; *The Concept of the Political*, 26, 38, 60, 120–21 (the last pages are of the German ed.); "Raum und Rom," 965; "Recht und Raum," 243; *On the Three Types of Juristic Thought*, 56, 73; *Hamlet or Hecuba*, 45.

205. See Schmitt, *Hamlet or Hecuba*, 45; *Political Theology*, 13–15; *The Concept of the Political*, 60; *Glossarium*, 277; Plessner, *Macht*, 192–93.

206. Schmitt's remarks on Kantian and Neokantian philosophy are found scattered throughout his works. On Kant, one may find them, e.g., in *Political Theology*, 14, 35; *Der Wert des Staates*, 27, 60–63; *The Concept of the Political*, 83–84, 90; "The Visibility," 47; *Political Romanticism*, 52–53; *The Nomos of the Earth*, 46–49; 168–71; *Constitutional Theory*, 113, 170–71, 183; *The Crisis*, 38; *On the Three Types of Juristic Thought*, 9, 11, 76, 78; *Glossarium*, 177–78, 370, 379; "Staatsethik," 152, 155, 163. On Ernst Cassirer, see *Glossarium*, 121; on Paul Natorp, see *Der Wert des Staates*, 63, 66–67; on Hermann Cohen, see *Der Wert des Staates*, 19, 63; on Hans Kelsen, see, e.g., *Political Theology*, 13–14, 18–22, 40–42; *On the Three Types of Juristic Thought*, 47–57; *Gesetz und Urteil*, 53–54.

207. See Schmitt, *Glossarium*, 121.

208. Here there is a functionalist moment. Cassirer speaks of an "activity of differentiation and connection," which is spontaneous and not derived from a substantial content. *Substance and Function* (Chicago: Open Court Publishing Company, 1923), 33; see Schmitt, *Glossarium*, 64, 238; *Political Romanticism*, 19, 84; *The Concept of the Political*, 60.

209. *Substance and Function* 20, 19.

210. See Schmitt, *Glossarium*, 136, 238, 277; *The Concept of the Political*, 60; *Political Theology*, 13–15; "The Plight," 56; *Political Romanticism*, 52; *Hamlet or Hecuba*, 45. Völker Neumann indicates that, in Schmitt's thought, "the concept occupies the place of the thing," and that, in his "conceptual realism," reality is subjected to the concept; *Carl Schmitt als Jurist*, 563. Likewise, Martin Gralher characterizes Schmitt's thought as a "static conceptual realism." "Antinomisches Denken und dilemmatische Kontrastdialektik—Warum Carl Schmitt kein Liberaler sein könnte," in *Carl Schmitt und die Liberalismuskritik*, ed. Klaus Hansen and Hans Lietzmann (Opladen: Leske & Budrich, 1988), 87. Schmitt in fact speaks of a "conceptual realism [*Begriffsrealismus*]" on his part (*Glossarium*, 80–81; see 77), in an explicit allusion, however, to conceptual articulations capable of understanding concrete existence. In *Glossarium* (81), he uses words similar to those in "The Plight of European Jurisprudence" in order to speak of the law as philosophy, a discipline different from one which is caught in "the alleys with no way out of general concepts." Neumann's and Gralher's claims may be valid regarding some of Schmitt's particular analyses. They are, however, difficult to apply to his

hermeneutical theory—a theory that, as we have seen, rejects the attempt to reduce the real to the pole of the ideal, and instead rests on an explicit thematization of the relation and tension of the hermeneutical poles, on a consideration of the dynamic and unfathomable character of existence. In some particular analyses it is indeed possible to interpret Schmitt as more inclined toward one of the poles, eventually that of the conceptual (see, for example, *Der Wert des Staates und die Bedeutung des Einzelnen*). However, his thematization of the problem of the relation and tension of the poles of understanding endows Schmitt's thought with a corrective criterion to avert the reductions of one pole to the other. As we shall see in the next section, in his main works, his analyses of the matter at hand are grounded precisely in this consideration of the poles of the real and the ideal. On Schmitt's attention to concrete reality in his conceptualizations, see Christian Meier: "Zu Carl Schmitts Begriffsbildung—Das Politische und der Nomos," in *Complexio Oppositorum*, ed. Helmuth Quaritsch (Berlin: Duncker & Humblot, 1988), 554–55, 573; Martin Loughlin, "Politinomy," in *The Oxford Handbook of Carl Schmitt*, ed. Jens Meierhenrich and Oliver Simons (New York: Oxford University Press, 2016), 583; Paul-Ludwig Weinacht, "Über Carl Schmitts Arbeit an Begriffen: Wort und Begriff des Staates," 75–76; Ernst Jünger, *Strahlungen I*, in *Sämtliche Werke* (Stuttgart: Klett-Cotta, 1998), vol. 2, 61; Helmut Quaritsch, *Positionen und Begriffe Carl Schmitts* (Berlin: Duncker & Humblot, 1995), 20–24; McCormick, *Carl Schmitt's Critique of Liberalism*, 16–17; Schmitt, "Gespräch über den Partisanen," 11.

211. Schmitt, *Der Wert des Staates*, 16–17, 74.

212. See Schmitt, *Der Wert des Staates*, 42, 80.

213. Bendersky links this work to Schmitt's early Neokantianism; see Joseph J. Bendersky, *Carl Schmitt. Theorist for the Reich* (Princeton, NJ: Princeton University Press, 1983), 10–11. Carlo Galli separates it from that position and emphasizes the mediating function that Schmitt attributes to the state; see *Genealogia*, 315–25.

214. A "contemplation of nature . . . to which the living together of human belongs, as far as it is merely a matter of the empirical and explanatory social sciences." Schmitt, *Der Wert des Staates*, 36.

215. See Schmitt, *Der Wert des Staates*, 36.

216. Schmitt, *Der Wert des Staates*, 74–75.

217. Schmitt, *Der Wert des Staates*, 99; see 98, 107.

218. Schmitt, *Der Wert des Staates*, 74–75.

219. Schmitt, *Der Wert des Staates*, 79.

220. Schmitt, *Der Wert des Staates*, 80.

221. Schmitt, *Der Wert des Staates*, 82. Schmitt acknowledges, moreover, a mediating character of the state. As "juridical subject," it possesses an abstract ideal implication; yet, as capable of realizing the law, it is also a "reality." The state, then, is a reality distinct from objects considered by a science of facts.

222. See McCormick, *Carl Schmitt's Critique of Liberalism*, 127; Schmitt, *Dictatorship*, xxxviii, xlv.
223. Schmitt, *Dictatorship*, xl, 179.
224. See Schmitt, *Dictatorship*, xxxix, 179.
225. Schmitt, *Dictatorship*, xlv.
226. See Schmitt, *Dictatorship*, xxxviii–xliv; McCormick, *Carl Schmitt's Critique of Liberalism*, 125–28; Bielefeldt, *Kampf und Entscheidung*, 27, 30; Eric A. Posner and Adrian Vermeule, "Demistifying Schmitt," in *The Oxford Handbook of Carl Schmitt*, ed. Jens Meierhenrich and Oliver Simons (New York: Oxford University Press, 2016), 613, 623–24; Jacques, "Law, Decision, Necessity," 114, 115, 117.
227. See Schmitt, *Political Theology*, 3, 12–13, 35.
228. See Schmitt, *Political Theology*, 36–37, 45–46.
229. See Schmitt, *The Crisis*, 8. On this text, see Kálman Pócza, *Parlamentarismus und politische Räpresentation. Carl Schmitt kontextualisiert* (Baden-Baden: Nomos, 2014); Stefan Hermanns, *Kritik am Parlamentarismus bei Carl Schmitt und die Utopie der Demokratie* (Frankfurt: Lang, 2011); Ellen Kennedy, "Carl Schmitt's Parlamentarismus in Its Historical Context," in Carl Schmitt, *The Crisis of Parliamentary Democracy* (Cambridge, MA and London: MIT Press, 1988), xiii–1; Jürgen Habermas, *Strukturwandel der Öffentlichkeit. Untersuchungen zu einer Kategorie der bürgerlichen Gesellschaft* (Darmstadt and Neuwied: Luchterland, 1962).
230. Schmitt, *The Crisis*, 35–36.
231. Schmitt, *The Crisis*, 44.
232. Schmitt, *The Crisis*, 9, 10, 14.
233. See Schmitt, *The Crisis*, 16–17.
234. Schmitt, *The Crisis*, 6.
235. Schmitt, *The Crisis*, 76.
236. See Schmitt, *The Crisis*, 42, 43, 48.
237. See Schmitt, *The Concept of the Political*, 26, 60.
238. See Schmitt, *The Concept of the Political*, 60.
239. See the first part of this chapter.
240. See Schmitt, *The Concept of the Political*, 26, 38, 60, 85, 95–96, 120–21 (this last reference according to the German ed.). *The Concept of the Political* offers a description of the historical evolution of Europe from a preponderantly substantialist to a preponderantly functionalist mentality, once again within the framework provided by the juridical understanding of existence. See *The Concept of the Political*, 80–96.
241. Schmitt, *Constitutional Theory*, 67–68.
242. Schmitt, *Constitutional Theory*, 62.
243. Schmitt, *Constitutional Theory*, 65.
244. Schmitt, *Constitutional Theory*, 59.
245. Schmitt, *Constitutional Theory*, 65.

246. Schmitt, *Constitutional Theory*, 76.
247. Schmitt, *Constitutional Theory*, 125.
248. Schmitt, *Constitutional Theory*, 126–28; see Ojakangas, *A Philosophy of Concrete Life*, 135–37.
249. See Schmitt, *Constitutional Theory*, 131.
250. Schmitt, *Constitutional Theory*, 249.
251. See Schmitt, *Constitutional Theory*, 93, 169–70, 249.
252. Schmitt, *Constitutional Theory*, 55.
253. Schmitt, *Constitutional Theory*, 239; see Ojakangas, *A Philosophy of Concrete Life*, 133–35, 137–39.
254. See Schmitt, *Constitutional Theory*, 302. Schmitt understands the form of institutionality as a "*complexio oppositorum.*" *Roman Catholicism*, 10–11. It is the articulation of a collective (in this case, the people), according to an idea, so that certain persons—the representatives—are able to express the whole. If one accepts the thesis of the Schmittian "sociology of concepts," that articulating idea must rest on the dominant conception of the world in the epoch in question; see *Political Theology*, 46. Only then can the people find expression in the institution and a unity be found among representatives and represented.
255. See Schmitt, *Constitutional Theory*, 127–28.
256. Schmitt, *Constitutional Theory*, 243.
257. Schmitt, *Legality and Legitimacy*, 4–5.
258. Schmitt, *Legality and Legitimacy*, 25.
259. Schmitt, *Legality and Legitimacy*, 3–4.
260. Schmitt, *Legality and Legitimacy*, 10–11.
261. Schmitt, *Legality and Legitimacy*, 23.
262. Schmitt, *Legality and Legitimacy*, 27; see 87, 92; *The Crisis*, 6; *Constitutional Theory*, 341–42.
263. Schmitt, *Legality and Legitimacy*, 28.
264. See Schmitt, *Legality and Legitimacy*, 30.
265. See Schmitt, *Legality and Legitimacy*, chaps. 3, 4, and 5.
266. Schmitt, *Legality and Legitimacy*, 94.
267. See Schmitt, *Legality and Legitimacy*, 4–11.
268. Schmitt, *Legality and Legitimacy*, 21–22.
269. Schmitt, *Legality and Legitimacy*, 27.
270. Although it is possible eventually to find elements later used by Schmitt in favor of his political activities in Berlin, and Schmitt highlights certain internal problems of the theory of the bourgeois state of law, in the pre-1933 period (including *Constitutional Theory* and *Legality and Legitimacy*), Schmitt is still distant from a totalitarian position; see J. Bendersky, *Carl Schmitt*, 29–30, 63, 93, 97, 99–100, 146. In *Constitutional Theory*, Schmitt considers the relevance of both the functional and the substantial aspects involved in the conformation of a constitutional order. The substantial aspects (i.e., the people, "identity") should

not overcome functional elaborations (representation, division of powers, fundamental rights, institutional guarantees). The institutional elaborations, however, must attend to the substantial elements, otherwise, Schmitt argues, they become fragile before the totalitarian threat. See Schmitt, *The Crisis*, 42–43, 48, 76; *Legality and Legitimacy*, 28.

271. See Schmitt, *On the Three Types of Juristic Thought*, 47–57, 73–74.
272. See Schmitt, *The Leviathan*, chaps.1 and 2.
273. Schmitt, *The Leviathan*, 31.
274. Schmitt, *The Leviathan*, 31.
275. Schmitt, *The Leviathan*, 33.
276. Schmitt, *The Leviathan*, 34.
277. Schmitt, *The Leviathan*, 34.
278. Schmitt, *The Leviathan*, 32–34.
279. See Schmitt, *The Leviathan*, 85.
280. Schmitt, *The Leviathan*, 56.
281. See Schmitt, *The Leviathan*, 57–63.
282. Schmitt, *Land and Sea*, 5.
283. See Schmitt, *Land and Sea*, 31–33.
284. See Schmitt, *Land and Sea*, 36.
285. Schmitt, *Land and Sea*, 47; see 48–49; "Staat als konkreter, an eine geschichtliche Epoche gebundener Begriff," in *Verfassungsrechtliche Aufsätze aus den Jahren 1924-1954: Materialien zu einer Verfassungslehre* (Berlin: Duncker & Humblot, 2003), 380. Schmitt attends to the importance of the "maritime existence" for the development of the "industrial revolution." *Dialogues*, 74, 75. Nonetheless, maritime space does not *constitute* technology, whose emergence as a form of rationality is independent of it. See Schmitt, *Dialogues*, 72, 76.
286. Schmitt, *Land and Sea*, 55–57.
287. See Schmitt, *Land and Sea*, 74.
288. See Schmitt, *Land and Sea*, 84.
289. See Schmitt, *Land and Sea*, 86.
290. Schmitt, *Land and Sea*, 90–91.
291. Schmitt, *Land and Sea*, 91. On the scope and limits of Schmitt's conception of the four elements, see Michael Marder, *Pyropolitics. When the World Is Ablaze* (London: Rowman & Littlefield, 2015), chap. 1.
292. Schmitt, *Land and Sea*, 92.
293. Schmitt, *Land and Sea*, 57.
294. Schmitt, *Land and Sea*, 93.
295. Schmitt, *The Nomos of the Earth*, part I, chap. 4. Schmitt links the notion of *nomos* to appropriation, division, distribution of the earth, and also to the "pasturage (*Weiden*)," cultivation, usage, and production. See *The Nomos of the Earth*, 70; "Appropriation/Distribution/Production," 326–27; "Nomos—Nahme—Name," 345; and "The New *Nomos* of the Earth," 351; the last three texts in *The*

Nomos of the Earth in the International Law of the Jus Publicum Europaeum; Land and Sea, 59–60, 93. On the importance of this concept in Schmitt's thought, see Montserrat Herrero López, *The Political Discourse of Carl Schmitt. A Mystic of Order* (London: Rowman & Littlefield, 2015).

296. Schmitt, *The Nomos of the Earth*, 46, 69, 80. Internally, it is an "initial division and distribution of the land." Externally, it implies that the "land-appropriating group is confronted with other land-appropriating or land-owning groups and powers." *The Nomos of the Earth*, 45.

297. See Schmitt, *The Nomos of the Earth*, 73, 82.

298. Schmitt, *The Nomos of the Earth*, 38 (translation modified).

299. Schmitt, *The Nomos of the Earth*, 39 (translation modified).

300. See Schmitt, *The Nomos of the Earth*, 42. The earth emerges bestowed with a "meaning" in a juridical sense: "she contains law within herself, as a reward for labor; she manifests law upon herself, as fixed boundaries; and she sustains law above herself, as public sign of order." The sea does not betray, on the contrary, such juridical character. It does not proportionally reward labor; it has no limits; and it does not allow for stable marks to be made upon it. *The Nomos of the Earth*, 42–43. In addition to that revelation, and although Schmitt does not say it in this part, there must be in the human being the capacity to distance itself from and to conceptualize what is revealed to it. Before that, it is not yet possible to speak of a *human* appropriation of the land.

301. See Schmitt, *The Nomos of the Earth*, 108–13, 121, 152–68.

302. Schmitt, *The Nomos of the Earth*, 120–22.

303. Schmitt, *The Nomos of the Earth*, 123.

304. See Schmitt, *The Nomos of the Earth*, 123–24, 140–44.

305. Schmitt, *The Nomos of the Earth*, 148; see 183.

306. Schmitt, *The Nomos of the Earth*, 172–73.

307. Schmitt, *The Nomos of the Earth*, 187; see 187, 189.

308. Schmitt, *The Nomos of the Earth*, 227.

309. See Schmitt, *The Nomos of the Earth*, 220–21, 226, 230, 239.

310. See Schmitt, *The Nomos of the Earth*, 223–24, 235–35, 241.

311. See Schmitt, *The Nomos of the Earth*, 234, 241–46.

312. Schmitt, *The Nomos of the Earth*, 227; see 253–57.

313. Schmitt, *The Nomos of the Earth*, 259–79.

314. Schmitt, *The Nomos of the Earth*, 283; see 280–83. It establishes a "line of self-isolation," which distinguishes the pure and uncontaminated "New World" from the corrupted "Old World." *The Nomos of the Earth*, 287, 289. This idea bears force in the nineteenth century, when the European spatial order was entering a crisis, and waves of migrants were abandoning (traveling to America) a Europe that wavered between reaction and shock. Before the "deep problematic that was manifesting itself as socialism, communism, atheism, anarchism, and nihilism," the dominant European thought opposed a reaction in the form of a "legitimist

or legalitarian" façade, while neglecting the thought of existentialist authors. *The Nomos of the Earth*, 290–92; see 293–99.

315. See Schmitt, *The Nomos of the Earth*, 309–22.
316. Schmitt, *The Nomos of the Earth*, 38.
317. Schmitt, *Hamlet or Hecuba*, 37.
318. Schmitt, *Hamlet or Hecuba*, 37.
319. Schmitt, *Hamlet or Hecuba*, 33; see 33–37.
320. Schmitt, *Hamlet or Hecuba*, 40, 45; see 49.
321. Schmitt, *Hamlet or Hecuba*, 45; see 40, 46.
322. See Schmitt, *Hamlet or Hecuba*, 44–46. Regarding the similarity between aesthetic understanding and legal understanding in this work by Schmitt, see David Pan, "Tragedy as Exception in Carl Schmitt's *Hamlet or Hecuba*," 732.
323. See Schmitt, *Theory of the Partisan*, 14.
324. Schmitt, *Theory of the Partisan*, 20; see 14, 16.
325. See Schmitt, *Theory of the Partisan*, 23–32, 35.
326. Schmitt, *Theory of the Partisan*, 69; see 68–72.
327. Schmitt, *Theory of the Partisan*, 72–74.
328. Schmitt, *Theory of the Partisan*, 74–76.
329. See Schmitt, *Theory of the Partisan*, 76–80.
330. See Schmitt, *Theory of the Partisan*, 92–93. Absolute enmity is facilitated, moreover, by another factor that Schmitt has already broached: namely, that "absolute weapons of mass destruction require an absolute enmity," for only on the condition that opponents are declared "to be totally criminal and inhuman" can such level of destruction arrive at any kind of justification. *Theory of the Partisan*, 93, 94.
331. Erik Peterson, *Der Monotheismus als politisches Problem. Ein Beitrag zur Geschichte der politischen Theologie im Imperium Romanum* (Leipzig: Jakob Hegner, 1935), 158 (footnote 168).
332. See Schmitt, *Political Theology II*, 103.
333. See chapter 2.
334. See Schmitt, *Political Theology II*, 95. "He [Peterson] made himself secure through a dogmatic theology." *Political Theology II*, 42. Peterson says: "Only because of dogma is theology separated from its association with that most dubious of academic disciplines, the so called Humanities." "One must have the courage to live once more in the sphere of dogma, and then one can be assured that people will be interested in theology again." *Was ist Theologie?* in *Theologische Traktate, Ausgewahlte Schriften*, ed. Barbara Nichtweiß (Würzburg: Echter, 1994), vol. 1, 16.
335. Schmitt, *Political Theology II*, 44–45; see 97.
336. Schmitt, *Political Theology II*, 57; see 66.
337. Schmitt, *Political Theology II*, 58.
338. See Schmitt, *Political Theology II*, 34. Schmitt also questions Peterson's thesis from within the boundaries of Christian theology itself, by means of a

reflection on the Trinity. He sets his mind on the notion of "*stasis*," to which Peterson refers—a *stasis* that is in this "Trinity." "*Stasis*"—says Schmitt, invoking Greek sources—"means in the first place quiescence, tranquility, standpoint, status. . . . But *stasis* also means, in the second place (political) *unrest*, movement, uproar and civil war." It is therefore possible to think of a source of "unrest, movement, uproar" in the Trinity. *Political Theology II*, 122–23. This understanding of *stasis* challenges Peterson's thesis. Schmitt writes: "At the heart of the doctrine of the Trinity we encounter a genuine politico-theological *stasiology*." *Political Theology II*, 123; see 126. This stasiology may be interpreted in juridical terms, as the tension between the old law and the incarnation; see Miguel Vatter, "The Political Theology of Carl Schmitt," in *The Oxford Handbook of Carl Schmitt*, ed. Jens Meierhenrich and Oliver Simons (New York: Oxford University Press, 2016), 260. The Trinity is considered here by Schmitt in a juridical way. It is for him a tension of unity and multiplicity. Schmitt distinguishes the Trinity from a unity that does not admit any difference or tension within, but also from a dualist structure like that of the gnostic, which cannot be brought into a unity. That is, there is—as in the juridical existence understood broadly—a pole unifying or ideal and a pole of the multiple or real, in addition to a tension and relation between both. One can then speak here of a Schmittian "juridization" of theology.

339. See Hans Blumenberg, *Die Legitimität der Neuzeit* (Frankfurt: Suhrkamp, 1966). On the discussion between Schmitt and Blumenberg, see Alexander Schmitz and Marcel Lepper (eds.), *Carl Schmitt—Hans Blumenberg. Briefwechsel 1971–1978 und weitere Materialien* (Frankfurt: Suhrkamp, 2007); Pini Ifergan, "Cutting to the Chase: Carl Schmitt and Hans Blumenberg on Political Theology and Secularization." *New German Critique* 111 (2010): 149–71; Alexander Schmitz, "Legitimacy of the Modern Age? Hans Blumenberg and Carl Schmitt," in *The Oxford Handbook of Carl Schmitt*, ed. Jens Meierhenrich and Oliver Simons (New York: Oxford University Press, 2016), 705–30; Celina Maria Bragagnolo, "Secularization, History and Political Theology: The Hans Blumenberg and Carl Schmitt Debate." *Journal of the Philosophy of History* 5 (2011): 84–104.

340. Schmitt, *Political Theology II*, 116.

341. Schmitt, *Political Theology II*, 117.

342. See Schmitt, *Political Theology II*, 118–20.

343. See Schmitt, *Political Theology II*, 120–21, 128–30.

Works Cited

Works by Schmitt

Schmitt, Carl. *Donoso Cortés in gesamteuropäischer Interpretation. Vier Aufsätze.* Cologne: Greven Verlag, 1950.

———. "Raum und Rom. Zur Phonetik des Wortes Raum." *Universitas* 6 (1951): 963–67.

———. "Recht und Raum." In *Tymbos für Wilhelm Ahlmann*, 241–51. Berlin: de Gruyter, 1951.

———. "Die Einheit der Welt." *Merkur* 47 (1952): 1–11.

———. "Die geschichtliche Struktur des heutigen Welt-Gegensatzes von Ost und West." In *Freundschaftliche Begegnungen. Festschrift für Ernst Jünger zum 60. Geburtstag*, edited by Armin Mohler, 149 52. Frankfurt: Klostermann, 1955.

———. *Gesetz und Urteil. Eine Untersuchung zum Problem der Rechtspraxis.* 2nd ed. Munich: Beck, 1969.

———. "Gespräch über den Partisanen." In *Guerilleros, Partisanen. Theorie und Praxis*, edited by Joachim Schickel, 9–29. Munich: Hanser, 1970.

———. *Political Romanticism.* Translated by Guy Oakes. Cambridge, MA: The MIT Press, 1986.

———. *Politische Romantik.* Berlin: Duncker & Humblot, 1998.

———. *Die Wendung zum diskriminierenden Kriegsbegriff.* Berlin: Duncker & Humblot, 1988.

———. *The Crisis of Parliamentary Democracy.* Translated by Ellen Kennedy. Cambridge, MA: The MIT Press, 1988.

———. "The Plight of European Jurisprudence." *Telos* 83 (1990): 35–70.

———. "Die Lage der europäischen Rechtswissenschaft." In *Verfassungsrechtliche Aufsätze aus den Jahren 1924–1954: Materialien zu einer Verfassungslehre*, 386–429. 4th ed. Berlin: Duncker & Humblot, 2003.

———. *Theodor Däublers "Nordlicht." Drei Studien über die Elemente, den Geist und die Aktualität des Werkes.* Berlin: Duncker & Humblot, 1991.

———. *On the Three Types of Juristic Thought*. Translated by Joseph Bendersky. Westport, CT: Praeger, 2004.

———. *Über die drei Arten des rechtswissenschaftlichen Denkens*. Berlin: Duncker & Humblot, 1993.

———. "Was habe ich getan?" In *Schmittiana. Beiträge zu Leben und Werk Carl Schmitts*, vol. 5, edited by Piet Tommissen, 13–19. Berlin: Duncker & Humblot, 1996.

———. *Roman Catholicism and Political Form*. Translated by Gary L. Ulmen. Westport, CT: Greenwood Press, 1996.

———. "The Visibility of the Church: A Scholastic Consideration." In *Roman Catholicism and Political Form*, edited by Gary L. Ulmen, 47–59. Westport, CT: Greenwood Press, 1996.

———. "Die Sichtbarkeit der Kirche: Eine scholastische Erwägung." *Summa: Eine Vierteljahresschrift* no. 2 (1917): 71–79.

———. "Staat als konkreter, an eine geschichtliche Epoche gebundener Begriff." In *Verfassungsrechtliche Aufsätze aus den Jahren 1924–1954: Materialien zu einer Verfassungslehre*, 375–85. 4th ed. Berlin: Duncker & Humblot, 2003.

———. "Das Problem der Legalität." In *Verfassungsrechtliche Aufsätze aus den Jahren 1924–1954: Materialien zu einer Verfassungslehre*, 440–51. 4th ed. Berlin: Duncker & Humblot, 2003.

———. *Legality and Legitimacy*. Translated by Jeffrey Seitzer. London and Durham, NC: Duke University Press, 2004.

———. *Der Wert des Staates und die Bedeutung des Einzelnen*. 2nd ed. Berlin: Duncker & Humblot, 2004.

———. *Political Theology. Four Chapters on the Concept of Sovereignty*. Translated by Georg Schwab. Chicago, IL: University of Chicago Press, 2005.

———. "Die Einheit der Welt (Vortrag)." In *Frieden oder Pazifismus? Arbeiten zum Völkerrecht und zur internationalen Politik 1924–1978*, edited by Günter Maschke, 841–52. Berlin: Duncker & Humblot, 2005.

———. *The Nomos of the Earth in the International Law of the Jus Publicum Europaeum*. Translated by Gary L. Ulmen. New York: Telos Press, 2006.

———. "The New *Nomos* of the Earth." In *The Nomos of the Earth in the International Law of the Jus Publicum Europaeum*, translated by Gary L. Ulmen, 351–55. New York: Telos Press, 2006.

———. "Nomos—Nahme—Name." In *The Nomos of the Earth in the International Law of the Jus Publicum Europaeum*, translated by Gary L. Ulmen, 336–50. New York: Telos Press, 2006.

———. "Appropriation/Distribution/Production: An Attempt to Determine from *Nomos* the Basic Questions of Every Social and Economic Order." In *The Nomos of the Earth in the International Law of the Jus Publicum Europaeum*, translated by Gary L. Ulmen, 324–35. New York: Telos Press, 2006.

———. *Theory of the Partisan. Intermediate Commentary on the Concept of the Political*, translated by Gary L. Ulmen. New York: Telos Press, 2007.

———. "Drei Möglichkeiten eines christlichen Geschichtsbildes." In *Carl Schmitt & Hans Blumenberg: Briefwechsel*, 161–66. Frankfurt: Suhrkamp, 2007.

———. *Constitutional Theory*. Translated by Jeffrey Seitzer. Durham, NC: Duke University Press, 2008.

———. *Hamlet or Hecuba. The Intrusion of the Time into the Play*. Translated by David Pan and Jennifer R. Rust. New York: Telos Press, 2009.

———. *The Concept of the Political*. Translated by Georg Schwab. Chicago, IL: University of Chicago Press, 2007.

———. *Der Begriff des Politischen*. Berlin: Duncker & Humblot, 1963.

———. *Der Begriff des Politischen*. Hamburg: Hanseatische Verlaganstalt, 1933.

———. *Political Theology II. The Myth of the Closure of any Political Theology*. Translated by Michael Hoelzl and Graham Ward. Malden, MA: Polity Press, 2008.

———. *The Leviathan in the State Theory of Thomas Hobbes. Meaning and Failure of a Political Symbol*. Translated by Georg Schwab and Erna Hilfstein. Chicago, IL: University of Chicago Press, 2008.

———. *Ex Captivitate Salus. Experiences, 1945–47*. Translated by Matthew Hannah. Cambridge, MA: Polity Press, 2015.

———. *Die Tyrannei der Werte*. Berlin: Duncker & Humblot, 2011.

———. "Zu Friedrich Meineckes 'Idee der Staatsräson.'" In *Positionen und Begriffe im Kampf mit Weimar—Genf—Versailles 1923–1939*, 51–59. 4th ed. Berlin: Duncker & Humblot, 2014.

———. "Der Gegensatz von Parlamentarismus und moderner Massendemokratie." In *Positionen und Begriffe im Kampf mit Weimar—Genf—Versailles 1923–1939*, 60–74. 4th ed. Berlin: Duncker & Humblot, 2014.

———. "Staatsethik und pluralistischer Staat." In *Positionen und Begriffe im Kampf mit Weimar—Genf—Versailles 1923–1939*, 151–65. 4th ed. Berlin: Duncker & Humblot, 2014.

———. *Land and Sea. A World-Historical Meditation*. Translated by Samuel Garret Zeitlin. New York: Telos Press, 2015.

———. *Glossarium. Aufzeichnungen aus den Jahren 1947 bis 1958*. 2nd ed. Berlin: Duncker & Humblot, 2015.

———. *Dictatorship. From the Origin of the Modern Concept of Sovereignty to Proletarian Class Struggle*. Translated by Michael Hoelzl and Graham Ward. Malden, MA: Polity Press, 2015.

———. *Dialogues on Power and Space*. Translated by Samuel Garrett Zeitlin. Malden, MA: Polity Press, 2015.

Other Works

Adam, Armin. *Rekonstruktion des Politischen. Carl Schmitt und die Krise der Staatlichkeit 1912–1933*. Weinheim: Wiley-VCH, 1992.

Agamben, Giorgio. *State of Exception*. Translated by Kevin Attell. Chicago, IL: University of Chicago Press, 2005.

———. *Homo Sacer: Sovereign Power and Bare Life*. Translated by Daniel Heller-Roazen. Stanford, CA: Stanford University Press, 1998.

Anselm of Canterbury. *The Mayor Works*, edited by Brian Davies and Gillian Evans. Oxford: Oxford University Press, 2008.

Aquinas, Thomas. *Summa Theologica*. Translated by Fathers of the English Dominican Province. New York: Benziger Brothers, 1948.

Arendt, Hannah. *Lectures on Kant's Political Philosophy*, edited by Ronald Beiner. Chicago, IL: University of Chicago Press, 1992.

Arps, Arne. "Rezension zu: Hugo Eduardo Herrera: Carl Schmitt als politischer Philosoph. Berlin 2010." *Portal für Politikwissenschaft*, April 13, 2011.

Augsberg, Ino. *Kassiber. Die Aufgabe der juristischen Hermeneutik*. Tübingen: Mohr Siebeck, 2016.

Austin, John Langshaw. *How to Do Things with Words*. Oxford: Clarendon Press, 1962.

Bargu, Banu. "Stasiology: Political Theology and the Figure of the Sacrificial Enemy." In *After Secular Law*, edited by Winnifried Fallers Sullivan, Robert A. Yelle, and Mateo Taussig-Rubbo, 140–59. Stanford, CA: Stanford University Press, 2011.

Bendersky, Joseph J. *Carl Schmitt. Theorist for the Reich*. Princeton, NJ: Princeton University Press, 1983.

Bernet, Rudolf. "Derrida and His Master's Voice." In *Derrida and Phenomenology*, edited by William R. Mckenna and J. Claude Evans, 1–21. Dordrecht: Springer, 1995.

Bielefeldt, Heiner. *Kampf und Entscheidung. Politischer Existentialismus bei Carl Schmitt, Helmuth Plessner und Karl Jaspers*. Würzburg: Königshausen & Neumann, 1994.

Blumenberg, Hans. *Die Legitimität der Neuzeit*. Frankfurt: Suhrkamp, 1966.

Böckenförde, Ernst-Wolfgang. "Konkretes Ordnungsdenken." In *Historisches Wörterbuch der Philosophie*, edited by Joachim Ritter and Karlfried Gründer. Vol. 6, 1312–13. Basel: Schwabe Verlag, 1984.

———. "Politische Theologie—Begriff und Bedeutung." *Neue Zürcher Zeitung*, May 30, 1981.

———. "The Concept of the Political: A Key to Understanding Carl Schmitt's Constitutional Theory." In *Law as Politics: Carl Schmitt's Critique of Liberalism*, edited by David Dyzenhaus, 37–55. Durham, NC: Duke University Press, 1998.

Bortoft, Henri. *Taking Appearance Seriously: The Dynamic Way of Seeing in Goethe and European Thought*. Croydon: Floris Books, 2012.

Bourdin, Bernard. "La modernité séculière a-t-elle besoin d'une théologie politique?" *Esprit* 372 (February 2011): 125–37.

Bowie, Andrew. *Schelling and Modern European Philosophy*. New York: Routledge, 1993.
Bragagnolo, Celina María. "Secularization, History and Political Theology: The Hans Blumenberg and Carl Schmitt Debate." *Journal of the Philosophy of History* 5 (2011): 84–104.
Caputo, John D. *Hermeneutics. Facts and Interpretation in the Age of Information*. London: Pelican, 2018.
Carrino, Agostino. "Carl Schmitt and European Juridical Science." In *The Challenge of Carl Schmitt*, edited by Chantal Mouffe, 180–94. London and New York: Verso, 1999.
Cassirer, Ernst. *Substance and Function*. Translated by W. C. Swabey and M. C. Swabey. Chicago, IL: Open Court, 1923.
Coillot-Thélène, Catherine. "Carl Schmitt versus Max Weber: Juridical Rationality and Economic Rationality." In *The Challenge of Carl Schmitt*, edited by Chantal Mouffe, 138–54. London and New York: Verso, 1999.
Conrad, Burkhard. "Das rhetorische Moment von politischer Theologie." *Zeitschrift für Politik* 54 (2007): 408–30.
Cristi, Renato. *Carl Schmitt and Authoritarian Liberalism*. Cardiff: University of Wales Press, 1998.
Croce, Mariano, and Salvatore, Andrea. *The Legal Theory of Carl Schmitt*. Oxford: Routledge, 2013.
Crockett, Clayton. *Radical Political Theology. Religion and Politics after Liberalism*. New York: Columbia University Press, 2011.
de Man, Paul. "Promises (Social Contract)." In *Allegories of Reading. Figural Language in Rousseau, Nietzsche, Rilke, and Proust*, edited by Martin McQuillan, 246–77. New Haven, CT: Yale University Press, 1979.
de Saussure, Ferdinand. *Course in General Linguistics*. Translated by Wade Baskin. New York: McGraw-Hill, 1966.
de Vries, Hent. *Religion and Violence: Perspectives from Kant to Derrida*. Baltimore, MD: Johns Hopkins University Press, 2002.
de Vries, Hent, and Lawrence Sullivan, eds. *Political Theologies: Public Religions in a Post-Secular World*. New York: Fordham University Press, 2006.
de Wilde, Marc. "Meeting Opposites: The Political Theologies of Walter Benjamin and Carl Schmitt." *Philosophy and Rhetoric* 44 (2011): 363–81.
Derrida, Jacques. "Speech and Phenomena: Introduction to the Problem of Signs in Husserl's Phenomenology." In *Speech and Phenomena and Other Essays on Husserl's Theory of Signs*, translated by David B. Allison, 3–104. Evanston, IL: Northwestern University Press, 1973.
———. "Differance." In *Speech and Phenomena and Other Essays on Husserl's Theory of Signs*, translated by David B. Allison, 129–69. Evanston, IL: Northwestern University Press, 1973.

———. "Implications: Interview with Henri Ronse." In *Positions*, translated by Alan Bass, 1–14. Chicago, IL: University of Chicago Press, 1981.

———. "Positions: Interview with Jean-Louis Houdebine and Guy Scarpetta." In *Positions*, translated by Alan Bass, 37–96. Chicago, IL: University of Chicago Press, 1981.

———. "The Linguistic Circle of Geneva." In *Margins of Philosophy*, translated by Alan Bass, 137–53. Chicago, IL: University of Chicago Press, 1982.

———. "Signature, Event, Context." In *Margins of Philosophy*, translated by Alan Bass, 307–30. Chicago, IL: University of Chicago Press, 1982.

———. *Memoires. For Paul de Man*. Translated by Avital Ronell and Eduardo Cadava. New York: Columbia University Press, 1989.

———. "Force of Law: The 'Mystical Foundation of Authority.'" *Cardozo Law Review* 11 (1990): 920–1045.

———. "Force of Law. The 'Mystical Foundation of Authority.'" In *Acts of Religion*, edited by Gil Anidjar, 230–98. New York: Routledge, 2002.

———. "Before the Law." In *Acts of Literature*, edited by Derek Attridge, 181–220. London: Routledge, 1992.

———. *Of Grammatology*. Translated by Gayatri Chakravorty Spivak. Baltimore, MD: Johns Hopkins University Press, 1997.

———. *Rogues: Two Essays on Reason*. Translated by Pascale-Anne Brault and Michael Nass. Stanford, CA: Stanford University Press, 2005.

———. "Force and Signification." In *Writing and Difference*, translated by Alan Bass, 1–35. London: Routledge 2001.

———. "Violence and Metaphysics: An Essay on the Thought of Emmanuel Levinas." In *Writing and Difference*, translated by Alan Bass, 97–192. London: Routledge 2001.

———. *The Politics of Friendship*. Translated by George Collins. London and New York: Verso, 2005.

———. *The Beast & the Sovereign I*. Translated by Geoffrey Bennington. Chicago, IL: University of Chicago Press, 2009.

———. *The Beast & the Sovereign II*. Translated by Geoffrey Bennington. Chicago, IL: University of Chicago Press, 2011.

Descartes, René. *Meditationes de prima philosophia*. In *Œuvres complètes*, edited by Charles Adam and Paul Tannery. Vol. 7. Paris: Vrin, 1996.

Doerr, F. "Besprechung des Buches Gesetz und Urteil von Carl Schmitt." *Zeitschrift für das Gesamte Handelsrecht und Konkursrecht* 73 (1913): 537–39.

Dotti, Jorge E. "*Filioque*. Una tenaz apología de la mediación teológico-política." In Carl Schmitt, *La tiranía de los valores*, 9–86. Buenos Aires: Hydra, 2009.

Doyon, Maxime. "The Transcendental Claim of Deconstruction." In *A Companion to Derrida*, edited by Zeynep Direk and Leonard Lawlor, 132–49. Oxford and Malden, MA: Wiley Blackwell, 2014.

Dreisholtkamp, Uwe. *Jacques Derrida*. Munich: Beck, 1999.
Dyzenhaus, David. "Why Carl Schmitt?" In *Law as Politics: Carl Schmitt's Critique of Liberalism*, edited by David Dyzenhaus, 1–20. Durham, NC: Duke University Press, 1998.
———. *Legality and Legitimacy: Carl Schmitt, Hans Kelsen and Hermann Heller in Weimar*. Oxford: Oxford University Press, 1997.
Eichhorn, Mathias. *Es wird regiert! Der Staat im Denken Karl Barths und Carl Schmitts in den Jahren 1919 bis 1938*. Berlin: Duncker & Humblot, 1994.
Fichte, Johann Gottlieb. *Wissenschaftslehre nova methodo*. In *Gesamtausgabe der Bayerischen Akademie der Wissenschaften*, edited by Erich Fuchs, Hans Gliwitzky, Reinhard Lauth, and Peter Schneider. Vol. 2, part 4. Stuttgart and Bad Cannstatt: Frommann-Holzboog, 1962.
Forsthoff, Ernst. *Rechtsstaat im Wandel. Verfassungsgeschichtliche Abhandlungen 1954–1973*. 2nd ed. Munich: Beck, 1976.
Frank, Manfred. *What Is Neostructuralism?* Translated by Sabine Wilke and Richard Gray. Minneapolis: University of Minnesota Press, 1984.
———. *Ansichten der Subjektivität*. Frankfurt: Suhrkamp, 2012.
Gadamer, Hans-Georg. *Truth and Method*. Translated and revised by Joel Weinsheimer and Donald G. Marshall. London: Bloomsbury, 2013.
———. "Grenzen der Sprache." In *Gesammelte Werke*. Vol. 8, 350–61. Tübingen: Mohr Siebeck, 1993.
Galli, Carlo. "Carl Schmitt's Anti-liberalism: Its Theoretical and Historical Sources and Its Philosophical and Political Meaning." *Cardozo Law Review* 21 (2000): 1597–1618.
———. *Genealogia della politica. Carl Schmitt e la crisi del pensiero politico moderno*. Bologna: Il Mulino, 1996.
———. *Janus Gaze: Essays on Carl Schmitt*. Translated by Amanda Minervini. Durham, NC: Duke University Press, 2015.
Garcia-Düttmann, Alexander. *Derrida und Ich. Das Problem der Dekonstruktion*. Bielefeld: Transcript Verlag, 2008.
Gasché, Rodolphe. *Inventions of Difference. On Jacques Derrida*. Cambridge, MA: Harvard University Press, 1995.
———. *The Tain of the Mirror: Derrida and the Philosophy of Reflection*. Cambridge, MA: Harvard University Press, 1986.
Gerlich, Siegfried. "Die Politische Theologie Carl Schmitts." *Sezession* (Themenheft Carl Schmitt) 42 (2011): 28–31.
Gralher, Martin. "Antinomisches Denken und dilemmatische Kontrastdialektik—Warum Carl Schmitt kein Liberaler sein könnte." In *Carl Schmitt und die Liberalismuskritik*, edited by Klaus Hansen and Hans Lietzmann, 81–92. Opladen: Leske & Budrich, 1988.
Groh, Ruth. *Arbeit an der Heillosigkeit der Welt—Zur politisch-theologischen Mythologie und Anthropologie Carl Schmitts*. Frankfurt: Suhrkamp, 1998.

———. *Carl Schmitt gnostischer Dualismus*. Berlin: Lit, 2014.
Grondin, Jean. *Introduction to Philosophical Hermeneutics*. Translated by Joel Weinsheimer.New Haven, CT: Yale University Press, 1994.
———. *The Philosophy of Gadamer*. Translated by Kathryn Plant. Montreal: McGill-Queen's University Press, 2003.
Gutting, Gary. "The Obscurity of 'Différance.'" In *A Companion to Derrida*, edited by Zeynep Dyrek and Leonard Lawlor, 72–88. Oxford and Malden, MA: Wiley Blackwell, 2014.
Habermas, Jürgen. *Strukturwandel der Öffentlichkeit. Untersuchungen zu einer Kategorie der bürgerlichen Gesellschaft*. Darmstadt and Neuwied: Luchterland, 1962.
Habfast, Ulrich. "Das normative Nichts. Eine Studie zum Dezisionismus in den frühen Schriften Carl Schmitts." PhD diss., University of Frankfurt, 2010.
Halldack, Felix. "Beschprechung der Schrift 'Gesetz und Urteil' von Carl Schmitt." *Kant-Studien* 17 (1912): 464–67.
Heidegger, Martin. *What Is Metaphysics?* In *Pathmarks*, translated by David Farrell Krell, 82–96. Cambridge: Cambridge University Press, 1998.
———. *Sein und Zeit*. 18th ed. Tübingen: Max Niemeyer, 2001.
———. *Beiträge zur Philosophie (Vom Ereignis)*. In *Gesamtausgabe 65*, edited by Friedrich-Wilhelm von Hermann. 2nd ed. Frankfurt: Klostermann, 1994.
———. *Vorträge und Aufsätze*. 9th ed. Stuttgart: Neske, 2000.
Henrich, Dieter. "Sebstbewusstsein. Kritische Einleitung in eine Theorie." In *Hermeneutik und Dialektik*, edited by Rüdiger Bubner, Konrad Cramer, and Reiner Wiehl. Vol. 1, 257–84, Tübingen: Mohr, 1970.
Hermanns, Stefan. *Kritik am Parlamentarismus bei Carl Schmitt und die Utopie der Demokratie*. Frankfurt: Lang, 2011.
Herrera, Hugo E. *Carl Schmitt als politischer Philosoph. Versuch einer Bestimmung seiner Stellung bezüglich der Tradition der praktischen Philosophie*. Berlin: Duncker & Humblot, 2010.
Herrero López, Montserrat. *The Political Discourse of Carl Schmitt: A Mystic of Order*. London: Rowman & Littlefield, 2015.
———. "Carl Schmitt als politischer Philosoph." *Philosophisches Jahrbuch* 120, no. 1 (2013): 196–97.
Hitschler, Daniel. *Zwischen Liberalismus und Existentialismus. Carl Schmitt im englischsprachigen Schrifttum*. Baden-Baden: Nomos, 2011.
Hitz, Thorsten. *Jacques Derridas praktische Philosophie*. Munich: W. Fink Verlag, 2005.
Hobbes, Thomas. *Leviathan*. Cambridge: Cambridge University Press, 1996.
Hobson, Marian. *Jacques Derrida*. London and New York: Routledge, 1998.
Hofmann, Hasso. *Legitimität gegen Legalität. Der Weg der politischen Philosophie Carl Schmitts*. 4th ed. Berlin: Duncker & Humblot, 2002.

Hogrebe, Wolfram. *Duplex. Strukturen der Intelligibilität*. Frankfurt: Klostermann, 2018.
Høibraaten, Helge. "Carl Schmitt, Henrik Ibsen und die Politische Theologie. Die Kronprätendenten, Kaiser und Galiläer und die Lehre vom Dritten Reich." In *Henrik Ibsen, Kaiser und Galiläer. Quellen—Interpretationen—Rezeptionen*, edited by Richard Faber and Helge Høibraaten, 233–93. Würzburg: Königshausen & Neumann, 2011.
Hooker, William. *Carl Schmitt's International Thought. Order and Orientation*. Cambridge: Cambridge University Press, 2009.
Husserl, Edmund. *The Crisis of European Sciences and Transcendental Phenomenology: An Introduction to Phenomenological Philosophy*. Translated by David Carr. Evanston, IL: Northwestern University Press, 1970.
Ifergan, Pini. "Cutting to the Chase: Carl Schmitt and Hans Blumenberg on Political Theology and Secularization." *New German Critique* 111 (2010): 149–71.
Jacques, Johanna. "Law, Decision, Necessity: Shifting the Burden of Responsibility." In *The Contemporary Relevance of Carl Schmitt: Law, Politics, Theology*, edited by Matilda Arvidsson, Leila Brännström, and Panu Minkkinen, 107–19. Oxford: Routledge, 2016.
Jellinek, Walter. "Besprechung der Schrift 'Gesetz und Urteil' von Carl Schmitt." *Archiv für öffentliches Recht* 23 (1914): 296–99.
Johnson, Christopher. *System and Writing in the Philosophy of Jacques Derrida*. Cambridge: Cambridge University Press, 1993.
Jünger, Ernst. "Strahlungen I." In *Sämtliche Werke*. Vol. 2. 2nd ed. Stuttgart: Klett-Cotta, 1998.
Kahn, Paul W. *Political Theology: Four New Chapters on the Concept of Sovereignty*. New York: Columbia University Press, 2011.
Kaiser, Joseph H. *Die Repräsentation organisierter Interessen*. Berlin: Duncker & Humblot, 1956.
Kalyvas, Andreas. *Democracy and the Politics of the Extraordinary: Max Weber, Carl Schmitt, and Hannah Arendt*. Cambridge: Cambridge University Press, 2008.
Kant, Immanuel. *Critique of Pure Reason*. Translated by Norman Kemp Smith. Hampshire and New York: Palgrave MacMillan 2007.
———. *Critique of the Power of Judgment*. Translated by Paul Guyer and Eric Matthews. Cambridge: Cambridge University Press, 2000.
Kennedy, Ellen. "Carl Schmitt's Parlamentarismus in Its Historical Context." In Carl Schmitt, *The Crisis of Parliamentary Democracy*, xiii–l. Cambridge, MA: The MIT Press, 1988.
Keohane, Kieran. "On the Political in the Wake: Carl Schmitt and James Joyce's Political Theologies." *Cultural Politics. An International Journal* 7, no. 2 (2011): 249–64.
Kiefer, L. "Begründung, Dezision und Politische Theologie." *Archiv für Rechts- und Sozialphilosophie* 76, no. 4 (1990): 480–82.

Kierdorf, Christian. *Carl Schmitts Idee einer politischen Theologie*. Berlin: Duncker & Humblot, 2015.
Kierkegaard, Søren. *Repetition: A Venture in Experimenting Psychology by Constantin Constantinus*. In *Kierkegaard's Writings*, edited by Howard V. Hong and Edna H. Hong. Vol. 6, 125–330. Princeton, NJ: Princeton University Press, 1983.
Kirchheimer, Otto. *Von der Weimarer Republik zum Faschismus. Die Auflösung der demokratischen Rechtsordnung*. Frankfurt: Suhrkamp, 1976.
Kodalle, Michael. *Politik als Macht und Mythos. Carl Schmitts "Politische Theologie."* Stuttgart: Kohlhammer, 1973.
Kondylis, Panajotis. "Jurisprudence, Ausnahmezustand und Entscheidung. Grundsätzliche Bemerkungen zu Carl Schmitts 'Politische Theologie.'" *Der Staat* 34 (1995): 325–57.
Koselleck, Reinhart. *Kritik und Krise. Eine Studie zur Pathogenese der bürgerlichen Welt*. Frankfurt: Suhrkamp, 1973.
Kramme, Rüdiger. *Helmuth Plessner und Carl Schmitt: eine historische Fallstudie zum Verhältnis von Anthropologie und Politik in der deutschen Philosophie der zwanziger Jahre*. Berlin: Duncker & Humblot, 1989.
Kuhn, Helmuth. *Der Staat. Eine philosophische Darstellung*. Munich: Kösel, 1967.
Lanchester, Fulco. "Un giurista davanti a se stesso. Intervista a Carl Schmitt." *Quaderni costituzionali* 3, no. 1 (1983): 5–34.
Larenz, Karl. *Methodenlehre der Rechtswissenschaft*. 6th ed. Berlin and New York: Springer, 1991.
Legrand, Pierre. "Derrida/Law: A Differend." In *A Companion to Derrida*, edited by Zeynep Dyrek and Leonard Lawlor, 581–604. Oxford and Malden, MA: Wiley Blackwell, 2014.
Lehnert, Erik. "Maschke, Herrera, Schmitt—Blick in neue Bücher." *Sezession* 41 (June 2011): 40–41.
Lilla, Mark. *The Reckless Mind: Intellectuals in Politics*. New York: New York Review of Books, 2001.
Loughlin, Martin. "Politinomy." In *The Oxford Handbook of Carl Schmitt*, edited by Jens Meierhenrich and Oliver Simons, 570–91. New York: Oxford University Press, 2016.
Lüdemann, Susanne. *Politics of Deconstruction: A New Introduction to Jacques Derrida*. Stanford, CA: Stanford University Press, 2014.
Maier, Hans. *Kritik der politischen Theologie*. Einsiedeln: Johannes Verlag, 1970.
Maimon, Salomon. *Essay on Transcendental Philosophy*. Translated by Nick Midgley, Henry Somers-Hall, Alistair Welchman, and Merten Reglitz. London and New York: Continuum, 2010.
Manderson, Desmond. *Kangaroo Courts and the Rule of Law: The Legacy of Modernism*. Oxford and New York: Routledge, 2012.
———. "Modernism, Polarity and the Rule of Law." *Yale Journal of Law and Humanities* 24, no. 2 (2012): 475–505.

Mansfield, Nick. "Derrida and the Culture Debate: Autoimmunity, Law and Decision." *Macquarie Law Journal* 6 (2006): 97–111.
Marder, Michael. *Groundless Existence. The Political Ontology of Carl Schmitt.* London and New York: Continuum, 2010.
———. *Pyropolitics. When the World Is Ablaze.* London: Rowman & Littlefield, 2015.
Maschke, Günther. "Carl Schmitt in den Händen der Nicht-Juristen." *Der Staat* 34 (1995): 104–29.
———. "Vorwort." In C. Schmitt, *Staat, Großraum, Nomos. Arbeiten aus den Jahren 1916–1969*, edited by Günther Maschke, xiii–xxvii. Berlin: Duncker & Humblot, 1995.
Mattutat, Liza. *Die vertrackte Urteilsform. Ein Argument zur Frage der Rechtsgeltung mit und gegen Hans Kelsen, Gustav Radbruch und Carl Schmitt.* Marburg: Tectum Verlag, 2016.
Maus, Ingeborg. *Bürgerliche Rechtstheorie und Faschismus. Zur sozialen Funktion und aktuellen Wirkung der Theorie Carl Schmitts.* Munich: Wilhelm Fink, 1980.
McCormick, John P. *Carl Schmitt's Critique of Liberalism. Against Politics as Technology.* Cambridge: Cambridge University Press, 1997.
———. "Derrida on Law; Or, Poststructuralism Gets Serious." *Political Theory* 29, no. 3 (2001): 395–423.
———. "Schmittian Positions on Law and Politics? CLS and Derrida." *Cardozo Law Review* 21, nos. 5–6 (2000): 1693–722.
———. "Three Ways of Thinking 'Critically' about the Law." *The American Political Science Review* 93, no. 2 (1999): 413–28.
Mehring, Reinhart. *Carl Schmitt.* Hamburg: Junius, 2001.
———. *Carl Schmitt: Denker im Widerstreit. Werk-Wirkung-Aktualität.* Freiburg: Verlag Karl Alber, 2017.
Meier, Christian. "Zu Carl Schmitts Begriffsbildung—Das Politische und der Nomos." In *Complexio Oppositorum*, edited by Helmuth Quaritsch, 537–56. Berlin: Duncker & Humblot, 1988.
Meier, Heinrich. *Leo Strauss and the Theologico-Political Problem.* Cambridge: Cambridge University Press, 2008.
———. *Carl Schmitt and Leo Strauss: The Hidden Dialogue.* Chicago, IL: University of Chicago Press, 1995.
———. *Carl Schmitt und Leo Strauss. Zu einem Dialog unter Abwesenden.* Stuttgart: Metzler, 1998.
———. *The Lesson of Carl Schmitt: Four Chapters on the Distinction between Political Theology and Political Philosophy.* Chicago, IL: University of Chicago Press, 2011.
Meierhenrich, Jens, and Oliver Simons. "'A Fanatic of Order in an Epoch of Confusing Turmoil:' The Political, Legal, and Cultural Thought of Carl Schmitt."

In *The Oxford Handbook of Carl Schmitt*, edited by Jens Meierhenrich and Oliver Simons, 3–70. New York: Oxford University Press, 2016.

Meierhenrich, Jens. "Fearing the Disorder of Things: The Development of Carl Schmitt's Institutional Theory, 1919–1942." In *The Oxford Handbook of Carl Schmitt*, edited by Jens Meierhenrich and Oliver Simons, 171–216. New York: Oxford University Press, 2016.

Meister Eckhart. "Die deutschen Werke vol. III." In *Die deutschen und lateinischen Werke*, edited by Joseph Quint. Stuttgart: Verlag W. Kohlhammer, 1976.

Mendieta, Eduardo. "Land and Sea." In *Spatiality, Sovereignty and Carl Schmitt: Geographies of the Nomos*, edited by Stephen Legg, 260–67. London: Routledge, 2011.

Mouffe, Chantal. *The Return of the Political*. London and New York: Verso, 1993.

———. "Carl Schmitt and the Paradox of Liberal Democracy." In *The Challenge of Carl Schmitt*, edited by Chantal Mouffe, 38–53. London and New York: Verso, 1999.

———. *On the Political*. London: Routledge, 2005.

Nault, François. "La fraternité. En lisant Derrida, Schmitt et la Bible." *Revue d'éthique et de théologie morale* 247 (2007): 29–52.

Neuhouser, Frederick. *Fichte's Theory of Subjectivity*. Cambridge: Cambridge University Press, 1990.

Neumann, Franz. *Wirtschaft, Staat, Demokratie. Aufsätze 1930–1954*, edited by Alfons Söllner. Frankfurt: Suhrkamp, 1978.

Neumann, Volker. *Carl Schmitt als Jurist*. Tübingen: Mohr Siebeck, 2015.

Nicoletti, Michele. *Trascendenza e potere: La teologia politica di Carl Schmitt*. Brescia: Morcelliana, 1990.

Nietzsche, Friedrich. *Twilight of the Idols*. Translated by Duncan Large. Oxford: Oxford University Press, 2008.

———. *Gay Science*. Edited by Bernard Williams. Cambridge: Cambridge University Press, 2001.

Noack, Paul. "Staatstheoretiker, Politischer Theologe—oder was sonst? Neue Bücher von und über Carl Schmitt." *Der Staat* 43 (1996): 195–207.

Oertmann, Paul. "Besprechung der Schrift 'Gesetz und Urteil' von Carl Schmitt." In *Literaturbeilage zur Deutschen Juristenzeitung* 18, no. 12 (1913): 817–18.

Ojakangas Mika. *A Philosophy of Concrete Life: Carl Schmitt and the Political Thought of Late Modernity*. Bern: Peter Lang, 2006.

Otto, Rudolf. *The Idea of the Holy*. London, Oxford, and New York: Oxford University Press, 1958.

Palmer, Richard E., *Hermeneutics: Interpretation Theory in Schleiermacher, Dilthey, Heidegger, and Gadamer*. Evanston, IL: Northwestern University Press, 1969.

Pan, David. "Tragedy as Exception in Carl Schmitt's *Hamlet or Hecuba*." In *The Oxford Handbook of Carl Schmitt*, edited by Jens Meierhenrich and Oliver Simons, 731–50. New York: Oxford University Press, 2016.

Paric, Danijel. *Anti-römischer Affekt. Carl Schmitts Interpretation der Erbsündenlehre und ihre wissenschaftliche Funktion.* Berlin: Lit, 2012.

Peterson, Erik. *Der Monotheismus als politisches Problem. Ein Beitrag zur Geschichte der politischen Theologie im Imperium Romanum.* Leipzig: Jakob Hegner, 1935.

———. "Was ist Theologie?" In *Theologische Traktate, Ausgewahlte Schriften,* edited by Barbara Nichtweiß. Vol. 1, 1–22. Würzburg: Echter, 1994.

Plessner, Helmuth. *Macht und menschliche Natur. Ein Versuch zur Anthropologie der geschichtlichen Weltansicht.* In *Gesammelte Werke V.* Frankfurt: Suhrkamp, 1981.

———. *Die Stufen des Organischen und der Mensch.* Berlin and New York: de Gruyter, 1975.

Pócza, Kálman. *Parlamentarismus und politische Räpresentation. Carl Schmitt kontextualisiert.* Baden-Baden: Nomos, 2014.

Posner, Eric A., and Adrian Vermeule. "Demistifying Schmitt." In *The Oxford Handbook of Carl Schmitt,* edited by Jens Meierhenrich and Oliver Simons, 612–24. New York: Oxford University Press, 2016.

Quaritsch, Helmut. *Positionen und Begriffe Carl Schmitts.* 3rd ed. Berlin: Duncker & Humblot, 1995.

Rae, Garin. *The Problem of Political Foundations in Carl Schmitt and Emmanuel Levinas.* London: Palgrave MacMillan, 2016.

Raffoul, Fraçois. "Heidegger and Derrida on Responsibility." In *A Companion to Derrida,* edited by Zeynep Dyrek and Leonard Lawlor, 412–29. Oxford and Malden, MA: Wiley Blackwell, 2014.

Rampazzo Bazzan, Marco. "Die Staatslehre Fichtes unter dem Aspekt der politischen Theologie nach Carl Schmitt." In *Der Eine oder der Andere: "Gott" in der klassischen deutschen Philosophie und im Denken der Gegenwart,* edited by Christopher Asmuth, 85–95. Tübingen: Mohr Siebeck, 2010.

Rasch, William. "Judgment: The Emergence of Legal Norms." *Cultural Critique* 57 (2004): 93–103.

Redaktion. "Rezensionen." *Archiv für die Geschichte des Widerstandes und der Arbeit* 20 (2016): 799–800.

Reisegger, Gerhoch. *Wege aus dem Globalisierungs-Chaos. Grundlagen für eine neue Wirtschaftsordnung.* Tübingen: Hohenrain, 2009.

Rissing, Thilo, and Michaela Rissing. *Politische Theologie. Schmitt-Derrida-Metz.* Munich: Wilhelm Fink, 2009.

Robbins, Jeffrey W. *Radical Democracy and Political Theology.* New York: Columbia University Press, 2011.

Rumpf, Helmut. *Carl Schmitt und Thomas Hobbes: Ideelle Beziehungen und aktuelle Bedeutung.* Berlin: Duncker & Humblot, 1972.

Rüthers, Bernd. *Die unbegrenzte Auslegung.* 7th ed. Tübingen: Mohr Siebeck, 2012.

Salter, Michael G. *Carl Schmitt: Law as Politics, Ideology and Strategic Myth.* Oxford: Routledge, 2012.

Sartori, Luigi, and Michelle Nicoletti. *Teologia Politica*. Bologna: Ed. Dehonia, 1991.
Schelling, Friedrich Wilhelm Joseph. "Vom Ich als Prinzip der Philosophie oder über das Unbedingte im menschlichen Wissen." In *Werke* (Historisch-kritische Ausgabe), edited by Thomas Buchheim, Jochem Hennigfeld, Wilhelm G. Jacobs, Jörg Hantzen, and Siegnert Peetz. Vol. 2. Stuttgart: Frommann-Holzboog, 1980.
Scheuerman, William E. *Carl Schmitt: The End of Law*. Oxford: Rowman & Littlefield, 1999.
Schleiermacher, Friedrich Daniel Ernst. *Hermeneutik und Kritik*, edited by Manfred Frank. Frankfurt: Suhrkamp, 1977.
Schlink, Bernhard. "Why Carl Schmitt?" *Rechtshistorisches Journal* 10 (1991): 160–76.
Schmitz, Alexander. "Legitimacy of the Modern Age? Hans Blumenberg and Carl Schmitt." In *The Oxford Handbook of Carl Schmitt*, edited by Jens Meierhenrich and Oliver Simons, 705–30. New York: Oxford University Press, 2016.
Schmitz, Alexander, and Marcel Lepper, eds. *Carl Schmitt—Hans Blumenberg: Briefwechsel 1971–1978 und weitere Materialien*. Frankfurt: Suhrkamp, 2007.
Schnur, Roman. *Revolution und Weltbürgerkrieg. Studien zur Ouvertüre nach 1789*. Berlin: Duncker & Humblot, 1983.
Schönberger, Christoph. "Werte als Gefahr für das Recht? Carl Schmitt und die Karlsruher Republik." In Carl Schmitt, *Die Tyrannei der Werte*, 57–91. Berlin: Duncker & Humblot, 2011.
Seubert, Harald. "Hugo Eduardo Herrera, Carl Schmitt als politischer Philosoph." *Zeitschrift für Geschichtswissenschaft* 59 (2011): 862–64.
———. "Eigene Fragen als Gestalt: Zu neuerer Literatur über Carl Schmitt." *Der Staat* 37 (1998): 435–60.
Simon, Rupert. *Die Begriffe des Politischen bei Carl Schmitt und Jacques Derrida*. Frankfurt: Peter Lang, 2006.
Sokoloff, William W. "Between Justice and Legality: Derrida on Decision." *Political Research Quarterly* 58, no. 2 (2005): 341–52.
Stirner, Max. *The Ego and His Own: Case of the Individual against Authority*. London and New York: Verso, 2014.
Stolleis, Michael. *Geschichte des Öffentlichen Rechts in Deutschland*. Vol. 4, 1995–1990. Munich: Beck, 2012.
Strauss, Leo. "Notes on Carl Schmitt: The Concept of the Political." In Heinrich Meier, *Carl Schmitt and Leo Strauss: The Hidden Dialogue*, 91–119. Chicago, IL: University of Chicago Press, 1995.
Taubes, Jacob, and Carl Schmitt. *Jacob Taubes—Carl Schmitt: Briefwechsel und Andere Materialien*, edited by Herbert Kopp-Oberstebrink, Thorsten Palzhoff, and Martin Treml. Munich: Fink, 2011.

Tillich, Paul. *Dynamics of Faith*. New York: Harper & Row, 1957.
———. *Theology of Culture*, edited by Robert C. Kimball. Oxford: Oxford University Press, 1959.
Türk, Johannes. "At the Limits of Rethoric. Authority, Commonplace, and the Role of Literature in Carl Schmitt." In *The Oxford Handbook of Carl Schmitt*, edited by Jens Meierhenrich and Oliver Simons, 751–75. New York: Oxford University Press, 2016.
Ulmen, Gary. *Politischer Mehrwert. Eine Studie über Max Weber und Carl Schmitt*. Weinheim: Wiley-VCH, 1991.
Vatter, Miguel. "The Idea of Public Reason and the Reason of State: Schmitt and Rawls on the Political." *Political Theory* 36 (2008): 239–71.
———. "The Political Theology of Carl Schmitt." In *The Oxford Handbook of Carl Schmitt*, edited by Jens Meierhenrich and Oliver Simons, 245–68. New York: Oxford University Press, 2016.
von Simson, Werner. "Carl Schmitt und der Staat unserer Tage." *Archiv des öffentlichen Rechts* 114 (1990): 185–220.
Wacker, Bernd, ed. *Die eigentlich katholische Verschärfung: Konfession, Theologie und Politik im Werk Carl Schmitts*. Munich: Fink, 1994.
Walsmann. "Besprechung des Buches 'Gesetz und Urteil' von Carl Schmitt." *Rheinische Zeitschrift für Zivil- und Prozessrecht* 5 (1913): 431–32.
Weber, Max. *The Protestant Ethic and the Spirit of Capitalism*. Translated by Talcott Parsons. London: Routledge, 2001.
———. *Economy and Society: An Outline of Interpretive Sociology*, edited by Guenther Roth and Claus Wittich. 2 vols. Berkeley: University of California Press, 1978.
———. "Parlament und Regierung im neugeordneten Deutschland." In *Gesammelte politische Schriften*, edited by Johannes Winckelmann, 306–443. Tübingen: Mohr Siebeck, 1988 (5th ed.).
Weber, Werner. *Spannungen und Kräfte im westdeutschen Verfassungssystem*. Berlin: Duncker & Humblot, 1970 (3rd ed.).
"W. I." "Besprechung der Schrift *Gesetz und Urteil* von Carl Schmitt." *Fischers Zeitschrift für Praxis und Gesetzgebung der Verwaltung* 42 (1913): 148–49.
Weinacht, Paul-Ludwig. "Über Carl Schmitts Arbeit an Begriffen. Wort und Begriff des Staates." In Paul-Ludwig Weinacht, *Staat—Staatsräson—Staatsbürger. Studien zur Begriffsgeschichte und zur politischen Theorie*, 67–90. Berlin: Duncker & Humblot, 2014.
Weinsheimer, Joel C. *Gadamer's Hermeneutics: A Reading of "Truth and Method."* New Haven, CT: Yale University Press, 1985.
Wiley, James. *Politics and the Concept of the Political: The Political Imagination*. New York: Routledge, 2016.
Willms, Bernard. "Carl Schmitt—Jüngster Klassiker des politischen Denkens?" In

Complexio Oppositorum. Über Carl Schmitt, edited by Helmut Quaritsch, 577–97. Berlin: Duncker & Humblot, 1988.

Wolin, Richard. *The Seduction of Unreason*. Princeton, NJ: Princeton University Press, 2004.

Zima, Peter V. *Theorie des Subjekts. Subjektivität und Identität zwischen Moderne und Postmoderne*. Tübingen: Francke Verlag, 2010.

Index

Adam, Armin, 154
aesthetics, 119n119
  aesthetic understanding, 77, 91–93, 130n250, 154n41, 171n322
Agamben, Giorgio, 132n263
alterity, 10–12, 14, 15, 18, 20, 25, 26, 28, 29, 32–36, 38, 39, 41, 42, 46, 54, 60, 83, 86, 87, 89, 91, 96, 97, 118n112, 126n218, 127n234
angst, anxiety, anguish, 16, 23, 50, 85, 96, 114n65, 119–20n135, 124n202
Anselm of Canterbury, 48, 136n30
Aquinas, Thomas, 48, 136n31
Arendt, Hannah, 154n41
Aristotle, 110n8
Arps, Arne, 109n1 (foreword)
Augsberg, Ino, 125n216
Austin, John Langshaw, 37, 128n240, 129n246
autonomy, 2, 12, 13, 34

Bakunin, Mikhail, 100
Bargu, Banu, 134n4
being-together in allocution, 13, 15, 42
Bendersky, Joseph J., 111n17, 157n114, 166n213, 168n270
Bernet, Rudolf, 124n205
Bielefeldt, Heiner, 131n257, 154n35, 167n226

Blumenberg, Hans, 108, 172n339
Böckenförde, Ernst-Wolfgang, 118n123, 135n27, 137n56, 141n110, 157n116, 158n122
Bortoft, Henri, 161n173, 161n174
Bossuet, Jacques-Bénigne, 68
Bourdin, Bernard, 134n4
Bowie, Andrew, 124n205, 124n208, 125n212, 164n192
Bragagnolo, Celina Maria, 172n339

Caputo, John D., 113n27, 116n89, 126n229, 128n237
Carrino, Agostino, 110n7
Cassirer, Ernst, 96–97, 165n206, 165n208
Catholicism, 63, 114n65, 138n69, 143n115, 144n116, 145–46n117
chaos, 22, 62, 84, 144n116
Christianity, 58, 62, 63, 106, 107, 144–45n116, 171–72n338
  Christian view of history, 144–45n116
Coillot-Thélène, Catherine, 140n97
community, 26, 67, 77, 89, 150n165
concepts, 10–15, 19, 22, 27–28, 33–34, 37–39, 43, 53–57, 62, 65, 69, 74, 78, 79, 81–88, 101, 108, 123n201, 139n86, 144n115, 145n117, 148n139, 165n210

190 Index

concepts *(continued)*
  abstract, 15–16, 28, 29, 33, 34, 41, 42, 80, 82, 87, 88, 89, 90, 95, 96, 160n160
  ambiguity of, 28, 74, 75, 81, 87
  concrete, 21, 28, 35, 38, 74, 75, 81, 82, 87–90, 121n166
  dynamism of, 14, 19, 28, 35, 74, 87
  empirical, 157n114
  existential, 42, 81, 88, 89
  juridical, 3, 40, 43, 57–60, 63, 94, 99, 139n95, 147n119
  metaphysical, 58–60, 139n95
  normative, 88
  political, 3, 45, 57, 59, 63, 140n106, 147n119
  spiritual, 63, 81
  theological, 45, 57, 58, 59, 63, 140n106, 147n119
conflict, 43, 55, 61, 62, 67–69, 93, 104–7, 133n279, 150n157, 151n165, 163n187, 172n338
  civil war, 163n187, 172n338
  war, 55, 61, 93, 104, 105–6, 151n165
Conrad, Burkhard, 134n4
constitution, 61, 93, 97, 101, 102, 103, 168n270
Cristi, Renato, 21, 117n109
Croce, Mariano, 111n20
Crockett, Clayton, 48, 136n34, 136n36, 140n106

death, 46, 49, 68, 115n73
de Maistre, Joseph, 68
de Man, Paul, 128n242
de Saussure, Ferdinand, 13, 113n35, 113n38
de Vries, Hent, 133n279, 135n27
de Wilde, Marc, 134n4
decision, 16, 29, 36, 39, 40, 55, 84, 85, 88, 98, 99, 125n218–26n226, 127n233, 148n139, 153n35
  concrete, 98

concrete historical, 62
existentially correct, 38
general, 77
interpretive, 21, 22, 28, 35, 36, 38, 43, 69, 74, 81, 84, 87–90, 92, 93, 101, 106, 126n218, 139n82
judicial, 76, 77, 121n166, 130n249, 130n250, 132n263, 160n163
juridical, 6, 11, 12, 15, 67, 74, 77, 117n112, 118n112, 132n263, 142n112, 160n163
just, 6, 12, 35, 36, 39, 64, 67, 74, 76, 90, 126n226, 128n234, 130n249, 143n112, 160n163
manipulative, 10, 11, 12, 36, 43, 55, 87, 88, 117n112
moral, 62, 148n139
political, 6, 130n249, 150–51n165
responsible, 12, 131n259
sovereign, 10, 11, 12, 15, 40, 41, 125n218, 131n251, 132n263
wrong, 127n233
decisionism, 15, 16, 36, 39, 40, 53, 64, 66, 67, 99, 103, 126n226, 127n233, 130n249
democracy, 100
Derrida, Jacques, 2–5, 9–16, 29–43, 46, 49, 50, 64, 75, 110n14, 111n1–3, 112n4–27, 113n28–37, 113n39–47, 114n48–50, 114n52–65, 122n178–80, 125n217–18, 126n223–25, 126n227, 126n229–33, 127n233–34, 128n234–39, 128n241–42, 129n242, 129n245, 129n247–49, 130n249, 131n258, 132n263–65, 133n266, 133n272–75, 133n277, 133n279, 153n21
Descartes, René, 48, 136n33
dictatorship, 40, 99, 122n182
  commisarial, 40, 99
  sovereign, 40
différance, 14, 29, 33, 114n53, 124n205

differences:
  play of, 13, 14, 33, 124n208
  system of, 14
Dilthey, Wilhelm, 68
Doerr, F., 154n35
dogma, 3, 45, 53, 58, 59, 61, 63, 64, 66, 67, 69, 107, 108, 136n36, 140n98, 144–45n116, 146–47n118, 147n119, 152n175, 165n203, 171n334
Donoso, Juan, 68, 140n101
Dotti, Jorge E., 142n110
Doyon, Maxime, 113n32
Dreisholtkamp, Uwe, 112n9, 113n42, 128n239
Dyzenhaus, David, 142n110

economy, 105, 106, 119n129, 158n125, 162n181
Eichhorn, Mathias, 134n4
enemy, 10, 11, 15, 16, 29, 36, 41, 42, 55, 67, 100, 105, 106, 107, 120n135, 149n147, 150n157, 150–51n165
event, 9, 10, 11, 16, 19, 20, 30, 46, 66, 116n89, 144n116, 148n139, 151n165
exception, 2, 3, 4, 5, 9, 10, 16, 19, 21–32, 34, 35, 50, 57, 59–60, 64, 65, 73, 80, 85, 86, 94–96, 108, 116n93, 117n108, 122n195, 128n234, 137n52, 148n139, 157n105, 158n127, 163n189, 164n199
  existential, 1, 5, 6, 17, 18, 19, 20–22, 25, 27, 28–32, 34, 37, 49, 50, 52, 53, 54, 57, 60, 65, 66, 80, 81, 83, 86, 96, 97, 116n93, 122n184, 132n263, 144–45n116, 148n139, 158n127
  juridical, 3, 11, 16, 20, 29, 30, 35, 39–41, 55, 80, 99, 117n112, 127n234, 131n251

political, 3, 11, 20, 30, 39–41, 55, 99, 107, 122n182, 131n258
  state of, 10, 11, 16, 29, 30, 32, 99, 132n263

faith, 3, 45, 46, 47–48, 49, 50, 52, 53, 57, 58–59, 60–61, 62–66, 69–70, 95, 96, 104, 137n49, 143n114, 143n115, 144n116, 146n117, 146–47n118, 147n119, 147n120, 149n147, 150–51n165, 152n175
Fichte, Johann Gottlieb, 68, 123n202, 125n211
Forsthoff, Ernst, 142n110
Frank, Manfred, 34, 124n207, 124n208, 125n209, 159n154
friend, 15, 16, 29, 41–42, 67, 100, 149n147
friendship prior to friendships, 12–13
functionalism, 1, 26, 33, 51–53, 78, 79, 82, 87, 88, 93, 95–97, 99, 102–4, 138n68, 144n115, 145n117, 165n208, 167n240

Gadamer, Hans-Georg, 74–75, 152n1–4, 153n5, 153n11–17, 158n126, 161n175, 163–64n191
Galli, Carlo, 117n110, 135n27, 149n153, 154n35, 160n166, 166n213
Garcia-Düttmann, Alexander, 126n233
Gasché, Rodolphe, 113n40, 114n50
Gerlich, Siegfried, 134n4
God, 46, 48, 54, 57, 62, 65–67, 131n258, 136n36, 137n50, 137n52, 144n116, 148n139, 149n147, 150–51n165
Gralher, Martin, 165n210
Groh, Ruth, 134n4, 141n108, 145n117
Grondin, Jean, 153n17, 158n125
Gutting, Gary, 114n51

Habermas, Jürgen, 167n229
Habfast, Ulrich, 154n35
Halldack, Felix, 154n35
Hegel, Georg Wilhelm Friedrich, 68, 125n209, 148–49n139
Heidegger, Martin, 46, 49, 50, 64, 82, 115n74, 117n107, 118n118, 119n128, 135n18, 136n35
Henrich, Dieter, 124n207
Hermanns, Stefan, 167n229
hermeneutics, 1, 2, 4, 5, 6, 27, 28, 56, 74–97, 98, 99, 101, 130n250, 156n98, 165–66n210
Herrero López, Montserrat, 109n1 (foreword), 170n295
Hitschler, Daniel, 142n110
Hitz, Thorsten, 126n233
Hobbes, Thomas, 68, 103–4, 149n155, 150n157
Hobson, Marian, 112n9, 128n238
Hofmann, Hasso, 64, 121n168, 122n184, 130n250, 133n4, 143n114, 147n122, 148n135, 154n35
Hogrebe, Wolfram, 164n197
Høibraaten, Helge, 134n4
Hooker, William, 151n165
Husserl, Edmund, 119n128, 136n45

ideal, the, 27, 36, 41, 42, 53, 57, 76, 78, 80, 81, 83–99, 101–3, 106, 108, 111n15, 121n166, 138n69, 145–46n117, 166n210
Ifergan, Pini, 172n339
immanence, 13, 21, 32, 46, 49–50, 51, 57–60, 64, 82, 85, 117n108, 136n36, 139n86
immanentism, 60, 108, 141n106

Jacques, Johanna, 131n251, 131n259, 167n226
Jellinek, Walter, 154n35

Johnson, Christopher, 112n9, 113n40, 128n238
Jünger, Ernst, 166n210
jurisprudence, 4, 28, 80, 82, 84, 106, 110n7, 141n106, 151n165, 156n98
justesse, 37–38, 128n242
justice, 11, 12, 16, 36, 37, 38, 39, 43, 55, 75, 90, 126n225, 128n234, 128n242, 129n248, 130n249, 131n261, 142n112

Kahn, Paul W., 134n4
Kaiser, Joseph H., 142n110
Kalyvas, Andreas, 142n110
Kant, Immanuel, 77, 79–80, 96, 130n250, 140n102, 154n41, 157n114, 165n206
Kennedy, Ellen, 167n229
Keohane, Kieran, 134n4
Kiefer, L., 154n36
Kierdorf, Christian, 134n4
Kierkegaard, Søren, 64, 116n93
Kirchheimer, Otto, 142n110
Kodalle, Michael, 135n27
Kondylis, Panajotis, 117n112
Koselleck, Reinhart, 142n110
Kramme, Rüdiger, 150n159
Kuhn, Helmuth, 142n110, 148n135

Lanchester, Fulco, 109n1 (introduction)
land, 104–6, 170n296
  land-appropriation, 105, 170n296, 170n300
language, 10–15, 29, 41, 42, 43, 73, 75, 78, 91, 124n206, 158n125, 161n181
  and *différance*, 33
  and law, 37–38, 132n263
  as human institution, 128n239
  game of, 14, 29

heteronomy of, 14, 32
originary violence of, 128n238
Larenz, Karl, 75, 153n18–20
Legrand, Pierre, 128n239
Lehnert, Erik, 109n1 (foreword)
Lenin, Vladimir, 107
Lepper, Marcel, 172n339
liberalism, 61, 99, 100, 106, 107
Lilla, Mark, 130n249, 134n4
Loughlin, Martin, 166n210
Lüdemann, Susanne, 112n22, 128n237, 128n239
Lyotard, Jean-François, 46, 49, 50

Machiavelli, Niccolò, 68, 149n153
Maier, Hans, 139n95
Maimon, Salomon, 155n71
Manderson, Desmond, 130n249, 131n261
Mansfield, Nick, 125n218
Mao, Tse-tung, 107
Marder, Michael, 64, 122n184, 130n250, 142n110, 147n121, 154n35, 164n191, 169n291
Maschke, Günther, 141n109, 151–52n165
Mattutat, Liza, 121n176
Maus, Ingeborg, 154n35
McCormick, John P., 111n15, 115n67, 115n71, 115n74, 122n182, 127–28n234, 129–30n249, 131n256, 146n118, 149n156, 154n35, 164n198, 166n210, 167n222, 167n226
meaning:
    displacement of, 28, 29, 76, 124n208
    divine, 5
    historical, 144n116, 164n191
    ideal, 75, 83, 88, 89, 121n166
    in language, 13–15, 32–33, 35, 37, 41, 158n125, 158n126
    new, 75, 161n178
    normative, 31, 62, 76, 77
    of existence, 1, 5, 6, 7, 16, 17, 18, 19, 20, 22–24, 25, 26, 27, 28, 30, 31, 32–33, 35, 42, 51, 53–54, 56, 60, 66, 67, 68, 69, 74, 67, 68, 69, 74, 76, 77, 80, 81, 82, 83, 84–85, 86, 87, 88, 89–93, 95, 96, 97, 98, 99, 105, 106, 116n89, 118n121, 127n233, 129n246, 132n263, 138n68, 138n69, 141n106, 147n118, 153n24
    of the earth, 105, 170n300
    of the rule, 18, 20, 28, 35, 38, 39, 43, 56, 74, 75, 77, 82, 83, 87–93, 94, 121n166, 160n165
    of the text, 75
    practical realm, 7, 17
    search for, 26, 84–85
    traditional, 88
Mehring, Reinhart, 142n110
Meier, Christian, 166n210
Meier, Heinrich, 2–3, 5, 6, 45–50, 60–71, 96, 110n9–13, 133n3–4, 134n5–7, 135n8–26, 135n28, 136n29, 136n36–38, 136n42, 137n52, 141n107–9, 142n111, 143n113–14, 145–46n117, 146–47n118, 147n119, 147n125–26, 147n128–30, 148n132–35, 148n139, 149n145–47, 150n162–64, 150–52n165, 152n166–75
Meierhenrich, Jens, 164n191, 164n197
Meister Eckhart, 48, 136n32
Mendieta, Eduardo, 119n128
metaphysics, 21, 46, 48, 58–60, 63, 107–8, 117n108, 137n50, 139n95, 139n97, 140n98, 140n101, 140n102
method, 1, 3, 4–5, 19, 22, 23, 27, 49, 51, 52, 56, 65, 97–98, 121n173
monarchy, 59, 140n101

moral, 49, 62, 70, 79, 119n129, 136n36, 148n139
   moral theology, 48, 53, 54
   moralization, 106, 151n165
Mouffe, Chantal, 141n110, 149n156
myth, 100, 161–62n181
   mythical thought, 100, 162n181
   mythical violence, 129n248, 133n279
   theory of myth 161–62n181

nation, 102
Nault, François, 134n4
Neuhouser, Frederick, 123n202
Neumann, Franz, 142n110
Neumann, Volker, 111n20, 130n250, 141n109, 142n110, 143n112, 154n35, 165n210
neutrality, 6, 22, 23, 26, 42, 68, 83, 84, 119n128
neutralization, 17, 23, 24, 26, 28, 42, 54, 68, 104, 145n117
Nicoletti, Michele, 117n110
Nietzsche, Friedrich, 119–20n135
Noack, Paul, 133–34n4, 141n109
norm, 4, 11, 27–31, 35, 38, 40, 57, 62, 67, 73, 76, 77, 84, 86, 91, 98, 99, 101, 102, 105, 108, 116n89, 118n112, 127n233, 127–28n234, 130n249, 131n261, 132n263, 142–43n112, 146–47n118, 163n189
normality, 3, 4, 5, 11, 12, 16, 19, 20, 21, 29, 30–31, 37, 39–40, 41, 51, 54, 57, 84, 107, 117–18n112, 131n258, 137n52, 138n69, 148n139
normativism, 61, 62, 64, 67, 70, 80, 99, 101, 103, 105, 117n112, 142–43n112
numinous, the, 95–96

occasionalism, 88

Oertmann, Paul, 153n35
Ojakangas Mika, 21, 30, 64, 117n108, 120n151, 122n183, 122n184, 142n110, 147n123, 148n139, 151n165, 162n181, 168n248, 168n253
order, 40, 41, 55, 62, 82, 84, 99, 103, 105, 131n251, 131n259, 144n116, 170n300
   constitutional, 168n270
   juridical, 40, 55, 56, 58, 61, 82, 84, 101, 103, 105, 106, 118n112, 129n245, 131n251, 132n263
   juridico-political, 40, 99, 101, 105
   of experience, 67
   of language, 43
   of meaning, 17, 84–85, 105, 138n68, 147n118
   of phenomenology, 9–11
   political, 82, 101, 105, 140n101
   social, 82
   spatial, 170n314
   theological, 106
other, the, 2, 5, 6, 9–16, 17, 20, 22, 24–29, 32–34, 38, 41–43, 46, 49, 51, 54–56, 66–69, 75, 80, 86, 89, 96, 97, 101, 118n112, 123–24n202, 125n218, 127n233, 138n68, 148n139, 150n157
Otto, Rudolf, 164n200-2

Palmer, Richard E., 157n110
Pan, David, 115n66, 163n189, 171n322
Paric, Danijel, 150n164
peace, 11, 55, 68
people, the, 6, 98, 101, 102, 103, 168n254, 168n270
Peterson, Eric, 107–8, 164–65n203, 171n331, 171n334, 171–72n338
philosophy, 3, 10, 14, 45–49, 60, 64, 139n97, 143n114, 148n139
   and juridical thought, xi, 76–97, 156n98, 165n210

Index 195

and theology, 2, 3, 45–49, 60, 64, 67, 69, 136n36, 143n114
existential, 122n184
juridical
of concrete life, 2, 5, 6, 19, 25, 57, 60, 73, 76–97, 99
political, 45–46, 136n36, 143n114, 152n175
practical, xi
transcendental, 14, 165n206
Plato, 49, 110n8
Plessner, Helmuth, 20, 21, 42, 68, 117n104, 117n107, 120n154, 121n160, 122n193, 123–24n202, 133n277, 141n110, 149n148, 150n158, 150n159, 158n128, 165n205
Pócza, Kálmán, 167n229
poles of understanding, 53–54, 55, 56, 66, 78, 83–93, 94, 95, 98, 102, 108, 111n15, 138n69, 145–46n117, 156n98, 166n210
politics, 3, 6, 107, 163n189
and law, 3, 6
and metaphysics, 108, 140n101
and theology, 151n165
of enmity, 15
pure, 71
political theology, 2–3, 45–50, 63–71, 107–8, 135n27, 136n36, 141n109, 143n114, 146n118, 149n147, 151–52n165
positivism, 61, 108, 132n261, 147n118
Posner, Eric A., 167n226
power, 25, 68, 144n116, 162n181
constitution-making, 101–2
of real life, 19, 30
of technology, 17, 25, 106
of the subject, 32, 34, 38, 91, 106
of unconsciousness, 33, 38, 126n218
political, 98, 99, 100, 117, 169n270, 170n296
sustaining, 116

progress, 24, 63
Proudhon, Pierre-Joseph, 100
Pufendorf, Samuel, 68

Quaritsch, Helmut, 166n210

Rae, Garin, 139–40n97
Raffoul, François, 112n27
Rampazzo Bazzan, Marco, 134n4
Rasch, William, 77, 121–22n177, 130n250, 153n10, 154n36, 154n38, 161n171, 164n193
Reisegger, Gerhoch, 134n4
religion, 63, 104
religious, 149n147
beliefs, 48, 52, 71
conditioning, 70, 145n117
conflict, 105, 163n187, 164n191
dispute, 104
dogma, 3
dogmatism, 147n119
experience, 47, 52, 96
faith, 45, 47–48, 58, 59, 66, 67, 155n66
motivations, xi, 63, 70
positions, 53, 55, 60, 61, 137n50
sphere, 107
tradition, 3
representation, 61, 102, 145–46n117, 169n270
revolution, 53, 99, 107
Rissing, Thilo, 114n65, 134n4
Rissing, Michaela, 114n65, 134n4
Robbins, Jeffrey W., 135n27
romanticism, 79, 132n261, 147n119, 155n66
Rumpf, Helmut, 149n156
Rüthers, Bernd, 118n123, 137n56, 142n110, 157n116, 158n121

Salan, Raoul, 107
Salter, Michael G., 164n191
Salvatore, Andrea, 111n20

Sartori, Luigi, 135n27
Schelling, Friedrich Wilhelm Joseph, 123n201, 125n209
Scheuerman, William E., 129n245, 154n35
Schleiermacher, Friedrich Daniel Ernst, 159n154
Schlink, Bernhard, 143n114
Schmitz, Alexander, 172n339
Schnur, Roman, 142n110
Schönberger, Christoph, 156n98
scientism, 58, 83, 136n45
Seubert, Harald, 109n1 (foreword), 134n4, 141n109, 143n114
seriousness, 2, 7, 91–92, 100, 118n121, 131n251, 164n191
signified/signifier, 13–14, 113n41
Simon, Rupert, 126n225, 130n249
Simons, Oliver, 164n191, 164n197
Socrates, 49, 110n8
Sokoloff, William W., 130n249
Spinoza, Baruch, 68
Stirner, Max, 128n239, 159n140
Stolleis, Michael, 141n109
Strauss, Leo, 136n36, 142n110, 152n175
socialism, 61, 162n181, 170n314
sociology of concepts, 58–60, 70, 99, 107, 140n101, 140–41n106, 147n119, 168n254
sovereignty, 10, 59
space, 22, 61, 104–6, 119n128
speech acts, 37–38, 129n246
Stalin, Joseph, 107
state, the, 55, 57, 61, 93, 102, 103, 104, 166n221
  Rechtsstaat, 101
subject, the, 2, 3, 9–12, 14–16, 21, 25–26, 29–30, 32–35, 38, 42, 51, 52–54, 56, 78, 82, 85–87, 89, 91, 93–97, 100–1, 112n10, 122n193, 123–24n202, 157n105

substantialism, 1, 4, 6, 33, 51–53, 55, 57, 62, 65, 96–97, 99, 100, 106, 137n49, 144n115, 167n240
subsumption, 1, 15, 28, 36, 38, 56, 67, 74, 76–77, 87, 93, 99, 116n89, 118n112, 121n166, 121n177, 126n218, 127n233, 128n234, 130n249, 142–43n112, 144n116, 160n163, 160n167

Taubes, Jacob, 133n2
technology, 9–43, 50–51, 54, 57, 62, 78, 104, 107, 115n74, 120n144, 132n261, 141n106, 143–44n115, 145n117, 146–47n118, 156n98, 169n285
theology, 45–71, 107–8, 135n27, 136n36, 141n109, 143n114, 146n118, 149n147, 151–52n165
Tillich, Paul, 48, 136n34
transcendence, 1, 5, 21–22, 32, 38, 46, 48–54, 56, 57, 59, 60, 64, 65, 85, 86, 87, 94, 96, 108, 117n107, 117n108, 118n118, 122n193, 136n36, 137n52, 138n69, 139n86, 158n131, 159n153
  and power, 33, 126n218
Türk, Johannes, 161–62n181

Ulmen, Gary, 154n35
understanding, xi, xii, 2, 4–7, 11–28, 30, 32, 34–36, 38, 40, 41–43
  aesthetic, 77, 91–93, 130n250, 154n41, 171n322
  juridical, xi, 2, 4–6, 11, 12, 16–31, 35–42, 73–97, 117–18n112, 121n166, 121n177, 130n249, 138n68, 161n178, 167n240
  technological, 5, 16–29, 31, 34, 50–56, 114n65, 115n74, 120n144, 132n261, 138n68, 141n106, 143–

Index 197

44n115, 145n117, 146–47n118, 156n98, 165n203, 169n285

values, 22, 61, 82–83, 84
Vatter, Miguel, 142n110, 160n166, 172n338
Vermeule, Adrian, 167n226
von Clausewitz, Carl, 107
von Simson, Werner, 143n114

Wacker, Bernd, 134n4
Walsmann, 154n35
Weber, Max, 17, 78, 115n72, 146n118

Weber, Werner, 142n110
Weinacht, Paul-Ludwig, 109n1 (foreword), 166n210
Weinsheimer, Joel C., 161n172
Wiley, James, 134n4
will to power, 23, 85, 158n125
Willms, Bernard, 142n110
Wolin, Richard, 130n249

Xenophon, 49

Zima, Peter V., 124n205

www.ingramcontent.com/pod-product-compliance
Lightning Source LLC
Chambersburg PA
CBHW020732240426
43665CB00052B/459